The New Hiscox Guide for Baptist Churches

Everett C. Goodwin

Judson Press ® Valley Forge

The New Hiscox Guide for Baptist Churches
© 1995
Judson Press, Valley Forge, PA 19482-0851

Library of Congress Cataloging-in-Publication Data
Goodwin, Everett C.
    The new Hiscox guide for Baptist churches / Everett C. Goodwin
        p.   cm.
    Includes bibliographical references and index.
    ISBN 0-8170-1215-X (alk. paper)
    1. Baptists—Doctrines. 2. Baptists—Government. I. Hiscox, Edward Thurston,
    1814-1901. New directory for Baptist churches.
    II. Title
    BX6331.2.G68 1995   286'.1—dc2095-5880

98 99 00 01 02   8 7 6 5 4 3 2
Printed in the U.S.A.

To My Father

Carlton Byron Goodwin

*As father, mentor, colleague, and friend he has modeled
Baptist life in spirit and in practice.*

Contents

Acknowledgments

The new millennium, which has currently captured every interest, will also bring the fifth century of recorded Baptist experience. Both the new millennium and the new century are likely to bring extraordinary challenges and as yet unimagined opportunities to Baptists. In the almost four centuries of Baptist experience until now, Baptist churches and institutions have grown and changed remarkably. Yet, particularly as we anticipate this new time, it remains humbling to consider those who have gone before us and whose experiences make this work both necessary and possible.

In my own case I am acutely aware of the many lives and experiences of Baptists and others which, having intersected with my own, helped shape this volume. They begin with the elderly woman who, during worship in the church of my childhood, quietly entertained my restless spirit in order that my father could preach undistracted and my mother worship with some decorum. They have included national religious and political leaders who found spiritual resources in church life that made their leadership more effective and kept their personal lives focused even in difficult times. And from earliest memory until now there has been a saintly procession of those for whom each day was a challenge for personal or economic survival, who nevertheless demonstrated ways to bring their faith and their church to the street corners of their daily lives. Among them are countless men and women who, as pastors, teachers, colleagues, and mentors in ministry, have enlivened and enriched my own perception and experience in ministry as a Baptist.

The first specific acknowledgments for this work must certainly go to Edward T. Hiscox from whose writings the first *Hiscox Guide* was developed, and to Frank T. Hoadley who edited the 1964 edition of the *Guide* which served as the source from which my own developed. I am especially grateful to Carol Franklin Sutton who suggested that this project and I might benefit one another, and to Judson Press for the opportunity to accomplish it. Both Kristy Arnesen Pullen and Mary Nicol of Judson Press were of invaluable assistance in the writing and editing phases of this project. Beverly Carlson of the American Baptist Historical Society, James Dunn of the Baptist Joint Committee of Public Affairs, and W. Stan Hastey of the Alliance of Baptists provided important information and perspective in developing sections of the text and resources. Edwin S. Gaustad read the manuscript and offered valuable suggestions prior to final editing. Any remaining inaccuracies or infelicities of expression that may be present are my own responsibility.

The Baptist Fellowship of Metropolitan Washington, D.C., provided for me a profound experience of spiritual community and a reference point for continuing Baptist vitality and formation during the research and writing phase of the manuscript. One of its members, Irene Conway, assumed the tedious but critical task of proofreading both the initial manuscript and later the page proofs. Another, Lawrence Sherman, provided me with a writing office in his historic Georgetown building. Its location, fifty feet from the urban Canal National Park incorporating the eighteenth-century canal and locks, and fifty feet from the center of modern Georgetown's professional and commercial cacophony, provided the perfect physical metaphor for spanning the time and culture change from Hiscox's day to our own.

To my wife, Jane, and our daughters, Libby and Leah, a special thanks for support and encouragement during a project that also symbolized new priorities and directions in ministry and activity. My deepest acknowledgment appears in dedication.

Everett C. Goodwin
Washington, D.C.

Introduction

This volume, *The New Hiscox Guide for Baptist Churches*, has a long and honorable lineage. In presenting it for use as a resource for church leadership and organization among Baptists and as a resource for others to learn about Baptists, I hope that it will fill, in part, the same need for which Hiscox originally wrote.

The writings of Edward T. Hiscox (1814–1901) have been popular among many thousands of Baptists in the United States and beyond for over 135 years. Many helpful works have appeared under Hiscox's name. His *Baptist Church Directory* was first published in 1859. During his lifetime, Dr. Hiscox made several revisions to keep his work current. He also published several smaller volumes whose purpose was to present some of the materials from the *Directory* that he believed would be useful in shorter form. Toward the end of his life, he returned to his manuscripts for a thorough revision, from which emerged two completely new books. These two works were similar in subject matter and content, but one was longer and treated the material more intensively than the other. The shorter version, known as *The Standard Manual for Baptist Churches*, was published in 1890, and the more comprehensive volume, *The New Directory for Baptist Churches*, appeared in 1894.

Both books were reprinted many times in the following decades with only a minimum of revisions. By midcentury, the printer's plates had become worn and reprint editions were, therefore, substandard in appearance. More importantly, however, the content had also begun to show its age. When Hiscox first wrote, the United

States was still essentially small town and rural in character, and most Baptist churches served such a population. When Hiscox first wrote, the Southern Baptist Convention was only thirteen years old, and by 1894, not yet two generations old. The Northern Baptist Convention (later the American Baptist Churches in the U.S.A.) was not to organize for another thirteen years after that. Interchurch agencies, parachurch organizations, and a whole complex of Baptist and Baptist-related institutions simply did not exist. The rise of modern denominations and institutions was still to come. When the revised work, *The Hiscox Guide for Baptist Churches*, appeared in 1964, its inclusion of information related to these institutional developments was much needed. Again, Hiscox's work found an enthusiastic audience, and his thoughts guided a new generation of Baptists in leadership, church life, and appreciation of Baptist principles.

By now, *The Hiscox Guide for Baptist Churches* has become something of a classic, and, despite its advancing age, it has continued as a primary source for consultation and guidance regarding many issues in Baptist life. However, even as demand for the work has continued, its aging character has become more evident despite revisions. Much has happened since Hiscox first set out to create a guide for Baptist life and work. For example, whole denominational structures and vast programs of mission outreach have been established. Church strategies for ministry have undergone several transformations, first in response to urbanization, then in response to the suburban development of metropolitan areas, then through several periods of growth among groups with varied languages and cultural backgrounds. Churches have experienced great change in their relationship to the cultures in which they live, and in their significance in the community.

In Hiscox's time, churches were likely to be more uniform in numerical size, assumption, and in the life experiences of their members. For example, in his day most churches would have listed memberships between twenty-five and two hundred fifty, a few would contain five hundred, and a very few city churches might list memberships approaching one thousand. Now, Baptists include small house churches of a dozen members and "megachurches" of five thousand, fifteen thousand, or even twenty-five thousand members.

While no one book can address the varied needs and experiences of all Baptist churches, it has seemed appropriate to expand Hiscox's experience to more adequately encompass present circumstances.

In one sense things have come full circle. Hiscox strongly emphasized the independence and autonomy of the local church. In presenting the 1964 revision, Frank T. Hoadley, its editor, wondered "whether Hiscox would have changed with the times or not" but concluded that the book carrying his name must reflect the changes denominational structures had brought to Baptist life. Ironically, it is clear that, at present, denominational structures are being reduced in size and resources, and the tide of leadership and activity is once again focused in the local church. Therefore, a book advancing Hiscox's purpose seems especially appropriate and timely. Also, in recent decades religious developments have resulted in the establishment of many churches using the name or designation *Baptist* that are not affiliated with historic Baptist organizations. It is my hope, therefore, that this work might acquaint these new branches on the Baptist tree with the deep roots that give it life.

Some changes in church and culture have continued at a rapid pace. For example, the ministry, especially, has experienced great change in the last hundred years. It has become both more professional and also more diverse. A profession that was once almost exclusively male has become open to the leadership of women in many Baptist churches, while the same subject is the focus of much debate in others. The ordained ministry of Hiscox's time was almost exclusively focused on preaching and on presiding over the concerns of a local congregation. Now in addition to that still primary role, the ministry is a highly subdivided profession serving varied program needs in churches, denominational structures, hospitals and helping institutions, and in a variety of other contexts. Demands on the ministry are extraordinarily high. Yet, many observe, the ministry is at a low ebb of confidence and support. Again, one book cannot be a single guide to pastoral leadership, but it has seemed important to encompass these transformations in presenting a new guide for a new time.

Over the years *The Hiscox Guide* became a classic because

Hiscox wrote to universal concerns and challenges. He spoke a prophetic word to our day, for example, when he first wrote: "Neither age, sex, race, past character, nor condition in life should serve to keep one out of the church, if the evidence be abundant and satisfactory that such a person be truly converted." In another early work he addressed the subject of spiritual growth, which has experienced an important renewed emphasis in our generation: "God may be as much glorified and the world as much blessed by the development of character and the increase of good works on the part of believers, as by the addition of converts." A work is truly a classic when it has the power to remind a later time of principles it might otherwise forget. In that regard Hiscox affirmed the need for professionalism in ministry by saying that "special leaders and teachers are needed for the pastorates of churches." But he preceded it by reminding his original audience, as we need to be reminded: "Every Christian is under obligation to preach the gospel according to his ability and opportunity." That is an especially important word as, in our time, we struggle to recover the ministry of the laity. The classic quality of the work endures because Hiscox stayed true to basic Baptist principles and because his counsel was invariably based on his understanding of Scripture rather than prevailing theories of management, common sense, or other transient sources of advice.

Recently, however, it was determined that simply revising the 1964 edition would be inadequate. Hiscox's important contribution needed to be restated in language as clear and helpful for our time and circumstances as it was originally in Hiscox's own time.

Attempting to rewrite a classic is a dangerous task. One temptation is to write a totally new book on the same subject. But such a book would not be a *Hiscox Guide*. Worse, it might fail to incorporate the very spirit and structure that has so well endured the passage of time. Another temptation was simply to revise, here and there, the most archaic language, to delete outdated considerations, and to add what seemed new and particularly relevant among missing material. That course, however, risked not taking the material seriously: first, by arbitrarily determining that what seems outmoded no longer has value and, second, by assuming that new material was valuable simply because it was more recent. It seemed that rewriting a book that was inspired by the Hiscox spirit and that closely followed his structure was the course most likely to re-create a usable and dynamic work.

In accepting the task of rewriting, I began by realizing that I was among the many potential readers who had never read Hiscox primarily because it seemed archaic and therefore not relevant to my ministry or church leadership concerns. I was curious, therefore, to discover what it was that had originally made the book so useful and sustained its value for so many over such a long period of time.

In reading the book, it seemed to me that Hiscox had done a remarkable thing for his time: he had attempted to give order to the varieties of Baptist experience—and had sought to give it along common lines of concern, while leaving aside issues and matters where diversity of theology, society, or traditions encouraged "Baptists to be Baptists"—that is, to follow independent and divergent directions. I determined, therefore, to write the present work "in the spirit of Hiscox" but to use the prism of my own observations and experience and the communication tools of language common to late-twentieth-century expression. In developing this approach, several principles emerged:

The basic text for this re-presentation is the 1964 *Guide,* which had already incorporated some more recent considerations. I rewrote every sentence instead of simply revising here and there. Occasionally a familiar phrase from Hiscox will strike the reader's ear, of course. And frequently it seemed useful to quote from him directly. Page references for these quotes are from the 1964 edition and are cited in parentheses. The use of occasional phrases from the earlier edition has been to remind the eye and ear of Hiscox's phrasing in order to keep his style present.

Very little material was actually abandoned. In fact, I discovered much sound advice and practice from the 1890s that we might do well to reconsider. Much material was reshaped and expanded. And in several chapters and sections, I added material regarding programs and procedures that have become prevalent since Hiscox lived.

Throughout the work I have used the Revised Standard Version (RSV) of the Bible instead of retaining Hiscox's use of the King

James Version (KJV). By that decision I meant no theological judgment or controversy—indeed, for many purposes I personally prefer the KJV to read and even more modern translations for study. Nevertheless, the RSV presents the text in language reminiscent of Hiscox's era, yet more familiar to modern ears.

In many cases, material that Hiscox added by means of footnote has been incorporated into the main text. Endnotes have been added to provide references or citations where needed or to expand on a subject in a slightly different direction or for some other purpose of additional information.

The appendices, particularly those representing Hiscox's views on Baptist history, baptism, and other matters, have been retained. Though in some churches practices and procedures have changed, these essays present a valuable historical point of reference. The chronology has been brought up-to-date, edited, and revised. The section on resources, while by no means exhaustive, provides contemporary resources as well as retains many older Baptist works.

Much has been said about the increasing secularity of our age. Clearly the church must face this challenge with renewed relevance and vitality. Moreover, many issues at present are causing division and debate within churches: the role of women in leadership, the use of inclusive language in worship and theological expression, the nature of worship and worship styles, the nature and authority of Scripture, matters of sexual identity and the ethics of sexual behavior, new shapes and arrangements of family living, the growing gap between the very wealthy and the very poor, great demands on church programs and ministry and, often, declining resources to meet them—these are just a few examples. What might Hiscox think of these things? On the one hand we cannot know, of course. Yet we can know that he would have asserted without hesitation that the things of this world will pass, but the Word of God shall remain forever. And we can know that in order to greet these challenges, as well as ones yet to find definition, Hiscox would advise us all to take heed of Christ's purpose for the church, to attend to effective Baptist organization and leadership, and to extend the ministry of the church with its roots firmly in the Scripture and its branches reaching toward men and women in need of the gospel's eternal truth.

This *New Hiscox Guide*, of course, carries no special authority other than what seems authoritative to the reader and is, therefore, formative in the lives of individuals and churches. It is certainly not the official publication of any specific Baptist denomination, convention, or fellowship, nor does it intend to endorse a particular theological interpretation or point of view. I am grateful that Judson Press has seen the value of continuing a primer and resource for Baptists under the Hiscox name, but this book's appearance under the imprint of Judson Press does not imply its endorsement or that of the American Baptist Churches in the U.S.A. The vision and concept of this book remains that of Hiscox; the specific expressions are now mine, as are any new errors or continuing confusions. Indeed, I welcome comments from readers that might correct or enhance my own awareness of the variety of Baptist principles and practices. Whether readers agree with Hiscox's thoughts or mine is not the first significance. I am confident that Hiscox would affirm my own hope that the end result of this book might be lively dialogue; clear thinking among Baptists of many churches, conventions, and traditions about the nature and purpose of the church; and renewed commitment to its ministry and its Lord.

It is, in short, my hope that this book will provide a continuing contribution to the good order and vitality of Baptist churches. Its specific usefulness may erode over time, as has that of its predecessors. In May 1893 Hiscox wrote in the preface to his *New Directory*, "The principles on which this manual is constructed are drawn from the New Testament, and never in our history was there so much need of such an exposition and guide for members in our church fellowship as there is today." A century later, we have the same need. I offer this volume in the hope that those same principles, grounded in Scripture and honed by the faith of continuing generations, will find new application for our time. And I offer it in the hope of our Lord Jesus Christ, in whose name we gather and for whose sake we labor.

Chapter I

The Nature of the Church

The concept of "church" is so familiar that no further definition would seem necessary. Yet because of its familiarity, it is a word that has come to have both a broad general definition as well as a specific and exacting one. For example, Americans generally recognize a church to be a community, gathering, or institution that is organized to fulfill a religious purpose and meets on some regular schedule for the worship of God. In fact, to a great many the word *church* simply implies a building where people gather for religious purposes.

A Christian church, however, especially from the perspective of Baptist conviction, is a much more specific and visible thing. For Baptists, a church is a community of persons who have individually experienced the regenerating grace of God; have been baptized on profession of faith in Christ; have united with others of like mind and spirit in covenant for worship, instruction, and the observance of Christian ordinances, as well as for witness, mission, and service as they understand the gospel to require; have accepted Christ as their supreme Lord and Guide; and accept the Bible, especially the New Testament, as a divinely inspired record and therefore a trustworthy, authoritative, and sufficient rule of faith and practice. The Baptist experience of the church also includes a significant measure of fellowship—the gathering together of members for mutual enjoyment, support, and guidance in the Holy Spirit.

Baptists generally limit the meaning of the word *church* to describe a specific, local community or organization. Therefore, they resist the notion that a large institutional or hierarchical and corporate structure could properly be called a "church." Neverthe-less, many Baptist individuals and churches join with other Chris-tians and churches in believing themselves to be a part of the universal church—the spiritual reality ordained by Christ, which is larger, more inclusive, and more mystical than any specific expres-sion of it.

The Word *Church:* Its Origin and Definition

Modern languages derive the word *church* from the Greek *kuriakon*. For example, the English word *church* has a clear pho-netic kinship to the Scottish word *kirk* or the German *kirche* or the Danish *kyrke* or the Swedish *kyrka*. Even the Russian *zerkow*, when pronounced, has a similar sound. *Kuriakon* means, literally, "be-longing to the Lord." *Kuriakon*, however, is not the word the New Testament texts use to refer to what we know as the church. The word from which *church* has been translated is *ekklesia*.

Ekklesia is formed from *ek*, meaning "from" or "out of" and *kaleo,* which means "called out from" or "to call." Its primary use was to define a company or an assembly of persons who were selected, called out, or separated from the larger social context. Like many New Testament words, it was borrowed from the secular, civil vocabulary. In Greek use, for example, *ekklesia* was defined as "an assembly of citizens called together for deliberative purposes; a legislative assembly called to discuss the affairs of state." Most importantly, it implied order, organization, and mutual under-standing of process and procedure. It described a group of persons who possessed the rights of citizenship and who had the privilege of discussing important matters of public concern and the right to enact and enforce laws designed for the public good.

The Greeks used the word to describe an empowered, responsi-ble group of citizens as distinct from the general public, a rowdy crowd, or an incidental gathering. In a parallel manner, the word *ekklesia* was adopted in the Scriptures to describe those persons who were called out from the world at large: elected, chosen, separated. The *eklektoi* are the elected, the faithful, and those called to be saints. They are the citizens of the "kingdom of Christ"; they are the participants of the church of the living God. They are those who have accepted the designation of "people of God." Though the church often seems shrouded in mystery, it is nevertheless defined by an ancient word that implies an organized company with laws, officers, and ordinances. It is a specific expression of a spiritual fellowship that functions best with an orderly consideration of important matters. Thus structured, it may effectively perform the specific service it is led to perform in the service of God.

Hiscox pointed out that the word *ekklesia* is found 115 times in the New Testament. In 110 cases it refers to the institution Christians know as "the church." The other five uses serve to prove the point of the original use of the word and help us fully to understand its origin.

In three instances it is used in its original Greek civil context to describe the assembly that gathered at Ephesus on the occasion when Paul and colleagues incited a riot (Acts 19:32,39,41). When we examine this experience, we see that the excited, violence-ready crowd is referred to as *oklos*—a confused, disorderly crowd (Acts 19:33). *Ekklesia* is the word used to describe the assembly to which the matter was temporarily referred, or the regular assembly, which was the official, scheduled council where such cases of disorder or misfeasance were routinely referred for review and adjudication (Acts 19:32,39,41).

In two other cases the word *ekklesia* is used in a specific sense to describe a ritual gathering or "congregation." In these instances the word functions to describe an assembly with a specific, sacred character. In Acts 7:38, for example, Stephen addresses his accusers and refers to ancient history by reminding them: "This is he who was in the congregation (*ekklesia*) in the wilderness, with the angel who spoke to him at Mount Sinai . . ." In a similar sense it appears again in Hebrews (2:12), where a citation from Psalm 22:22 says: "I will proclaim thy name to my brethren, in the midst of the congregation I will praise thee." In both of these cases the word *ekklesia*, translated as "congregation," underlines the ancient theology of the covenant in which the seed of Abraham constituted a people called out and separated from all others, who were organized under a polity peculiarly their own, and with distinct ordinances, laws, and services. In a sense, these two uses reclaim an ancient Hebrew understanding in a specific Christian reinterpretation.

The word *ekklesia* is used in two other ways to define the Christian concept of the church in the New Testament. First, it frequently appears in a primary form, close to Greek civil usage, to designate a visible, local congregation of Christian believers who meet for worship, instruction, and service. Second, it is used in a figurative metaphorical sense to describe the invisible, universal congregation that includes all of God's people in heaven and on earth. In this use, *ekklesia* defines a spiritual reality that has no specific existence in time and space. Therefore, the visible, local church is the only tangible manifestation of the invisible, universal church.

Hiscox pointed out that of the 110 instances in which *ekklesia* is translated as "church," more than ninety are of the first usage—that is, defining visible, local congregations or communities of believers. The primary use of the word is therefore rooted in a very specific reference. Yet even these uses carry with them a sense of connection with the whole *ekklesia*—the whole church—of God: "Paul called the elders of the church," "the church of God at Corinth," "the seven churches of Asia," "the church of Ephesus," "the churches of Galatia," and so on. These are all specific, bounded, defined, human-expressed examples of *ekklesia*.

When Paul admonished husbands to love their wives as "Christ loved the church, and gave himself up for her . . . that he might present the church to himself in splendor . . ." (Ephesians 5:25,27), his use of *ekklesia* does not refer to a specific body of believers but to the mystical whole: all the people of God; the saved, universal, indivisible church. When Jesus made his great affirmation of the church by saying, "On this rock I will build my church, and the powers of death shall not prevail against it," (Matthew 16:18), *ekklesia*—the church—takes on a specific form with the character of eternal presence. In several other expressions—"through the church the manifold wisdom of God might now be made known" (Ephesians 3:10); "He [Christ] is the head of the body, the church" (Colossians 1:18)—reference is to the entirety of all Christ's church and not to a specific manifestation.

But whether in specific form, or whether as a reference to the great church universal, the word *church—ekklesia*—is a scripturally rooted term. Therefore, the concept and form of the church is a strong New Testament theme.

The Church in the New Testament

The shape of the church is briefly addressed in the New Testament, although neither specifically enough nor frequently enough to imply a specific charter to any particular form. In the book of the Acts especially, we catch glimpses and insights of how the first believers organized their communities, interpreted their experiences, and established their procedures.

For example, at Pentecost (Acts 2:1-21) we see the first Christians receive the empowerment of the Spirit. In the preaching and healing of Peter and John (Acts 3:1–4:22), we observe how the disciples began to follow the direction Jesus had given them. The dramatic account of Ananias and Sapphira reveals something of their early experiments in communal living and in the distribution of property (Acts 5:1-11). This story and its dramatic conclusion also demonstrates that their decisions and activities came at the price of some uncertainty: "And great fear came upon the whole church, and upon all who heard of these things" (Acts 5:11).

These early days of the church's experience sponsored the decisions that shaped the basic outlines to come. Two decisions in particular gave strong definition to the character of the church. The first is the new revelation by which Peter was led to expand the boundaries of the church's membership to include Gentiles (Acts 10:1–11:18). By his response to this new understanding that he should not "call any man common or unclean" (Acts 10:28), the church began to overleap the Jewish origins of the gospel and invite the whole world to hear the remarkable message of Christ. The second key decision came in response to "murmurings" between Hellenist and Jewish factions about the care of widows (Acts 6:1-6). The organizational decisions they made in response to these practical spiritual concerns began the process of internal organization for church community life in both worship and fellowship.

It is in the Epistles, however, and particularly those contributed by the apostle Paul, that we experience the church as a living, dynamic, developing expression of Christ's presence and purpose. In those pages we encounter the church of relationships and redemption. And it is by analogy and metaphor that Paul and other Epistle writers reveal its mystery. Analogies and metaphors describe rather than define, invoke rather than assert. Our understanding of church is therefore enriched by them rather than prescribed.

Yet Paul was writing to real communities of believers—not constructing abstract theory or giving generic advice. The images of the church that result are shaped by their real confusion, concern, and, frequently, painful conflict. It is, for example, to the Ephesians that he describes the relationship of Christ to his church in physical terms of the human body: "[he] has made him the head over all things for the church, which is his body, the fulness of him who fills all in all" (Ephesians 1:22-23). Christ is the head and the church is the body. This analogy is one that Paul used frequently and applied both to the church universal and invisible and to the church specific, local, and visible. By so describing it, he implied the head to be the source of intelligence, the derivation of laws, and the organizer of resources to enable the body of the church to understand, intend, and carry out his will. The church as the body is enlivened by the presence of Christ. The church as the body is to be obedient to the will of Christ. The church as the body is to benefit by the wise direction of the understanding of Christ.

Again, to the Ephesians, Paul said, "Husbands, love your wives, as Christ loved the church and gave himself up for her" (Ephesians 5:25). Here Paul takes the analogy of the body and adds to it the metaphor of a relationship. The result is an understanding of community that focuses on the highest and most ideal relationship illustrated by a happy and enduring marriage: a husband and wife whose intimate, tender, affectionate, supportive, and sacred responses to one another are mutually fulfilling.

Husbands and wives, limbs and torso, timbers and beams—these are the profound, tangible relationships that by analogy the New Testament describes the nature of the church. "If I am delayed," said Paul to Timothy, "you may know how one ought to behave in the household of God, . . . the pillar and bulwark of the truth" (1 Timothy 3:15). Built into the bulwark of a foundation, the pillars support the upper portion of the building. The earth, literally the foundation, holds the weight of the whole construction. Paul's logic seems to suggest that while the only foundation for the faith of the saints and the hope of souls is Christ, still, in a very important sense, the church is the bulwark of all Christian aspirations: witness and mission, education and spiritual development, evangelization and outreach. It was for these ends that the church was instituted, and it is in serving these purposes that the church is identified in its most complete and healthy form.

It is this "construction" model that Paul uses again and again to encourage the order that leads to strength in the church. Of himself and other apostles he said, "We are God's servants, working together; you are God's field, God's building. . . . Do you not know that you are God's temple and that God's Spirit dwells in you?" (1 Corinthians 3:9,16). Baptists believe that each redeemed life is Christ's temple. But even more so the community of the redeemed represents the temple. When Paul wrote to the Corinthian church—factionalized, friction-weary, and fatigued—he urged them to reclaim the vision of the temple and to understand anew their own role as one expression of it. They are a temple holy to God, he claims, and they dare not defile this sanctuary, which has been formed of their faith and their purpose.

The analogy of buildings and structures takes on its power when we step back but one pace to view it. The church is not just any building. It is not merely a dwelling. It is not primarily a place of commerce. It is a temple. As one among many human organizations, it would neither claim nor deserve a role different from any other human institution. But the abiding presence of the Spirit within it gives the church its importance and the reason for its existence. The strength of its timbers and beams is derived from a foundation in Christ that cannot be shaken.

Ultimately, however, analogies and metaphors about human bodies and physical construction were not sufficient to encompass the church's dynamic relationship to Christ. And to emphasize these aspects, Paul turned to a variety of human relationships.

We have already seen how marriage encouraged one such understanding. On other occasions, he used the image of the whole household. "So then, whenever we have an opportunity, let us work for the good to all, and especially for those of the family of faith," he said to the Galatians (6:10). Jesus' Palestine fostered large, extended familes. Middle Eastern custom was to be generous in extending hospitality even to strangers. But to members of the family, hospitality was not an act of choice but of obligation. And here Paul affirms that within the church there should be and is the relationship of brother and sister, father and mother, children, cousins, and in-laws—the extended family of Christ in faith. Mutual affection should rule, therefore, and members should care for each other's good, bear one another's burdens, and guide one another in pathways of Christian growth.

The only other point of identity equal to the bonds of family was the definition of one's citizenship. In a world dominated by Roman conquest, the citizenship one held might often determine not only mere privilege but life itself. In the world of the Bible, as in our own, being a stranger and a foreigner put one in a vulnerable position. Hospitality might be extended and received. But the barriers of unfamiliarity and suspicion could still exist. Against this distant relationship Paul says, "So then you are no longer strangers and aliens, but you are citizens with the saints and also members of the household of God" (Ephesians 2:19). It is a double metaphor. The church is compared to a nation, and those who are members of it are its citizens—a nation with no equal and a citizenship of unsurpassed privilege. And Christians are adopted into this nation as naturalized citizens where otherwise they were mere sojourners, visitors, or strangers without status. In a narrower sense, those within this nation are members of the household of God—members of God's family, enjoying an intimate and sacred relationship not only with God but with one another.

Ultimately not even the New Testament is able fully to define or to describe the church. It is of God, after all, and things of God are, in this life, beyond complete knowledge. For that reason, some of the most powerful scriptural images of the church are clothed in the greatest mystery. Like an organist at the keys of a great cathedral organ, searching for additional stops to add more tone, more color, and more sound to a great and climactic work, analogies and metaphors mix and magnify one another. In Revelation, for example, we see just such a commingling of images. It is the church triumphant, and yet the church in service; it is the church the great and beautiful bride of Christ, and still again, the church as evidence of the Holy City of God: "And I saw the holy city, the new Jerusalem, coming down out of heaven from God, prepared as a

bride adorned for her husband. . . . Then one of the seven angels
. . . said to me, 'Come, I will show you the bride, the wife of the
Lamb.' And in the spirit he carried me away to a great, high
mountain and showed me the holy city Jerusalem coming down out
of heaven from God" (Revelation 21:2,9,10).

What is the meaning of this vision? It is left for each person in
faith to wrestle with it. But with Hiscox we can conjecture that the
purity, beauty, and glory of the redeemed are implied in the bridal
relationship; that the affection of the Lamb, who is also the Bridegroom, is expressed in his joy at the reception of his bride, so
beautiful, for whom he had suffered so much and waited so long,
that he might "present the church to himself in splendor, without
spot or wrinkle or any such thing" (Ephesians 5:27); that the
glimpse of the city, populated by the glorified saints, may imply the
transcendent glory of the final habitation in which the church
triumphant shall be both creative and orderly, at once blissful and
dynamic, all under the joyous and loving reign of the Lord, the King
eternal, immortal, and invisible. We cannot know for sure. Visions
are not meant to have exact interpretations. They are intended to
inspire and to lift up the sights and the expectations of those who
see them.

So the scriptural teaching about the church can describe its
physical presence, its spiritual purpose and reality, the relationships
of those within it, and its role to those outside of it. But in the end,
the Scriptures most importantly call us to comprehend the church's
sacred fellowship as one of redemptive purpose which, by the
mercy of God, was sent to bring life to a lost world and to sustain
the life of faith in a faithless generation: the generation of the
apostles and our generation.

Historic Definitions of the Church

The generations that came after the era of the New Testament
experiences also made multiple contributions to the definition of
the church. There were many opportunities for shaping the institutional and structural character of the church because the New
Testament had not given the church a specific charter or form.
Likewise, the analogies and metaphors that Paul and the other

writers of the Epistles used to describe the church often lacked the theological precision some later Christians decided was necessary. Thus, the experiences of Christians—sometimes their common experience as they engaged with the world, and sometimes their personal experiences as they wrestled with one another—came to further define specific expressions of the church and the human perception of the church universal.

In the first several centuries of its life, the church was first shaped by its desire to grow and expand. Hardly had it begun, however, than it was equally shaped by persecution, first from the Jewish authorities of whom Paul (Saul) was an early example, and then more significantly from Rome. Then, just as much of the church was adapting to the reality of a hostile environment, it became the official religious structure of the Roman Empire in the age of Constantine. Rapidly, then, the church was redefined in terms appropriate to unite in purpose and to conform in structure with the most extensive empire the world has known.

The story of the development of the church in its many expressions is a dynamic and fascinating one. For Baptists who desire to understand both the ancient origins of the church and their own unique character in relation to it, whole libraries exist for exploration.

Of course, most Christians, ancient and modern, have tended ultimately to become dogmatic and to insist that their unique definition of the church is the true church. Most often the specific definition of theological truth and its effect on the church was expressed in a specific creed or confession. Hiscox astutely noted that as Christian people shape the truth of their faith, "all assume to start with the New Testament idea. But, as they proceed, they more and more diverge, and complicate the primitive simplicity with their ecclesiastical surroundings, their educational prepossessions, or with what trusted authority decides a church ought to be . . ." (p. 17).[1] The student of church history knows that Christian brothers and sisters have fought both figuratively and literally to prevail with their theology or ecclesiology. Indeed, the great historic creeds of the church (the Nicene Creed, Apostles' Creed, Athanasian Creed, and so on) are all examples of "compromises" or statements designed to end conflict or confusion between Christian factions. Ironically, these creeds or compromises have shaped the specific varieties of churches in very profound ways.

When Hiscox first wrote, he believed it would be helpful to identify some of the language that helped shape church forms and practices. He noted that the Latin and Greek churches phrased their definitions of the church in careful terms and cited several examples to demonstrate this practice:

> *The Latin Church:* "[The church is] the company of Christians knit together by the profession of the same faith, and the communion of the same sacraments, under the government of lawful pastors, and especially of the Roman bishop, as the only vicar of Christ on earth."—*Bellarmine De Eccl. Mil., III, 2*
>
> *The Greek Church:* "The church is a divinely instituted community of men united by the orthodox faith, the law of God, the hierarchy, and the sacraments." —*Full Catec. of the Orthodox Est. Church*

The words are carefully crafted. The Latin church stresses universality and the preeminence of the Roman bishop. The Greek or Byzantine church stresses orthodoxy of faith and a corporate hierarchy. A history of verbal debate and armed conflict attests to the certitude with which they were expressed.

Baptists trace their own specific origins to a later period, however, and derive from the great redefinitions of the church that the Reformation sponsored in general, and from the Calvinist theological formulations in particular. Hiscox, again, extracted the definitive descriptions of the church from the trail of creeds and confessions that preceded Baptist experience:

> *The Church of England:* "A congregation of faithful men, in which the pure Word of God is preached, and the sacraments duly administered according to Christ's ordinances, in all those things that of necessity are requisite to the same."—*Thirty-nine Articles, Art. XIX*
>
> *The Augsburg Confession:* "A congregation of saints, in which the gospel is purely preached, and the sacraments are rightly administered."—*Aug. Conf., Art. VII*
>
> *The Helvetic Confession:* "The church is a community of believers, or saints, gathered out of the world, whose

distinction is to know and to worship, through the Word
and by the Spirit, the true God in Christ the Savior."
—*Helv. Conf., Art. XVII*

The Belgic Confession: "A true congregation or assembly of all faithful Christians, who look for their salvation
only from Jesus Christ, as being washed by his blood
and sanctified by his Spirit."—*Belg. Conf., Art. XXVII*

The Saxon Confession: "A congregation of men embracing the gospel of Christ, and rightly using the sacraments."—*The Saxon Conf., Art. XII*

The Scottish Confession: "The church is a society of
the elect of all ages and countries both Jews and Gentiles; this is the catholic, or universal church. This
church is invisible, and known only to God."—*Scot.
Conf., Art. XVI*

The Westminster Assembly gave this definition amidst
the great religious turmoil in seventeenth-century England: "Particular churches in the primitive times were
made up of visible saints, viz., of such as being of age,
professing faith in Christ, according to the rules of faith
and life taught by Christ and his apostles, and of their
children."—*Wst. Assem. Directory*

Placed in this order, each of these statements brings us a step
closer conceptually to the understanding of the church that the
Baptist movement eventually articulated. The strong individualism
that characterizes Baptists—what some of the early among our
Baptist forebears called "soul liberty"—has prevented Baptists
from being creedal people. At most, Baptists participate in creedal
and confessional statements as an exercise in education or in a
provisional way. Still, even movements of spiritual individualists
have their charters. And Baptists have produced some definitive
historical documents that have guided them in their formation of
churches and spiritual relationships.

Among the earliest was the *London Confession of Faith*,
which was issued by seven Baptist churches in London in 1644.
It was a document in response to charges and accusations made
toward them by their opponents and detractors. This was the
volatile period in which the English Civil War placed a high
premium on precise definitions of ideology and position. This

confession therefore defines the church in this way:

> Christ hath here on earth a spiritual kingdom which is the church, which he hath purchased and redeemed to himself, as a peculiar inheritance: which church . . . is a company of visible saints, called and separated from the world by the Word and Spirit of God, to the visible profession of the faith of the gospel; being baptized into that faith, and joined to the Lord, and each other, by mutual agreement, in the practical enjoyment of the ordinances commanded by Christ their head and king.—*Art. XXXIII* (adapted from William L. Lumpkin, ed., *Baptist Confessions of Faith* [Valley Forge, Pa.: Judson Press, 1959], 165).

A generation later, Baptists in England benefited from the restoration of stability in civil life. Therefore, in 1677, a statement entitled the *Second London Confession* was adopted by the assembled representatives of a number of Baptist congregations meeting in London. It was most likely based on the 1644 London Confession. In 1689 England began a great period of Protestant good feelings under the newly established king and queen, William and Mary. That same year, ministers and delegates representing over one hundred "baptized churches" met in the General Assembly and adopted a statement that was a revised version of the 1677 document. It stated this of the church:

> The Lord Jesus Christ calleth out of the world unto himself, through the ministry of his word, by his Spirit, those that are given unto him by his Father, that they may walk before him in all the ways of obedience, which he prescribeth to them in his Word. Those thus called he commandeth to walk together in particular societies, or churches, for their mutual edification; and the due performance of that public worship which he requireth of them in the world. The members of these churches are saints by calling, visibly manifesting and evidencing . . . their obedience unto that call of Christ; and do willingly consent to walk together according to the appointment of Christ, giving up themselves, to the Lord and one another by the will of God, in professed subjection to the ordinances of the gospel.—*Chap. XXVI, secs. 5,6 (Lumpkin, 286).*

This confession served for over a century as the most frequently used assertion of the fundamentals of Baptist belief and practice.

While Baptists at worship did not frequently "recite" aspects of the confession as a ritual, it was often the basis for determining fellowship between members, churches, and groups of churches. It also was frequently a point of reference for Baptist bodies desiring to construct their own statements. For example, in 1742 the Philadelphia Association adopted this same confession, with some revisions. In the United States it therefore became known as the *Philadelphia Confession.*

Then, in 1833, Baptists in the United States adopted a statement entitled the *New Hampshire Confession.* Its general assertions, and especially those concerning the church, have stood as the classic statement of Baptist perspective on the shape and structure of the church for over 150 years. It speaks of the church in concise terms:

> A visible church of Christ is a congregation of baptized believers, associated by covenant in the faith and fellowship of the gospel; observing the ordinances of Christ, governed by his laws, and exercising the gifts, rights, and privileges invested in them by his word.—*Art. xiii (Lumpkin, 365).*

The New Hampshire Confession contributed concepts and phrases about the church that have appeared in countless Baptist church constitutions, covenants, and statements. It has not been a static document, however; it has been much revised by organizations and individuals, including Hiscox. (The citation above is from the 1833 text. Hiscox's version of the entire New Hampshire Confession is included as appendix B.) Nor was the New Hampshire Confession the last attempt by Baptists of many groupings, organizations, and identities to set forth a statement of belief and church organization. Still, even now in the late twentieth century, as Baptist life and organization experience profound changes and shifts, the New Hampshire Confession remains a foundational document to which a great many Baptists return in letter or in spirit to find common ground.

The Authority of Churches

All communities and corporations must find the appropriate balance of authority, responsibility, and individual freedom. Ideally, all associations should possess as much authority as needed to carry out their responsibilities or their purposes and to lead and direct their members within the limits of their constitutional relationships. Authority is also needed to allow organizations to provide for the continuing health of the body and to enable it to respond to such demands as the law or the larger community might require of it. Authority in general, therefore, is divided into *external* authority, which is granted or imposed by the civil order, and *internal* authority, which is defined, granted, and consented by the participants in that community.

But churches have an additional challenge: to balance the authority of human associations with the unique and specific authority that, by faith, they believe is founded in God. Churches must have the right to exercise and the power to enforce the authority that is derived from constitutions and laws. It is, of course, to the benefit of peace, order, and effectiveness that the provisions of such authority should be clear and exercised faithfully and consistently. They must have the humility to respect and to forbear the power that is God's alone to exercise. This power may be clarified only through study, reflection, and prayer.

Historically, churches have derived their spiritual authority from three primary sources: the Scriptures, traditions (history), and hierarchies. Some churches in some places have at times also derived their authority, even in matters of faith and mission, from the state. Responding to Jesus' challenge to make a clear distinction between that which is Caesar's and that which is God's has been the defining tension for much of the history of the whole church and for many individual churches and Christians.

Baptist churches have claimed to derive their authority in matters of faith from personal experience, believing that faith begins first in the heart; from the Scriptures, believing them to be the revealed Word of God; and from Christ, believing him to be the head of the church. This authority cannot be granted by legislatures, courts of civil or criminal jurisdiction, or powerful men or women of government, wealth, or lineage. Baptists further believe that this power cannot be granted or annulled from any ecclesiastical source either. Baptists believe, in short, that the authority that comes of faith begins in the individual, is made evident in the community of the church, and extends to whatever larger extension of ecclesiastical structure they might create only by consent.

Thus, in the ordering of their internal affairs, Baptists derive their authority from a voluntary compact or covenant among believers and participants who consent to it. In such a voluntary association, each individual surrenders to the larger body a part of his or her personal freedom of action in the belief that the greater good of both the individual and the whole fellowship will result. In Baptist churches such voluntary compacts are entered into by individuals who believe that the authority of the church is created by wisdom in dealing with matters of community concern and by the presence of the Spirit among them.

This internal authority is, therefore, always to be grounded in constitutional provisions that reflect the will of Christ and the presence of the Holy Spirit as they have experienced it. Such authority can only be exercised on its own members. A church brings the moral force of persuasion, of consistent behavior, and of the witness of Christian character to bear on all who will receive it. Nevertheless, with regard to exercising authority over individuals, it cannot interfere with any except those who are in willing fellowship. As Paul said to the Corinthian church, "For what have I to do with judging outsiders? Is it not those inside the church whom you are to judge?" (1 Corinthians 5:12).

Baptists have also historically believed that a church can only exercise spiritual authority over its own members. With regard to the personal rights and responsibilities of church members as members of society, it can only exhort and give guidance, never interfere. It cannot dictate what they shall eat or drink or wear; it cannot determine what business they engage in or what profession they practice, what associations and connections they shall enjoy, or what privileges they might exercise—except, of course, that in all these things they may ask of members to do nothing inconsistent with their profession of faith as Christians and nothing that will damage the credibility and witness of the gospel of Christ.

In urging one another to use their influence for good, or to refrain from tempting others to do evil or condone evil, or in defining those things that may bring reproach upon the name and purpose of Christ, Christians often confront differences of belief and commitment. The encounters Christians experience in resolving such differences may often be places of personal and community growth for churches. They are also often times of controversy and division. Limiting the church's authority to moral and spiritual concerns is an inefficient method of running an organization. On the other hand, Baptists believe it is the only way that true spiritual authority can be exercised.

The understanding that a church cannot dominate the faith or conscience of its members is a demonstration of humility in the face of God's authority. Baptists, for whom the notion of "soul liberty" is a foundation stone, must grant ultimate liberty to one another— and the ultimate judgment to God alone. Nevertheless, churches may agree on basic tenets of behavior and expression that are binding upon all who consent to them. Should the definition of tenets change on the part of either the majority or the individual, those in disagreement are free to reject any expression of authority in implementing them or, in extreme cases, are free to break the bonds of covenant in the fellowship and to seek fellowship in another church.

Just as a church is limited in its assertion of authority over its members, churches may not exercise discipline upon another, or for another, or interfere in any way with actions of other churches. Baptists have always held relations of fellowship and courtesy with one another and between churches. Some Baptist churches join together for the common support of missions and other programs with the common purpose of extending the gospel. Churches dismiss members from one to another and receive members from other Baptist congregations into their fellowship. Ministers and professional church leaders serve from one church to another, with a common recognition of credentials and character. Churches may enjoy fellowship in great variety. Baptist churches may respect the assertion of authority in other churches or in the denominations or fellowships with which they are affiliated, but they are not bound by them.

Church and State

For Baptists, the issue of the source and role of authority is specifically clarified in their historic view of the relationship between the church and the civil order. The medieval world and many historic churches had assumed a unity of political and spiritual or ecclesiastical power. Baptists, however, have from their earliest moments asserted that political authority and spiritual authority are separate and distinct and that each disrupts and ultimately destroys the other if that distinction is not kept. Therefore, Baptists developed and maintained the principle of strict separation of church and state.

This principle rests on foundations of experience, biblical interpretation, and the articulation of a clear philosophy that has guided Baptists in their review of contact between church and state. It is a story too lengthy and too significant to fully encompass here. Nevertheless, every Baptist should understand its significance.

The early experience of Baptist people shaped early Baptist thinking on this subject. Baptists are derived from many sources. In the United States they have come from Europe and England, from Asia and Africa, from South and Central America. Through mission efforts, Baptists are found in every corner of the world. A common bond between Baptists has been their familiarity with disadvantage and oppression. Whether as English Baptists fleeing the political power of Stuart kings, Africans who came to the early colonies in chains and found solace and liberation in Christ, Swedes trying to be free from the king's desire for conquest and conscripted armies to accomplish it, or central Europeans hungering for the freedom to worship beyond the capricious whims of local princes, Baptists have often been victims of state power.

As reformers, Baptists also frequently incurred the wrath of established church leaders. Those leaders, supported by structures of taxation, law, and enforcement, often persecuted Baptists for their opinions, sermons, and activities. In the early American colonies, established churches were supported by taxes, and the right to vote was frequently tied to church membership. Baptists, therefore, often paid the expensive price of political and spiritual disenfranchisement as well as the loss of tax benefit simply by being Baptists. Moreover, they were often persecuted if they did not pay the required tax. Baptist leaders among the colonial people—such as the iconoclastic preacher Roger Williams in Massachusetts and Rhode Island, the patient but persistent pastor Isaac Backus in his leadership throughout New England, John Leland in Virginia, and many others—made a strong witness against such treatment in order to win the right to worship and to organize churches as they believed God had directed them. They spent their entire lives working for change and for the freedom to be Baptists. Ultimately, their courage and statesmanship influenced the shaping of the Constitution of the United States and especially its First Amendment.[2]

The historic experience of Baptists, therefore, has shaped a strong commitment to preserving the freedoms so carefully won both in America and in other lands. And the struggle to achieve this freedom has sensitized many Baptists to desire to protect the same freedom for others, regardless of how different in belief and practice others might be. But in addition to experience, Baptists are people of biblical faith and cherish an ability to apply biblical principles to contemporary human affairs. The biblical interpretation and philosophical position among Baptists may be summarized:

> The Christian church was instituted by Christ who charged it with its mission, imbued it with its vision, and empowered it by the presence of the Spirit. It is Christ who continues as its head. Baptists believe that each local church constitutes a body politic in a spiritual realm, and that the local church is one small but specific manifestation of the body politic in the kingdom of God. The church is therefore in the world but not of it; it is required to maintain its existence, discharge its functions, and continue its witness in all conditions of life, social and civil, and to proclaim the gospel under all forms of human government.

At the same time, members of the church are citizens living everywhere under some form of civil government. In some places and times this citizenship brings them rights, privileges, and immunities. In other places and times such citizenship brings them obligations, difficulty, and distress. As a matter of reality, citizenship requires allegiance to the nation or government under which they live. But there is one exception: no civil allegiance may interfere with their obedience to the will of God and the claims of Christ. And if human laws and the demands of human governments are in opposition to this claim from a greater authority, if they interfere in any way with rights of conscience or religious faith, with the freedom of belief and worship, then God is to be obeyed and not the civil order.

Baptists believe that spiritual truth is propositional and empowered only by faith, not impositional and empowered by human law. Therefore, Baptists respect the beliefs and obligations of others who approach God in a different way and by a different belief, regardless of how erroneous they might believe them to be. Baptists are frequently subject to misinterpretation because they may jump to the defense of some unlikely gatherings of people, not because they agree with their theology or faith but because they sympathize with their right to believe as they have been led. In fact, Baptists have often been tightly allied with groups with whom they profoundly disagree in all other matters except their right to express their belief. In this way, Baptists attempt to be faithful to Jesus' own admonition to "render to Caesar the things that are Caesar's, and to God the things that are God's" (Mark 12:17).

Baptists avoid irresponsible and extreme libertarian behavior, believing that Christians should be productive and law-abiding citizens. In short, Baptists believe that government and religion should both be left free to do what each does best: "Be subject for the Lord's sake to every human institution, whether it be to the emperor as supreme, or to governors as sent by him to punish those who do wrong and to praise those who do right. For it is God's will that by doing right you should put to silence the ignorance of foolish men" (1 Peter 2:13-15). Yet, for Baptists, human citizenship is always defined in comparison to the standards of citizenship in Christ's kingdom. By the grace of Christ, we are free and called to live in the love of Christ. "Live as free men, yet without using your freedom as a pretext for evil; but live as servants of God" (1 Peter 2:16).

The principle of separation of church and state has never been easy. In some ages and times Baptists have suffered greatly at the hands of others who have sought to coerce them. In other ages, in their zeal to do right and to set the example for others, Baptists have sought to impose the will of their view of morality and their vision of God's kingdom on others. Yet despite its difficulty, this principle is one of the greatest gifts Baptists have to offer in faith and discipleship. It is a particularly valuable doctrine amidst the great diversity and pluralism of the late twentieth century. By preserving Baptist freedom in the Spirit, we preserve it for others; by demanding that others be granted this freedom, Baptists preserve it for themselves.[3]

The Church in the World

In previous times, a church might be the only community in which a church member shared his or her time, resources, or commitments. Offering a witness in the world was, under those conditions, primarily a matter of the church and its members speaking on behalf of their belief and their implications for the world around them. In the contemporary world, church members are often affiliated with other organizations and may share in the fellowship of communities other than the church. The successful pursuit of business, professions, and occupations virtually require such connections. Also, the desire to increase knowledge and skill or to enjoy recreation will normally bring church members into contact with many others. Such relationships may bring great satisfaction to the persons involved and may, in fact, offer an opportunity for the presence of the church and its message to be expanded. And frequently these contacts allow for the church to ally its resources with those of other individuals and organizations for community betterment, social justice, more effective communication and understanding between citizens of a civil community, and more. When the church (or its individual members) develops such relationships, it has an opportunity to witness in the world.

Nevertheless, the church as a community and its members as persons need always to remember that no other organization is inspired by such high ideals, and no other community is yoked in service to Christ. Therefore, fellowship in such other associations should always be consistent with the purposes of Christian commitment, or at the very least, not in conflict with them.

The churches, and the Christians who represent them, are called to service in the world for the purpose of bringing Christ's word of redemption and the witness of its mission. To remain faithful is often difficult. Churches are influenced by the structures of the world's institutions, exhibit the coloration of the world's fads, and reflect the world's habits. It is therefore always important that the church avoid feeling at peace with the world but instead remember that its purpose is to call forth a regenerated humanity, in order to populate the "assembly of the first-born who are enrolled in heaven" and to bring them before "a judge who is God of all" and into the presence of "the spirits of just men made perfect" (Hebrews 12:23).

Jesus came to redeem humankind and in doing so founded the church. He knew what was in human beings. He understood the world he came to save. He moved comfortably in the world and showed compassion for its inhabitants. But he never confused his purposes with the ambitions of the world, and in the end, the world rejected him.

The church must be faithful to its Lord and live toward the same purpose and the same end. That means quite simply that every effort at social justice and virtue, every goal of moral and ethical purity, should be seen at its highest and best in the church of God. Those who are expressly called out to be the "light of the world" and the "salt of the earth" should not fall below the standard of goodness in the secular world. God's people, who have been given spiritual resources, should use them to focus the higher vision of God's kingdom and give witness to that vision by being an example of it as a church in their own community.

Starting a New Church

Jesus founded the church universal. Specific churches have all been founded in his name by believers seeking to expand the universal church in response to the Great Commission and in the desire to build up the body of which Christ is the head. Baptist churches are constituted by a voluntary covenant on the part of those who wish to become its members and are willing to undertake its support and encourage its development.

Baptist churches are autonomous and independent. Therefore, they represent a variety of styles of governance and are variously constituted. The New Testament is the only necessary constitution of a church with regard to faith and practice. It is a general practice, however, for churches to develop constitutions and bylaws. This practice has developed in order to conduct business in an orderly fashion—and often in order to satisfy legal requirements of state or regional governments with regard to incorporation as a legal entity. In starting a new church, those responsible should always take care to interpret the New Testament principles in official documents and to formulate them in response to specific needs of the church. Those who constitute the church, as well as those who later join the church, should be made familiar with these documents and their provisions and should be in general agreement with them. As a general rule, church constitutions, once established, should be reviewed, revised, and amended as often as needed, and constitutions and/or bylaws should be thoroughly revised or rewritten about every ten years. This practice will encourage the church to remember and redefine its purpose as a part of the body of Christ and will also encourage it to maintain principles of operation consistent with current opportunities for ministry.

New churches are constituted for a variety reasons: in response to need in a new community, to minister to increased population in an established community, or where no suitable church may be found. A new church may be the result of an individual church's desire to extend the work of Christ, or it may be the work of an association of churches. It may be in response to the need for a ministry to meet the unique needs of recent immigrant populations or communities whose primary language is different from the majority. Sometimes a new church emerges from a division of opinion about doctrine or mission in a previous church. In the latter case, those proposing a new church must exercise deep, prayerful discipline to discern whether a new church is truly of Christ or whether it is instead a symptom of human failing and sin. Whatever its impetus, a church should always be the result of the presence of the Spirit prompting and guiding a gathering of believers to build a community in Jesus' name. Those contemplating the establishment of a church should approach their purpose with prayer, with due consideration of both the spiritual and practical resources necessary for the task, and in consultation and counsel with other churches or church leaders of similar belief and commitment.

Churches may fail for many reasons. But new churches shall surely fail if they are not born of the Spirit and if they do not "count the cost."

Once having determined to establish a church, the process by which new churches are constituted is straightforward. Churches belonging to an association or denomination may find helpful advice from denominational offices or fellow pastors. For purposes of legal definition, taxation, and other considerations of the civil community in which the church will be located, it is imperative also to consult the laws regarding the incorporation of religious or nonprofit organizations. Most churches will conserve resources and hasten their work by consulting reliable legal counsel in these matters. With such assistance, new church establishment should follow a steady course.

First, those desiring to establish the church should meet regularly for worship, reflection, and prayer prior to constituting the church. Again and again they should test their purpose, seek counsel, and seek the guidance of the Spirit.

Second, having made final commitment to their task, leaders should establish a responsible committee to develop official documents, such as constitutions, covenants, or articles of procedure. Persons designated for this task may find several of the works cited in Appendix G, "For Further Study," especially helpful. The book *A Baptist Manual of Polity and Practice* by Norman H. Maring and Winthrop S. Hudson (Valley Forge, Pa: Judson Press, 1962) may help in forming new Baptist church structures. In addition, a wide variety of literature published by other denominations and by commercial publishers may be of help in defining church programs, processes, and procedures.) If the church desires to define articles of faith, whether a historic statement or one of their own composing, this is the proper time to develop it.

Third, those members who will be joining by letter of transfer from another church should arrange for their letters to be sent for the purpose of constituting the new church. Otherwise, there should be a predetermined procedure for receiving those not transferring by letter but by means of baptism, Christian experience, or other means of statement. If the constituting members establish the new church as chartering members, they should send for letters of transfer from previous churches or inform a previous church of the action taken.

Fourth, an official constituting meeting should be announced and publicized. This meeting should be first a worship experience with prayer, Scripture, and praise preceding the business. During the business session, a temporary presiding officer should be elected until duly elected, constitutional officers may assume their duties. The constituting act should be properly executed by a vote or other means of unanimous consent. A model for a statement of consent might be:

> Resolved, that, guided as we believe by the Holy Spirit, and relying on the blessing of God, we do here and now by this act constitute ourselves a church of Jesus Christ to perform his service and to be governed by his will, as revealed in the New Testament.

Following this action, other documents as previously developed (constitution, bylaws, covenants, articles of faith) should be considered and approved. In all of these actions, the greatest strength of fellowship and commitment will result if sufficient time for discussion is allowed. When consensus has been achieved, then the permanent officers of the church, as described in the constitution, should be elected. If a pastor has not already been selected and voted as part of the act of constitution, a committee should be delegated to recommend pastoral leadership. This meeting should then conclude with a hymn and prayer for the further guidance, support, and blessing of the new church.

Fifth, the leadership of the new church should exercise extreme diligence in carrying out the provisions and procedures of the constitution and bylaws in order to establish good habits of operation. Likewise, they should prayerfully communicate their actions to the congregation and also seek the prayer and communication of the congregational members.

Sixth, Baptist churches that desire to affiliate with a denominational structure or an association should petition the denomination or association for recognition and acceptance into membership, if such identity has not previously been determined by the act of constitution. The association or denomination will have its own procedures to follow in responding to such a petition. Most often it will include an examination of the church's doctrines, an inquiry into the reasons and circumstances for its organization, a review of the church's status of incorporation and tax status, a familiarization of the new church with the procedures and practices of the denomination or association, and, ultimately, a vote by the official body of the association with a subsequent ritual for welcoming and rejoicing in the fellowship of the new church.

Seventh, in the early months and years of its life as a church, a new church should diligently establish its goals, programs, and procedures with a strong sense of the mind and presence of Christ, and likewise should establish effective processes of review. This is good practice for any church. But in the first years, a new church will be establishing practices that will become either the traditions that lead to success or the bad habits that lead to failure.

In every activity involved in starting a new church, reverence, awe, and praise should be at the center. Starting a new church, like attending a human birth, is powerful evidence of God's continuing creation and Christ's empowering presence.

Disbanding a Church

It is the church universal and the gospel the church embodies that is eternal, not a specific church itself. It is therefore sometimes necessary to abandon a church organization. It is helpful to remember that the records of faithful churches of the past—from the New Testament days until now—have lived on to inspire and challenge long after the particular churches themselves have ceased to exist. Nevertheless, disbanding a church is a matter that should be approached with the utmost care, reverence, and regard for what it has accomplished and what it means to the many whose lives it has touched. And great care should also be exercised in the stewardship of its remaining assets and resources, including its members. Hiscox said, "It is always a matter of serious concern thus to remove the candlestick out of its place, and such a course should be determined on only after long consideration, much prayer, and consultation with wise and unbiased brethren" (p. 32).

There are often alternatives to disbanding a church. For example, a church may need to close temporarily. This is sometimes effective when a church has been badly fractured because of division and dissension that has left the body dysfunctional and unable to progress. It is also occasionally effective with churches where long-standing traditions have ceased to be meaningful to the community in which the church seeks to serve, and when those who revere the traditions are too few to continue. A "new start" after a period of closure may enable a new congregation and new leadership to revitalize an old institution.

Another alternative may be a merger with another church. This is particularly effective where population changes and other circumstances have made two or more churches redundant and individually unable to be properly supported. A new and merged congregation may be able to carry on the traditions and purposes of its predecessors with new vision and vitality. Sometimes, where issues of doctrine do not prohibit and where the cordiality of fellowship will allow it, a merger or "federation" of churches of different denominational traditions may also be possible.

Nevertheless, there are times when complete disbanding is the only responsible alternative. The decision to undertake such a serious step may be recommended by leaders of the church or even by denominational representatives or respected colleagues in faith in other churches. For a Baptist church, the only responsible body to make the decision, however, is the congregation itself—after prayer, reflection, and contemplation. Whenever possible, even a majority of the membership should proceed cautiously if a minority desires to continue. What has been created and has lived in sacred trust should not be abandoned callously.

If disbanding is ultimately chosen, several simple guidelines may be helpful.

First, each member has a right to be assisted by time and encouragement to join another church. The moral, social, spiritual, and other values of church membership should not be neglected. Therefore, letters of transfer should be executed prior to the disbanding so that no member will be deprived of fellowship. In addition, a neighboring church should be selected for the transfer of the records of membership for persons unable to be contacted or those who have failed to choose a new congregation.

Second, matters of property should also be considered. This applies not only to buildings and furnishings but also especially to memorial gifts of tangible character (such as windows, organs, furnishings, and materials) and money given or bequested for particular purposes. Disposal, transfer, and redirection should be defined carefully to preserve both personal feelings and the principles by which such things were originally received. Local, state, and even federal laws will need to be considered, and the counsel of an attorney will undoubtedly be helpful to assure that assets continue to be used according to the spirit of their original purpose.

Third, if an old church is to be disbanded but some of the same members shall be part of constituting a new church in the same location, especially in the same building, careful determination must be made with regard to whether the new congregation may claim the history, traditions, and property of the disbanded church.

Fourth, provision for church records should be made with the historical society of the association or denomination with which the church has been affiliated. Barring such a possibility, another church might be designated as the repository of records, or, alternatively, the library of a college, university, or research library with appreciation for the church's history might be selected.[4]

Finally, when all matters of membership, property, and obligation have been attended, a service of disbandment should be announced. This service should celebrate the memories and achievements of the church, give thanks for God's many blessings bestowed during the life of the church, provide ample expression of sorrow and grief at the passing of this specific expression of the church, and seek God's guidance and blessing for the members who must now move on to a new church and a new fellowship.

As a part of the service, a business session should be called. (No official act of the church may have standing after it has been disbanded.) After verifying that all considerations of membership, property, and obligation have been concluded, then a resolution, preceded by any preface of remembrance deemed appropriate, should be offered: "That we do here and now, by this act, disband as a church, and cease to exist as a corporate and covenant organization." Following a vote on this resolution, which should be duly recorded as the final official act of the clerk of the church, a benediction should be spoken, and a concluding hymn, such as "Blest Be the Tie That Binds," might be sung.

Specific churches have life cycles, and therefore birth, death, and the stages in between should be celebrated and lived as blessings from God. A church being born is a joyous sight, while a church dying is an occasion for sadness. Yet the church universal was born of the Spirit through the saving acts of Jesus Christ. Of that church there shall be no end, except in the consummation when Christ and his whole church in heaven and on earth shall be joined with him for eternity.

NOTES

1. Page numbers in parentheses here and throughout this book refer to material quoted directly or referred to from Edward T. Hiscox, *The Hiscox Guide for Baptist Churches* (Valley Forge, Pa.: Judson Press, 1964).

2. The story of the early Baptists' struggle against state-connected religious structures is dramatic and interesting and has attracted the attention of many scholars, Baptist and otherwise. Suggestions for further reading are included in the bibliographical resources in appendix F.

3. Today Baptists of several denominations join together in support of the Baptist Joint Committee on Public Affairs (200 Maryland Ave., NE, Washington, D.C. 20002). While the work of the Baptist Joint Committee encompasses additional issues, its primary task is to review legislation and judicial process from the perspective of the separation of church and state and to protect the spiritual rights of individuals. They are frequently recognized as leading experts on issues related to the First Amendment. Many Baptist groups are also participants in another organization, Americans United for Separation of Church and State (1816 Jefferson Place, N.W., Washington D.C. 20036). This organization is a coalition of Baptists and other religious groups, in addition to several nonreligious organizations, devoted to the preservation of First Amendment rights.

4. An alternative is to consult with the historical society or agency of the church's denomination or association. One example is the American Baptist Historical Society with administrative offices in Valley Forge, Pennsylvania. Another is the Southern Baptist Historical Commission in Nashville, Tennessee. Other Baptist denominations have similar organizations that may assist a church in determining the appropriate location for its minutes and historical papers.

Chapter II

The Membership of the Church

The church universal is built on spiritual foundations, and its Head is Christ. The standards for inclusion in that body are determined by Christ alone, and membership is exclusively by his grace. A particular church gives evidence of the universal church and points to its presence. But a specific church is bounded by human definition. Membership in it, therefore, is established by human understanding as it interprets the mind of Christ and the evidence of the Scriptures.

We have established that a church is a voluntary society. The relationship between its members and between individual members and Christ is described, therefore, as a voluntary covenant. It is central to Baptist belief that no external force or authority should or can compel covenants of membership either to be formed or dissolved. Equally, the church should not and cannot compel one to unite with it, and an individual cannot compel the body to receive him or her into fellowship.

But the concerns of church membership are more extensive than that. For a believer, there is no obligation or compulsion to belong to a particular church. There is, however, a spiritual obligation to belong to *some* church. It is spiritually good to belong. For a believer not to belong to a church is to sacrifice one channel of grace. For the church to be deprived of the presence of even one believer results in a weakened church and a weakened witness: the truth of the gospel is less likely to be communicated, and the light of Christ's presence is less likely to be shared. This is a particularly important issue in every generation, and particularly so now when many persons who profess faith do not confess an obligation or do not profess a desire to be in spiritual fellowship with others in a church community.

Conversely, one should not seek membership in a church for other motives than that of the fellowship and witness of Christ. This is a particularly important consideration in a time in which church membership seems often to be for institutional or social connections. Church membership primarily for social purposes, or for the advancement of a profession, community standing, or a cause other than the gospel profanes the church. Just as the church is weakened by the absence of believers who choose not to belong, it is weakened by those who belong for the wrong reasons.

Membership is a matter of both spiritual freedom and discipline. A person of faith is free to choose the fellowship with which to unite and is urged to exercise that freedom in order to be spiritually renewed, directed, and strengthened. But equally, a believer is obliged to unite with others in the yoke of Christian fellowship and service. It is, therefore, a matter of gravity, not to be entered into lightly, but with prayer, reverence, and the companionship of the Spirit. The conditions, modes, and practices of membership deserve to be carefully considered and understood.

Conditions of Membership

Membership in the universal church is by the grace of Christ. But particular churches generally desire visible requirements for membership and frequently establish constitutional provisions to define them. In fact, they may be required to do so to satisfy laws and conventional understandings regarding institutional obligations. We live in a transient culture, with the result that many persons are slow to make lasting commitments. Membership should encourage commitment to community. We live in a mobile culture where individuals occasionally belong to more than one church, choosing to maintain a full membership in one community and a temporary or transient one in one or more others. Membership should therefore encourage a definition of the nature of commitment being made. Churches, therefore, frequently establish categories of membership that impose certain conditions regarding qualifications of residency, activity, commitment, or service.

The kinds and conditions of such qualifications may vary from church to church. And they may reflect theological and social variations from one region to another and also the degree of tolerance for diversity within specific congregations. In considering such qualifications and standards, churches should strive to be consistent with the Scriptures and with the spirit of the gospel. When he approached this subject, Hiscox asserted that there were four qualifications for participation in the spiritual fellowship, for membership in the universal church of Christ. His categories require little translation over time. He noted these qualifications to be: (1) a regenerate heart, (2) a confession of faith, (3) the reception of baptism, and (4) a Christian life (p. 36).

A Regenerate Heart

If a church is to be distinguished from other gatherings and associations of men and women, there must be a quality that distinguishes its members. It first must have a regenerate membership—a fellowship of persons who have been spiritually transformed and who perceive their transformation as being of Christ and for Christ's purposes. "Truly, truly, I say to you," said Jesus to Nicodemus, "unless one is born anew, he cannot see the kingdom of God" (John 3:3). In many churches this first condition has been forgotten or neglected. The result is that such churches are greatly weakened by members whose motivation is uncertain. A church must insist on a regenerate spirit.

Some suggest that the only requirements for church membership are a good moral character, a reputation of worthiness, or, even, a good intention. Worthiness and good character are valuable qualities; God uses worthy and good men and women. But an apparent good moral character may have shallow roots: it may spring from a child's desire to please parents, a desire to receive community approval, or a discipline that has trained one to do right and avoid wrong as reflexive behavior. But one who desires to be a part of the company of the faithful should be rooted in Christ—of Christ, for Christ, and with Christ. Christian character and moral worthiness within a church can flow from no other source.

The New Testament insists on this point. Both Jesus and his

apostles were clear that Christ's kingdom was not of this world and that those who belonged to it were such as are born of the Spirit. The earliest Christians, those of Jewish origin and those of Gentile origins, were "called out" from the broader company of people. They were not necessarily superior in moral understanding, nor were they always of unblemished past records. Indeed, it was often quite the contrary, as the personal history of no less than the apostle Paul demonstrates. *But they were transformed.* They were individuals who confessed faith in Christ and who could communicate by their confession how an encounter with Christ had changed them. When the church was empowered at Pentecost (Acts 2:1-47), the church did not grow in size and strength by gathering in all who were dazzled by the day's events or who were in human sympathy with a cause. Instead, it was the "saved"—the transformed—who brought vitality to the church. It was the same in Samaria and in Antioch, at Ephesus and Corinth and Philippi—everywhere the church grew.

For this reason the New Testament often referred to such persons as "saints." Such references do not highlight the unusual goodness of particular persons but instead point to the whole company of those whose lives had been changed in response to Christ. For example, the church at Rome was addressed "to all God's beloved in Rome, who are called to be saints" (Romans 1:7). In the same letter, Paul defined the nature of those who had been transformed. In their former condition they were "slaves of sin," but now, they were "set free from sin and have become slaves of God" with the result that the return was to be "sanctification and its end, eternal life" (Romans 6:20,22). Even to the members of the cantankerous, conflicted, and confused church at Corinth he wrote: "To those sanctified in Christ Jesus, called to be saints together with all those who in every place call on the name of our Lord Jesus Christ . . ." (1 Corinthians 1:2).

Peter, who like Paul was living evidence of the power of regeneration, gave us that wonderful description and affirmation of the transformed life: "Be yourselves built into a spiritual house, to be a holy priesthood. . . . You are a chosen race, a royal priesthood, a holy nation, God's own people, that you may declare the wonderful deeds of him who called you out of darkness into his marvelous light" (1 Peter 2:5,9).

Churches may be tempted to establish many standards for membership. But no standard should neglect to remember that the church is for God's purposes, and that its members are to proclaim and effect those purposes, and to that end, God empowers and transforms the true members of his church by the grace of Christ. Those who are identified in the spiritual community of Christ—who make up the churches of Christ—are those who have experienced a call to come out of darkness into light, to abandon evil for good, and to give up allegiance to all but God's purposes.

A Confession of Faith

In Romans 10:10 Paul asserted that "man believes with his heart and so is justified, and he confesses with his lips and so is saved." The modern language of psychology affirms the principle of which Paul wrote when it speaks of the need for personalities to be "integrated"—that is, for persons to be consistent in who they are, rather than to believe one thing and do another, or to assert one set of standards and yet live by another.

For a Christian, the ability to confess one's faith is critical: it is the means by which we communicate to others what has taken place within.

Confession of faith is relevant for church membership in two ways. First, it reinforces the individual in his or her need to be consistent, to be integrated in private faith and public expression. Second, it enables fellow Christians—other church members—both to be able to be confident in one another, to know that all have experienced the same transformation, and to be strengthened by the knowledge that all are working together for the same Lord and the same purpose.

Churches can devalue a confession of faith as a part of membership by making of it a ritual or by neglecting it altogether. Sometimes this is because they do not wish to take the time for it or because they do not wish to "embarrass" a candidate for membership or because the congregation does not wish to participate in it. A failure to encourage a confession of faith in some personal, meaningful way weakens the bond of fellowship in Christ. That bond is built in common experience—all the more important in an age of diversity and uncertain community. By sharing in the verbal articulation of one's transforming experiences, the Christian community is bound together in common hope, common experience, and in the common center of their new life. By participating in such an experience, the one seeking admission to membership gives evidence that he or she has been born of the Spirit, and also reminds those who are already members that this transforming experience continues to define their own participation in a community in faith.

A church will find moments of shared confession to be spiritually renewing and rewarding times. Whether it is in shared moments before baptism, or as part of a small group experience preparatory to membership, or as a public moment before the congregation votes, confession of faith focuses on the most important qualification of the candidate. It also has the power to restore the character of the church. Sometimes there are circumstances of personality or character, or time may be difficult to arrange for the whole congregation's participation. In such cases shared moments of confession may be experienced by a small group delegated by the deacons, the pastor, or some other appropriate group who may then communicate with the congregation a summary of the confession.

A Voluntary Baptism

Baptism is a physical and visible symbol of the confession of faith. The Scriptures tell us that by the same symbol, Jesus demonstrated his own faith and began an intense period of preparation for his ministry and work. It is the act that gives form to the experience of transformation and the testimony of confession.

In one sense baptism is a ritual or ceremonial qualification for membership. But it is a deeper symbol than simple ritual. Among Baptists, baptism is almost universally performed by immersion. It is an act that symbolizes death and resurrection, cleansing, restoration, and renewal. Baptists do not believe, as some Christians assert, that baptism itself is an act of sanctification. Nevertheless, the scriptural record is clear that as believers confessed their faith and were baptized, they became members of the church.

The power of the symbol of baptism should be respected. It should be reserved for those alone who have determined that new life is possible for them, and that they have experienced its beginning in an inward way. For this reason, Baptists should be cautious in encouraging children or adolescents to seek baptism before they are ready. It is also important that those being baptized, as well as those participating in the ritual by encouragement and observation, should remember that baptism is scriptural evidence of the beginning of new life in the Spirit, and not the end. It should not, therefore, suggest completion of maturity in faith but rather the beginning of that quest.

In an age when many persons join churches that are different from the church of their childhood, or when many adults return to church participation and membership after an absence, Baptist churches are occasionally confronted with the issue of whether to honor baptisms performed in other denominational traditions or in modes other than immersion. This is an issue to be considered carefully and prayerfully by each church in each circumstance. Spiritual origins in faith should be honored. Yet often baptism can be a powerful symbol of restored commitment and evidence of new life in both individuals and in the church. Likewise, those who request baptism as adults, having been baptized as children in the same or a different manner, can experience a positive spiritual effect in redefining and asserting a renewed understanding of the transforming spirit. Baptism should always be treated as the powerful symbol that it is.

A Christian Life

When Hiscox first addressed this scriptural qualification for membership in the church, he said simply, "This condition is obvious" (p. 39). It is hard to suggest otherwise. Yet on this subject whole books are written. The challenge of discerning exactly what is the life of Christ in each person is demanding. But in the most fundamental sense, we need simply to say that a faith expressed in words must be matched by deeds expressed in acts of living. The inward journey must find its expression in outward arrivals.

At the same time, churches must be careful not to reject members merely on the basis of past behavior or deeds. As new believers, they may be ignorant of many things that the church can help them to know. To one returning from a time of lapsed faith or, like the prodigal son, from a time of lapsed judgment and behavior, the church should extend the open arms of fellowship and the encouraging presence of love. The church is, as has been often quoted, "a hospital for sinners, and not a museum of saints."

The church desiring to set standards for Christian life appropriate to membership might well study Colossians 3:1-17. There we are admonished to "set your minds on things that are above, not on things that are on earth. For you have died, and your life is hid with Christ in God. . . . Whatever you do, in word or deed, do everything in the name of the Lord Jesus, giving thanks to God the Father through him" (3:2,17). The Christian life is one established on the highest expectations—not by the arrogance of ability to meet them by our own virtue but by the expectation that in our aspiration to be in relationship to Christ, we shall, grace by grace, be endowed with the ability to do his will. That is the Christian life appropriate to new and old members alike.

Categories of Membership

Church membership should have specific meaning. Yet in many churches it is ambiguous or misleading. For example, in a new, small church it has a very specific meaning of belonging and responsibility. In a large, old, institutional church, it may mean many different things to different people. In new churches membership lists are fresh and new, and most of the members are present every Sunday for worship. In established churches, membership lists are often inaccurate and contain names of absent or passive members who have not attended in years or whose level of involvement in the life of the congregation is minimal.

Ideally, churches should have one standard of membership to be applied to all and against which membership is frequently evaluated and records kept clear. Yet this is often not realistic. Participants in church life have differing levels of available time, commitment, or energy for involvement, and active members are often reluctant to recommend the removal of inactive or uninvolved members. In addition, the level of commitment and leadership that can be expected from spiritually mature members may be different from that reasonably to be received from new or spiritually unformed members. Therefore, it may be prudent for a church to have more than one category of membership.

For example, some churches have experimented with categories of membership that are based on levels of commitment of time for spiritual growth and service in mission. Some others require a new covenant of membership each year, with those who confirm the covenant providing the pool from which leadership is drawn.[1] Any categorization of membership that distinguishes between varieties of membership in this way requires great discipline and diligence in order to be meaningful and to function toward strengthening the church, and not dividing it. Most churches have used distinctions similar to the following with some success in maintaining a meaningful understanding of membership over the years:

1. *Full Membership:* Full or regular membership in the church should be reserved for those resident members who fulfill a defined expectation regarding involvement in the programs and fellowship of the church and who contribute to the church in a manner appropriate to the church's needs and their personal means. Some churches may wish also to establish that this category of membership may be contingent upon certain standards of Bible knowledge, mode of baptism, or other qualifications. Full membership brings with it full access to all church programs and full opportunity for leadership and participation in all aspects of church life. Membership records should be reviewed annually, and members not fulfilling the conditions of this membership category should be moved to another category after a reasonable attempt to communicate with the person in question. Some churches have adopted a covenant style of membership—that is, the covenant of the church or a specific covenant of membership expectation is reaffirmed periodically.[2] Churches that use a process of reaffirmation will reserve full membership only for those who periodically affirm the covenant of renewal.

2. *Nonresident Membership:* Nonresident membership often serves as a designation of membership for those who might otherwise meet the requirements of full membership but who live at such distance from the church that regular participation is not possible. Frequent communication with nonresident members should be encouraged. Nonresident members should be encouraged to pray regularly for the church and to make at least symbolic financial contributions for its support. It is the practice of some churches to restrict the privilege of voting on some issues among nonresident members. The rationale is that they are unlikely to have a full knowledge of the dynamics of those issues due to their prolonged absence from the fellowship.

3. *Associate Membership:* Associate membership is frequently a means by which some churches attempt to deal with multiple memberships. College students, military personnel, and others who may reside in the community for a temporary period often may desire to unite with a church but not give up membership in the church to which they belong in their permanent community. Also, a person may wish to retain membership in another church for reasons of family continuity or history. Associate membership expressed in one church allows for a primary, full membership to continue in another. Some churches also use associate membership for those who were baptized according to the rites of a different denomination and who wish to retain that connection. Persons in this category are restricted by some churches from voting on certain church issues or from service on some boards or committees of the church.

4. *Watchcare Fellowship:* Watchcare fellowship is a category available to churches who wish to include in the spiritual community participants who are not yet ready or able fully to join the fellowship by reason of age, spiritual conviction, or other considerations. It may also be a convenient way by which members of different denominational backgrounds or faiths may be included in the fellowship of the church. This category is particularly useful in churches where persons of different cultures, communities, or confessions are frequently present, or where the spouses of full members desire to be noted in some official capacity within the church. Such participants should never be counted as members or reported as such in denominational reports. They may, however, prove to be a rich source for new members in the future or a resource for continuing dialogue about faith concerns. College and university students and other temporary residents may find watchcare fellowship a more convenient category of membership than associate membership.

5. *Inactive Membership:* Inactive membership is a category into which those who were once active members may be placed. Often such a list will include members who have moved away and for whom no current address is known. This is a file that should be frequently reviewed. First, it is a source from which members may be encouraged to become active once again. It is also a category into which members should unhesitatingly be assigned when, after a suitable period of review, they are deemed unresponsive in the life of the church. Needless to say, no member should ever be received into the church in this category!

Modes of Admission

Baptists have admitted members by a variety of ways and rituals. Whatever the manner of admission, some form of ritual or significant moment is recommended in order to ensure that the fellowship of believers has formally met and has officially extended a welcome to the new member. It is also important in order for the new member to experience a bond with the fellowship from that moment, and for membership to be perceived as a significant status. In every case, prior to admission to membership the congregation should have been given an opportunity to express their approval and assent to the new member. Often this is by means of a formal congregational vote upon recommendation by the diaconate. Admission must not be by decision of board of committee or pastor alone.

Three modes of admission have been used with consistency and frequency:

1. *Baptism:* Upon profession of faith in Jesus Christ, a person may be admitted to the fellowship of the church by baptism. This is the mode universally recommended for those professing their faith for the first time. It is the example set by Jesus (see Mark 1:9, Matthew 3:13). First the candidate must make known his or her desire to be baptized and to unite with the church. Following the procedures established by the congregation (such as an opportunity to profess faith), such a candidate may proceed to baptism. Baptism should always lead to membership in a church community, whenever possible. However, there may be valid personal and spiritual reasons why one may be baptized first before all procedural steps leading to membership have been accomplished or before a vote of the congregation may be held. Occasionally one may have been baptized previously and still request baptism again. Such requests should be honored as an affirmation of growing spiritual sensitivity and maturity, even though the candidate may be qualified to be admitted to the fellowship by other means.

2. *Letter:* In a mobile culture, it is an unusual church member who does not need at some point to change church membership by reason of a move to a new location. Members should, in fact, be encouraged to take their primary church membership to a congregation located where they are able to be active. (They might, if they wish, retain an associate membership if such provision is available in the church from which they depart.)

A letter of transfer is the means by which one church communicates to another that a person has standing as a member and is qualified to be received into the fellowship of another church. It is also the way by which the receiving church may communicate to a previous church that a member has moved beyond a reasonable radius of fellowship. Letters of transfer are normally issued from church to church, although in unusual cases a letter may be issued to the member to be taken with him or her to whatever new church might later be determined.

Letters of transfer should not be taken lightly and should, in fact, amount to a kind of fellowship recommendation. The receiving congregation should still vote or express assent to the new member, either after the letter has been received or conditionally "upon the promise" of a letter.

3. *Experience:* Many churches allow for members to be received by "Christian experience," which is an affirmation of a life already affirmed in Christian spiritual growth. This mode of admission is used most often in two cases: first, for those who by some means have lost record of their membership, or who belonged to a church which has since disbanded or merged, or when communication is not practicable. The second case is among churches that recognize the validity of baptism in a non-Baptist denomination, whether by immersion or otherwise. Here the designation of Christian experience is a means of affirming a Christian pilgrimage begun in another tradition that now continues in the present church. In any case, a member admitted by experience should be encouraged to share an account of his or her spiritual journey and experience and be voted or affirmed by the congregation, as in the case of baptism or transfer.

In addition to these three traditional modes, some churches also recognize persons in their fellowship "by affiliation" or "by association." These modes generally recognize the participatory status of persons who do not desire or who are not qualified for formal membership but who do desire some formal connection with the church. One example is described above under the category of "Watchcare." Others might include students residing temporarily in a community, persons desiring temporary communication with the church while on temporary professional assignment, and members of the community who may wish to communicate with the church, share its fellowship, or even support its work but who do not desire to become members.

Modes of Dismission

In the modern world many Christians are used to frequent travel and long commutes—sometimes involving global travel. For that reason, older practices of insisting that members relocate their church membership as soon as they arrive in a new location is neither necessary nor even wise. Nevertheless, a church is a community of faith. It has a reasonable expectation that its members should be a part of its support, vitality, and fellowship. When that is not the case, for whatever reason, members should be encouraged to change memberships. As Hiscox originally stated, "Christians should not live outside the fold of the Good Shepherd, but within the shelter of this fellowship" (p. 43). Sometimes, members have become so inactive, or so evidently not a part of the fellowship, that the relationship between them and the church should be dissolved.

The relationship between members and their church should be dissolved in one of three ways:

1. *By letter.* A member may request a letter by which he or she may gain admission to another fellowship, or, more frequently, the new church with which the person has united may request a letter. Such letters should be granted in a timely manner following the vote of the congregation.

2. By Exclusion. Exclusion may be an action, taken upon a vote of the congregation after recommendation by the diaconate, that separates the church from an individual as a member. This action might be taken for several reasons, but never without reflection and prayer. Most often it would follow the determination of the church that the member was not worthy to continue in relationship because of failure to exercise appropriate membership responsibilities or because the life of the person indicated a consistent manner of living in defiance of the spirit of the gospel. An act of exclusion should always leave open the possibility of restoration.[3]

3. By Death. The death of members, of course, dissolves their particular relationship to a church here on earth and opens the hope of their unity with the whole church of God in eternity. Many churches find it helpful to have an annual service of remembrance during which all members who have died during the preceding year are remembered as their names are removed from the rolls. Appropriate occasions include the first Sunday of the new year or, for churches that follow a liturgical calendar, the Sunday nearest to All Saints Day.[4]

Membership Procedures and Discipline

It is important for the constitution, bylaws, or other statements of church operating procedures to clearly establish procedures by which members are to be received and dismissed. Some churches fail to grow simply because it is not clear how members may be added. Alternatively, churches frequently develop large inactive memberships because they fail to review the membership roles and to activate, transfer, or dismiss unresponsive members. And churches increasingly exhibit the symptoms of dysfunctional organizations, experience unresolvable conflict, or become paralyzed when they are unwilling to exercise appropriate discipline among members who function in a manner other than in the spirit of Christian love and cooperation.

The process of governing membership procedures is most often assigned to the diaconate of the congregation, though occasionally special membership committees are established. The responsible body within the church should be charged with receiving new members in an orderly fashion and in making sure that proper procedures are observed. Important moments such as hearing a faith confession, sharing baptism, and receiving new members with the hand of fellowship must be arranged by such a body in cooperation with the pastor. In reviewing candidates for membership, this committee should be mindful that membership is intended as a means for the building up of the church and for the maturing of the individual believer. Therefore, it ought not to establish severe tests of doctrine but rather should serve to encourage and assist growth in knowlege and spirit for the new member.

In an age of cultural diversity, a church must assure that age, sex, race, past character, or present condition in life are not barriers to church membership. If these or other issues seem to create barriers, the responsible body within the church should be charged to help bridge them by encouraging dialogue between the prospective member and the congregation. This might well include appointing a sensitive and trusted small group of persons to hear the candidate's profession of faith and to help interpret his or her experience to others.

In an age of theological diversity and, to say the least, frequent theological conflict, it is to be expected that each church might establish some means of defining the boundaries of acceptable doctrine among its members. Nevertheless, the advice that Hiscox first gave on this matter remains valuable and helpful:

> ... as to faith and practice, members of the same church should hold and act alike, since harmony in the body is of the greatest importance. But it would be unreasonable to demand or expect that considerable numbers of persons, differing in education, habits of thought, constitution of mind, and independent opinions, could attain perfect uniformity of belief in all matters of Christian truth. This would be impracticable, and in minor matters large Christian liberty should be allowed (p. 40).

In the most harmonious of churches, there are occasions when discipline among members must be exercised. Failure to do so may encourage illness within the fellowship and a weakening of both personal faith and the strength of the church. Conflict is unavoidable and, if handled in forthright and honest ways, can be productive.

Still, there are sometimes individuals or groups within a congregation whose personal needs, spiritual immaturity, or private agendas can become disruptive and even fatal to the harmony and purpose of the church. Constant criticism of the pastor and other leaders, insistence upon one's own way, disruption of meetings, self-righteous judgment, gossip, slander, and personal attacks are unacceptable in church fellowship. Likewise, destructive public behavior or poisoned relationships between church members can bring doubt on the credibility of the church.

Appropriate means must be developed to counsel with such persons in the manner and spirit of Christ. (See, for example, Matthew 18:15.) A responsible body within the church, usually the deacons, should be charged with the responsibility to counsel with persons exhibiting such behavior, with the desire of rebuilding the harmony of the fellowship and the exemplary integrity of individual lives. But when such means fail, the same group must not fail to act as mediators between wounded parties, to recommend "probationary" actions or, in extreme cases, to urge for exclusion and dismissal. In all such cases, however, the Spirit of Christ must be the guide, and the hope of reconciliation must be retained.

Church membership is a sacred trust between those who voluntarily covenant together, and also between the gathered fellowship and Christ, the Head of the church. In its best and most harmonious form, it has no equal on earth. The greatest of care and of prayer must be expended that it aspire to that standard. Members are the only significant resource of a church. They should be gathered, led and fed, and healed by the example of the Good Shepherd and the Great Physician.

NOTES

1. The theme for a covenant service for the new year should be that of confession, repentance, and rededication. Resources are available in a historic covenant service first created by John Wesley and in many worship resource guides. The Lord's Supper is often a powerful, central act of such a service, as the community of believers seeks to rededicate themselves in commitment, service, and fellowship for the following year.

2. Some churches, for example, renew the church covenant in an explicit

form as part of a New Year's service of Communion and covenant renewal. Members who affirm the covenant agree to certain expectations as members and are listed, as a result, as the full, resident, active members of the congregation. Others are noted as associate or other categories of members and not qualified for positions of leadership in the church during that year. In order to include all who desire to affirm the covenant, the process is continued during the month of January, and members may confirm the covenant by mail if they are away during that period.

3. Careful records should be kept of members who are dismissed by exclusion because of some length of inactivity, and particularly if the church has not been able to contact them personally. If, at a later date, the excluded member becomes active again or requests a letter of transfer, the church may wish to restore the member to the records for the purpose of the transfer or for the purpose of revitalizing his or her membership activity.

4. Churches that choose the new year as a means of remembering those deceased in the previous year might include a commemoration of their names at the service of Communion in a covenant service. Likewise, on the first Sunday of November, those churches that enjoy borrowing from the traditions of other denominations may find rich resources for such remembrance in the *Book of Common Prayer* and in other worship resource books.

Chapter III

The Christian Ministry—Ordination and Pastoral Leadership

Ministry is an activity of the whole people of God. Within a church, it is both an opportunity and a responsibility of the entire membership. For Baptists especially, the vitality of the ministry of the laity has always been the key to the success of churches. Nevertheless, from the very beginning of the church, certain of its members have been set apart to exercise leadership as shepherds, to perform specific acts of ministry, and to be specially equipped to build up the church. Among Baptists, such persons have been set apart by ordination or by commission. These ministers are the most visible in the church. They are also most often the church leaders who represent the church to the world.

Since Hiscox first wrote, the world has changed remarkably. Of necessity styles and focuses of ministry have changed with it. Yet the calling, qualifications, and commitment of the church's ordained ministry remains an irreplaceable resource in fulfilling Christ's work. In some segments of Christ's church, bishops or councils determine those who will minister in particular churches. It is argued that an "overshepherd" can match ministers and churches in ways to complement, compensate, and challenge both the church and the minister. Baptists at times follow such a principle through the counsel and leadership of regional ministers or denominational officials. But because each church is independent, churches and ministers ultimately select each other, and the church votes or otherwise affirms the call of its ministers.

This practice heightens the church's own unique sense of destiny and determination. It also brings temptations. Where people have the freedom of the choice of pastors, for example, they are likely to choose them on their own level. The same is true of ministers who will tend to gravitate to churches meeting their own preferences and standards. Hiscox said that "the old prophet's declaration, 'like people, like priest,' is as true now as when Hosea uttered it." And he was right. Therefore, when Baptists consider the question of ministerial relationships and leadership, and when ministers consider their potential fields of service, both must strive to maintain the high standards of the gospel. Ideally a church should expect its ministers to call the people to aspire to the mind and spirit of Christ, and ministers, by persistent, faithful effort, can by God's grace help their people become more and more molded into Christ's image and likeness.

The origins of the ministry go deep into the earliest recorded events of the Bible. The priestly traditions of the Hebrew people, however corrupt they ultimately became, recognized the need for people to be guided into the presence of God. The prophetic tradition reformed the role of godly agents and introduced the rustic analogy of the people as a flock, "led, fed and guarded by shepherds, called pastors" (p. 46). Jesus himself built upon this image when he confessed himself to be the Good Shepherd who gave not only protection but life to his sheep. The apostles and other leaders of the early church looked back to this image in establishing their first leadership roles.

Yet it is Christ himself who models the ministry of the church. And both churches and ordained ministers alike must not shrink from acknowledging this model and this connection. At the beginning of his ministry, Jesus ordained the twelve disciples and sent them out to preach (Mark 3:14). Later, he appointed the seventy and sent them out, "two by two, into every town and place where he himself was about to come" (Luke 10:1). His final instructions to his followers were to "go therefore and make disciples of all nations, baptizing them in the name of the Father and of the Son and of the Holy Spirit, teaching them to observe all that I have commanded you; and lo, I am with you always, to the close of the age" (Matthew 28:19-20).

Therefore, as churches determine those whom they will set apart to lead them in ministry and be shepherds among them, they do so at the instruction of Christ, and do so seeking no less than to re-create the image of Christ among them. They should, therefore, seek the Spirit of Christ to guide those they ordain and to empower them for the ministry they would perform. Among Baptists, it is the practice for churches to elect ministers. But as they do, let them be humbly aware that it must be God who prepares them and the Spirit who calls forth their gifts and defines their ministry. Those whom the people follow and support, then, should strive to be representatives of Christ in spirit and in purpose.

The Purpose of the Ordained Ministry

Like the idea of a church, the general purpose of an ordained ministry might seem self-evident. However, in our time, ministers are variously charged to be chief executives of churches, shepherds of administrative procedures, preachers, teachers, caregivers, worship leaders, visitors to the sick and the lonely, and community leaders charged with upholding moral values. All these are legitimate functions of the ministry and are authenticated by long tradition. But the central purpose of the ministry is defined quite specifically in the Gospels: to accomplish the conversion of men and women, and then to provide their instruction and empowerment in their faith in Christ and his gospel. That is the heart of the Great Commission (Matthew 28:19-20).

The complexity of modern life sponsors the temptation for ordained ministry to be about the work of many other things. Some would argue that evangelistic preaching is the only thing: the goal of conversion is all that matters. Others would argue that teaching and preserving right doctrine are the thing: only right faith leads to effective salvation. Still others expect that ministers must be managers and administrators of divine things. Modern churches—responding to the temptation of "success" in worldly terms—bless nearly every activity as a ministry and install a minister to make it succeed. In this way, much of the ministry of the church is inevitably exposed as business cloaked in a very thin disguise. Ministry, under those circumstances, loses its purpose.

In writing to the Ephesians, Paul said that Christ gave gifts, some to be apostles, prophets, evangelists, pastors, and teachers (Ephesians 4:11). Ministry can be effected in many personalities. But Paul was careful to remind the Ephesians—and us—of the purpose of all these works: "for building up the body of Christ, until we all attain to the unity of the faith and of the knowledge of the Son of God, to mature manhood, to the measure of the stature of the fullness of Christ" (Ephesians 4:12-13). There can be no avoiding it: the purpose of the ministry is not to be displayed in mimicking the business of the world or in merely keeping the members of the church busy. It is defined, rather, in calling and encouraging Christians who aspire to the likeness of Christ, and in challenging a church to aspire to be a living example of his work and witness.

When ministers keep that in focus as their calling, and when churches insist upon that as their purpose, unbelievers will be converted, and believers will advance in the maturity of their faith.

The Gifts of Ministry

The purpose of ministry is specific and focused. The gifts that bring ministry to life may be many and diverse. For the Corinthians Paul listed a great many gifts: utterance of wisdom and the utterance of knowledge; faith by the Spirit, and faith to effect healing; the working of miracles; and the interpretation of tongues (1 Corinthians 12:4-11). In a modern age we might say that these mean the ability to speak, to teach, and to administer; to possess the gift of compassion and concern for the needs of others; to exercise the gift of discernment and judgment; and to demonstrate the ability to heal by prayer, by empathy, and by comfort. There are, of course, many more.

Not all ministers possess gifts in equal measure. In fact, many ministers are exceptionally effective in the use of one or two highly developed gifts. For example, some ministers are great preachers, while others are highly effective teachers. But not all teachers are good preachers, nor are all preachers good teachers. Some ministers are gifted in providing pastoral care and guidance, while others are able administrators and managers. Ministers should, for the purpose of their own spiritual and professional growth, seek to grow in the development and use of less evident gifts. But their ministry will likely be most effective if their best gifts can be identified and developed to best use.

Not all who seek to minister are endowed with effective skills for ministry. Christians are often led to believe that the best among Christians will become ordained ministers. Sometimes one has remarkable gifts to witness in the world, to lead as laity, to administer the affairs of a church, but should not seek ordination. Likewise, it is tragic when one obviously gifted for ministry is not identified and encouraged to develop his or her gifts for ministry. This is particularly the case in an age that has experienced unparalleled growth in vocations, professions, and occupations. Many persons gifted for ministry pursue worthy vocations but do not respond to the opportunity to serve Christ in a specific way. The church is poorer for their absence.

It is, therefore, one of the great responsibilities of the present church to identify talents for ministry among its members and among those in contact with it—and having identified them, to encourage them and provide for their development. In this way the church of the present assures leadership for the church of the future.

The Call to Ministry

Ministry is not an occupation for which individuals are simply recruited, however, regardless of how gifted they may be. One can possess great ability in the use of language, have a keen intellect, exhibit personal piety and godly behavior, and even demonstrate a strong desire to do good. One thing more is needed. In the same way that a regenerate heart is required for true membership in the church, a minister must experience something that can only be properly described as a divine call to that service: "One does not take the honor upon himself, but he is called by God, just as Aaron was" (Hebrews 5:4).

The true nature of a call to ministry is often a mystery both to the one called and to those who observe it. At times, God's choices even seem unsuitable by human standards. The result of it is more certain, for those who are called approach the work of ministry from a deep, abiding, and unalterable conviction that such is the will of God for them. Those who are called exhibit the mark of the Holy

Spirit upon their soul. Those called may freely state that they might have preferred a different work, one that might have brought greater wealth, more excitement, or greater recognition, but that they could not make such a choice. Those called to ministry are not required to confess that there is nothing else they *could* do. Rather, they are called to confess that there is nothing else, by the grace of God, that they *would* do.

If the exact nature of a call is impossible to describe fully, there is nevertheless a pattern in the experience of those who are called. One being called may experience the presence of the Holy Spirit wrestling with her, demanding, coercing, and cajoling a new perspective about God's will for her. One who is called often remembers a sacred moment or a holy place where, like Jacob, he responded to say, "Surely the LORD is in this place" (Genesis 28:16). The call can seem sudden, like the young Samuel being awakened from his sleep finally to respond, "Speak, for thy servant hears" (1 Samuel 3:10). Calls are experienced in great and dramatic episodes, as when Isaiah, surrounded by seraphim and standing on shaking foundations, heard the Lord say, "Whom shall I send?" and responded dramatically by saying, "Here am I! send me" (Isaiah 6:1-8). A call may also follow a time of quiet reflection. In fact, even dramatic calls are often preceded by lengthy periods of reflection and prayer. But a call in any form lays a heavenly claim upon an earthly service in an unmistakable way.

Ministers respond to calls in different ways.[1] For some, a response is instantaneous and decisive, never to be raised for evaluation or question again. For others, response is slow and prolonged, as other directions and purposes of life are tested and tried, yet the Spirit returns to call them back from other purposes and plans. For some, testing the call is, as with Jeremiah, a lifelong exercise of reevaluation and even controversy with God. Such persons may return time and again to complain bitterly on their knees, "O LORD, thou hast deceived me, and I was deceived; thou art stronger than I, and thou hast prevailed. I have become a laughingstock all the day" (Jeremiah 20:7). For still others, a call to serve God may come in the midst of a life and career already in progress, as with the disciples who were called from their labors and professions. Or it may cause an almost complete reorienting of values and purposes, as with Paul on the Damascus road (Acts 9:1-22). It may even come to lives that, until that moment, exhibited little to encourage anyone to think God could make use of them, as was the case with both Peter and Paul. One who experiences a call comes to a recognition that the hand of the Lord is upon him or her and a response is required.

The strongest calls seem often to come to those who seem most to resist. But as individuals wrestle with the Spirit, as conviction works slowly in their souls, new insight emerges, new direction takes shape, new dreams are ignited. The evidence of response can finally be found in the certainty of a conviction to serve, in the presence of a mind and spirit able to discern the truth of the gospel and to make it clear to others, and in a desire to become qualified to serve in the way the Lord has called them.

A call to ministry brings opportunity and responsibility to the church: those whom the Lord calls to ministry the church is called to encourage. And only those who are called are true candidates for the effective ministry of the church. To prepare them for their leadership and their ministry in the church, the church has a responsibility to be in partnership with them in acquiring the training, qualifications, and experience by which their gifts may be made suitable for God's work.

Qualifications for Ministry

The first qualification for ministry is a *calling*. A minister ultimately derives his or her authority from that same source, and not on the basis of education, approval by church council, state authority, or any other external means. Nevertheless, God rarely calls ministers to serve in isolation and consistently calls the people of the church to work in community. The overwhelming testimony of the Scriptures is that by discernment, empowerment, support, and collegial relationships, churches and those who minister should work together. Therefore, it is appropriate that churches and church organizations establish standards and expectations for ministry that they then must help ministers to achieve and to maintain. Though we are to imitate Christ and to minister in his example, only Christ alone is perfect, and no minister should be held capable of exceeding the ministry of Christ. Churches that desire perfection in ministers should remember that perfection in faith and in ministry is the journey and experience of a lifetime. Ministry should grow in spirit and in strength during that lifetime, and churches should encourage and empower that growth.

Ministers should be also be qualified to grow in *spirit*. The Scriptures contain many examples of spiritual qualifications. In 1 Timothy, for example, temperance, sensibility, hospitality, and gentleness are singled out as standards for ministry (1 Timothy 3:1-5). To these Titus adds that one should be a "lover of goodness," "upright," "self-controlled," and able to "hold firm to the sure word as taught" (Titus 1:7-9). The qualification of being able to grow in the Spirit is perhaps first and greatest simply because it is the first and most important work of any minister to call others to growth in the Spirit and to lead them in it.

Ministers should be qualified to grow in *character*. The language of our age would say they should strive to be physically fit and emotionally healthy. In the Scriptures, Titus reminds us that ministers should not be "arrogant," "quick-tempered," "violent," or "greedy for gain" (Titus 1:7-9). Timothy adds that the Lord's servants should not be abusive, slanderers, swollen with conceit, or lovers of pleasure rather than God (1 Timothy 3:2-4), but instead "kindly to everyone, an apt teacher, forebearing, correcting his opponents with gentleness" (2 Timothy 2:24-25). These are high expectations, and were we to hold everyone we might empower for ministry to meet them entirely, the church would be without leadership in human form! They are, nevertheless, the standards of character toward which ministers are to develop. The commitment to confront the flaws of character within, and to grow and progress toward their improvement, is a major qualification for ministry.

Ministers should be qualified to grow in *knowledge*, *skill*, and *proficiency* in the specific tasks of the ministry to which they are called. Intellectual capability may not be the first qualification for ministry. But the ministry demands the best of the mind and skill of those who exercise it. Academic preparation appropriate to the demands of the work and the expectations of the community is necessary. (Many Baptist denominations, for example, require graduation from college and some form of seminary training for a standard ordination.) The specific requirements may be different from church to church and from denomination to denomination. But all ministers should be willing to meet and desire to exceed such standards for the effectiveness of their ministry. And knowledge should not end as a ministry begins. Ministry should be built on academic preparation and on a continuing commitment to education throughout a ministry.

Ministers should be qualified to grow in *experience*. As in any profession or service, skill, effectiveness, and ability should grow as experience provides mastery of new, more complex, and more demanding opportunities. In determining qualifications in a minister and in encouraging qualifications to be met, churches and ministers should work together, that mastery might provide growing confidence and ability for doing God's work more consistently and effectively. The apostle Paul, for example, often referred to his calling, to his character, and to his training as a way of establishing his credentials in writing to the New Testament churches. But ultimately it was his experience—experience in suffering, in meeting the challenges, in working through the variety of the means of grace among these first Christians—that he called upon to establish and maintain the qualifications for his continued ministry among them. (See, for example, 2 Corinthians 11-12 for one of Paul's many references to experience as a means of ministerial qualification.)

Finally, ministers should be qualified to grow in *grace*. It is what Hiscox referred to in saying that ministers "should be . . . courteous, gentle, generous, and kind to all" (p. 52). It is certainly what Paul meant when he unfailingly closed his letters by saying, "May the Lord of peace himself give you peace" (2 Thessalonians 3:16) or simply "live in peace" (2 Corinthians 13:11) or "My love be with you all in Christ Jesus" (1 Corinthians 16:24). Despite Paul's frequent need to use the language and tones of admonition and criticism, grace was always evident when he closed with such benedictory tones as: "The grace of the Lord Jesus Christ and the love of God and the fellowship of the Holy Spirit be with you all" (2 Corinthians 13:14). Growth in grace is the sign that a minister is remaining faithful to his or her calling.

The Ordination of Ministers

Ministers who have experienced a call, who meet the qualifications for ministry, and who desire to be recognized for ministry within the church should seek to be ordained. Ordination is not exclusively a matter of institutional authority, for the empowerment for ministry comes from God. Neither is it a matter of human rights and privileges, for if anything, ordination marks one for greater service, not less. It should be observed, in fact, that the spirit of sanctity and the high ceremony for setting ministers apart by ordination has no specific parallel or source in the Scriptures. By long tradition in the church, however, it has become the act by which the church affirms the calling and preparation of individuals for the ministry by participating with them in a partnership of recognition, support, and covenant for the ministry they will undertake. In that spirit, churches should hold ordination both in process and in ceremony as among the highest acts of its corporate activity and worship.

The New Testament origins of the word *ordination* come from the process of choosing, electing, or appointing one to the specific office of bishop or pastor. It does not refer to a ceremonial process. Therefore, while the service of worship in which the ceremony of ordination is celebrated may be a moment of joy and great inspiration for a church community, it is the process and the procedure of ordination that has the greatest validity. It is, therefore, important for churches and church leaders to be familiar with that process.

Baptist traditions regarding the independence of each congregation place ordination in the jurisdiction of the local church. Nevertheless, many Baptist associations, fellowships, and denominations have established standards for ordination and have agreed upon procedures for ordination to be administered. In order for ordination to be recognized beyond the local church, therefore, churches sponsoring a candidate for ordination are advised to consult the procedures of their affiliated fellowship.

The Ordination Process

The process of ordination should begin with the candidate. When a candidate has experienced a call and has satisfied established requirements, he or she should seek the counsel of the church of which he or she is a member. (In some cases this might be the church to which the candidate has been called to be a minister, but not always.) Generally the candidate should consult first with the pastor or other senior official of the congregation, and then arrange to meet with the appropriate board, usually the diaconate. In some congregations and traditions, the candidate may previously have been "licensed" for ministry, and in others licensing may be a required step prior to ordination. If the latter is the case, then the diaconate will first determine whether they wish to license the candidate. Following that, they shall examine the candidate themselves, if no others are to be involved. Even if the church desires to ordain a minister without reference to a fellowship or association, it is nonetheless a long-standing Baptist practice to invite pastors and representatives from other churches to participate in the ordination examination.

When a church has well-defined denominational affiliations, the diaconate should recommend to the congregation that an ordination council be called in accordance with established denominational procedures. This council would be made up of representatives of churches in the association and may include a "standing committee" of that organization. Where established procedures exist, they should govern the proceedings. If no procedures exist, a chairperson should be designated and the agenda for the proceedings established. The council, when scheduled and gathered, will first review whether basic requirements for ordination have been met regarding the candidate's training and credentials and affirm that it is the intent of the church to ordain the candidate. If the basic requirements of membership, training, or other qualifications are met, it will proceed to examine the candidate. This examination should include three major areas:

1. *Christian Experience:* Council members may ask questions regarding the spiritual awakening of the candidate and request a brief narrative of the candidate's sense of regeneration and growing spiritual maturity. A review of how the candidate's life experiences and education have prepared her or him for ministry might also be included.

2. *Call to Ministry:* The council should expect the candidate to articulate the manner in which he or she has experienced a call to ministry and how the response has led to seeking ordination. In addition, if ordination is taking place in response to a specific call to ministry, the council may desire to hear how that ministry will fulfill the candidate's call.

3. *Views of Christian Doctrine:* The council should engage the candidate in conversation regarding his or her theological perspectives and beliefs. The purpose of this is to determine whether the ordinand has considered the major issues of Christian faith and formed a personal perspective in faith from which to exercise ministry. As such discussions among Baptists nearly always generate debate, councils should strive to honor independent opinions and perspectives. Candidates should not be expected to adhere to a particular scriptural interpretation or doctrine unless such beliefs are a stated part of the church or denomination's covenant. Candidates should, however, be required to articulate thoughtful and clear expressions of faith and belief.

Specific topics for conversation and review at an ordination council meeting are specified as the result of denominational expectations and standards. It is also common practice to have the candidate present some of the material in the form of a paper or written statement. This practice encourages concise articulation but should not encourage the council to become an academic seminar. When conversation with the candidate is finished, a general discussion should follow, with an emphasis on evaluating his or her suitability for ministry. (The candidate may be excused for all or part of this activity.) If there are serious reservations regarding the candidate, they should be stated openly, and reasons should be presented. If concerns are great enough, the candidate might be invited to respond to the concerns. When, in the judgment of the chairperson, the discussion has been completed, a vote should be taken on a resolution similar to this: "Resolved, that this ordination council, having examined the candidate, recommends that he or she be set apart for ministry on behalf of the church and in Christ's name, and therefore also recommend that the church proceed to a public service of ordination." The council should then conclude with prayer.

In the course of an ordination council, there may arise valid reasons of qualification, character, or spiritual maturity that might suggest that a candidate should be discouraged from seeking ordination, or at least to delay further consideration of it. If such is the case, the council must face these issues. The pain of the moment may well spare both the candidate and the church from future anguish or a failed ministry.

Regardless of the council's final vote, it is a matter of advice to the church that has requested it. If the council votes not to recommend the candidate, the church still has the right to proceed with ordination. But in doing so, it must assume responsibility that it is acting counter to the advice of the larger community and should have strong and valid reasons for proceeding with ordination. In addition, the church that ordains a minister without the affirmation of a wider fellowship should be aware that the ordination may not be recognized as valid beyond the specific fellowship of that church.

The Ordination Ceremony

After the ordination council has recommended the candidate to the congregation, a committee should be designated to arrange for a suitable ceremony. An ordination should be a time of great rejoicing and also of serious commitment. Often it is an occasion to which other churches and guests should be invited and the best hospitality of the church extended. The preparation committee should coordinate the several aspects of the occasion with the diaconate, the worship committee, the pastor, and the hospitality committee.

The ordination service may follow many outlines or patterns of order for worship. In general, the service should be consistent with the worship style of the congregation and incorporate aspects of particular importance to the ordinand.

In addition to elements common to any Christian worship service, such as hymns, prayers, and one or more Scripture readings, an ordination service should include these specific elements:

A Charge to the Candidate: Usually an address regarding the responsibilities and opportunities of ministry offered by an ordained minister, often one who is especially close to the candidate, such as a teacher, former pastor, or friend.

A Charge to the Church: An address or brief sermon reminding members of their opportunity and responsibility to support and encourage the ministry of the ordinand. If the ordinand will be serving some other church, the present congregation shall nonetheless serve as a symbol of the congregation or community in which ministry will be offered.

The Act of Ordination: Often a moment when other ordained ministers are invited to lay hands on the candidate while a prayer of ordination is offered. In some churches, some or all members of the congregation are also invited to participate in the laying on of hands. This is a practice particularly consistent with Baptist beliefs regarding the priesthood of the believer and the equality of Christian community. It serves to emphasize the recognition and support of the candidate by the whole church.

The Reception of the Candidate: By the hand of fellowship extended by an ordained minister, and when the ordination is in a church the newly ordained minister will serve, extended also by a leader of the church. The presentation of a symbolic gift to the ordinand symbolizes support and empowerment for ministry. (A Bible is often a suitable gift to symbolize the basis of ministry. Other gifts might include a portable Communion set, a particularly significant book, or a pulpit robe in churches where they are used.)

A Response by the Newly Ordained Minister: Usually a very brief statement of thanksgiving. Sometimes such a response might lead into a service of Communion led by the newly ordained minister. This is particularly appropriate if the ordaining church is one in which the minister will be serving in pastoral ministry.

The Benediction: Usually spoken by the new minister.

Following the service, a time of hospitality and celebration should encourage all present to be mindful of God's presence among their celebration and to be grateful for new ministry being provided and raised up in their fellowship. During the reception, greetings and communications from community and denominational leaders might be read, and commendations and words of appreciation for participants in the service should also be shared.

The Renewal of Ordination

After a minister has been ordained, there is no biblical or theological requirement for him or her to be ordained again regardless of changes in place of service. Nevertheless, Baptist polity and traditions do invite the renewal of the spirit and purpose of ordination on some occasions.

First, if an ordained minister has left the active service of ministry for some length of time, especially if the absence has been because of uncertainty about the nature or call of his or her ministry or because of some unhappy experience in ministry, a service of renewal of ordination vows may be significant in refocusing the ministry ahead.

Second, when a minister moves to a new field of service, whether to a different church or to a different kind of ministry, a "service of installation" often serves to refocus the commitments and empowerment of ordination for a new place and new circumstances.

Third, occasionally ministers originally ordained in a different denomination desire to unite among a Baptist fellowship and to seek a ministry there. Denominational and fellowship guidelines differ on the necessity of reordination—sometimes it is officially only a matter for credentials to be reviewed and established. Nevertheless, an ordination ceremony in this circumstance often can recharge a sense of ministry among new people with a different history and tradition.

Among Baptists, ordination has generally been understood to focus one to a vocation in ministry and not to a peculiar status. Therefore, Baptist churches have not generally ordained persons without a specific ministry to pursue. Ordination should be considered the beginning of a ministry that immediately takes focus in a specific role or office.

Ministerial Offices

Unlike some other Christian organizational structures, Baptists do not generally have highly developed offices organized into historical hierarchies and traditional forms. Those denominations that have enumerated "offices" trace their development to medieval life or to early Reformation expressions of church life. Baptists, on

the other hand, are a post-Reformation expression of the church and
have prized simplicity and functionality in leadership roles. Nevertheless, during the last several decades, Baptist churches, institutions, and structures have proliferated. In churches, schools, and
colleges, in denominational and associational structures, and in
missions, ministers serve in a variety of roles, offices, and responsibilities. For good or ill, church life has taken on the corporate
character and complexity of the world around it. Many churches
have grown large and have multiple staff members. The result is
that ministry is impossible to define in a single concept. It is
therefore important to identify ministry according to the roles it
performs, the responsibilities it carries, and the accountability that
gives it a channel of direction.

The New Testament provides only rudimentary definitions of
ministerial offices. It was a simpler age then, and the church was
very young. For example, in the Scriptures, the term *episcopos*,
which is most often translated as "bishop," and *presbyteros*, which
is commonly translated as "elder," are used interchangeably. The
episcopos was an overseer or supervisor. Among Greek Christians
especially, *episcopos* came to be applied to the pastoral role, as one
who had oversight of the flock and who supervised the congregation in spiritual concerns. The term *presbyteros*, or "elder," was
more likely derived from synagogical usage and was employed by
Jewish Christians likewise to refer to the person given responsibility to be the "caretaker" of synagogical or community concerns. A
third term found in the New Testament is *diakonos*, which means
"servant" or "minister," that is, one who serves or ministers to
others. In Baptist churches diaconal ministry is a role to which lay
members are most often elected. But among hierarchical traditions,
deacons are often ordained members of the clergy and have a
specific, if subordinate, priestly role.

The New Testament introduces two other words that appear in
relative isolation and are applied to Jesus. One is the term *poimen*,
which means "pastor" or "shepherd" (John 10:1-18). Jesus also
used this image of himself as a role model for spiritual leadership
in other teachings, such as the image of the lost sheep (Matthew
18:12-14). Translated to the church, the shepherd's "pastoral" role
is to sustain the church by leading, guiding, and guarding the flock

committed to his care. The other word is *hierus*, which means "priest" and is found in Hebrews 4:14–5:10. Its use in that context is to connect Jesus' role in redemption to the ancient faith and theology of atonement of the Hebrews.

A first distinction regarding offices or roles, therefore, is to note that pastoral and ministerial roles are related but not identical. As Hiscox put it, "A pastor is a minister, but a minister is not necessarily a pastor" (p. 57). This is a particularly significant distinction to properly identify and manage the variety of roles in large churches and in denominational or mission corporate structures. Much confusion results in larger congregations, for example, where every member of the ordained ministry staff is referred to as "pastor."

Such role confusion can undermine the proper authority and role of the one who is charged with the responsibility of being *the* pastor, and, ironically, also confuses the roles of others who minister on the staff under his or her guidance.

To clarify, the minister is the herald, the *kerux*, who preaches the gospel, who proclaims glad tidings to men and women. A minister may also be *diakonos*, the servant who meets the needs of others by his or her leadership, compassion, expertise, or skill. The pastor is the *poimen*, the designated one "in charge," whose ultimate responsibility is to care for the whole flock. Ministers may be evangelists, healers, workers for righteousness, administrators, caregivers—and in many other roles unique to particular church jobs and functions. But unless he or she has care of a church, a minister is not a pastor.

On the other hand, every minister may have pastoral relationships with few or many. And in the life of a large congregation, although there is one pastor, each minister may have many pastoral relationships or serve as a pastor to a small group or a segment of the whole congregation. (A good example is a youth minister or a visitation minister, both of whom have unique pastoral roles to defined populations within a church's life.) For example, James was the pastor of the church in Jerusalem. Other apostles, however, such as Paul, Cephas, or Barnabas, preached the gospel from place to place. They often planted churches but did not remain to pastor churches. They were theologians and educators, but they did not remain in one congregation to guide and care for the faith and belief of a particular flock.

Life in present congregations has often produced multiple roles of ministry for both ordained ministers and elected lay officers and leaders. It is helpful for the good order and care of church life to understand and appreciate the roles and offices ordained ministers may perform.

Pastor

The role of the pastor is that of general oversight and care of the church. In a church where only one ordained minister is present, that minister must function as pastor above all other roles. As pastor, he or she will preach to proclaim the Good News, to win souls for Christ, to expand the spiritual sensitivity of the congregation, to proclaim the day of the Lord. Not all pastors excel in the pulpit, yet preaching must not be neglected. As Hiscox so insightfully put it, "sound gospel sermons, ably prepared and earnestly delivered, constitute the only kind of pulpit service which can long commend itself to the consciences of the people" (p. 58).

But pastoral ministry cannot end in the pulpit. The pastor must also be an administrator, caring for the orderly processes and mundane concerns of congregational life together. Not all pastors are able administrators, but every pastor can identify administrative gifts in others, encourage their assistance, and by that means encourage the well-being of the flock. Likewise, the pastor must be an educator, providing opportunities for clear understanding of the gospel and its meaning for salvation, effective living, and growth in grace. Pastors are not uniformly gifted teachers, but as with preaching, attention to preparation and communication will not fail to strengthen a congregation's understanding.

Pastoral ministry must include compassion and caregiving. The pastor must be a sympathizing and empathizing friend to all, striving to be helpful wherever help may be needed. She must be sensitive to those who need to be visited because they are lonely and to the necessity of reaching out to those who seem most distant. The pastor must stand equally with the prominent and rich as they evaluate their responsibilities and with the poor and obscure as they face the challenges of each day. Only by knowing the context of daily life and by being present to the joys and sorrows of the congregation will a pastor have the knowledge of the heart necessary to minister effectively. Not all pastors have the gift of empathy, and modern life makes visitation and personal contact increasingly difficult, but persistence and a flexibility in finding ways to be in contact will open doors to pastoral care.

There is nothing in the life of the church that should be beyond the concern, care, responsibility, and leadership of the pastor. For example, the constitution of the church may designate a layperson to receive and disburse funds, but the pastor is nevertheless the chief steward of the church. Traditions and organizational principles may designate the superintendent to organize the Sunday school, but the pastor is the principal and headmaster of the church as an educational institution.

The pastor is charged with ultimate spiritual care and authority in the life of the congregation. This does not mean, however, that the pastoral role should be authoritarian or that only the pastor has spiritual insight. Quite the opposite. The effective pastor must work collegially with the congregation whenever possible and must identify and encourage the gifts within the congregation's members, both to reduce the burden of his or her own responsibilities and to enhance the strength of the congregation. Often the best evidence of effective pastoral leadership over time is a church in which a vitality of faith is so evident and effectiveness of operations is so smooth that it appears at first glance that the pastor has no significant role to play.

Associate and Assistant Ministers

When churches have achieved large size and complex programs, they often have one or more ordained ministers in addition to the pastor. In such churches the pastor's role must include pastoral supervision of these ministers. The roles of the ministers must be clear, and the relationship of pastor, staff ministers, and congregation must be well defined in order for the congregation to be an effective church. It is most effective if ministers other than the pastor are perceived by the congregation as being extensions of the pastor's role and responsibilities. It is equally important that the ministers understand themselves in that manner. If staff ministers perceive themselves to be independent and separate from the pastor's general responsibility for the congregation, confusion, competition, and, often, relationships destructive to church health will surely result.

When additional ministers are engaged to expand the leadership and ministry in a congregation, it should be as the result of careful planning. Ministers should be added to the church's staff to accomplish a particular ministry, expand a particular program, or assist the pastor in specific areas of responsibility. Careful articulation of expectations, responsibility, authority, and supervision will help assure effective ministry by the staff member and also will encourage harmonious staff relationships. Evangelism, ministry to youth, Christian education, administration, and music leadership are common areas where the pastor's effectiveness can be extended by the presence of additional ministers. Often educational expectations and specific experience are required of ministers to fulfill those ministries. Staff ministers are often titled "assistant" or "associate" depending upon their level of skill and experience, the amount of supervision they require, and the level of responsibility they exercise in the position. Generally, the title "assistant" implies less experience and less responsibility than the designation "associate." In some churches, the title "associate" designates a minister who belongs to the church, but who has no duties or remuneration.

Missioners and Special-Purpose Ministers

In addition to associate or assistant ministers, churches and church agencies may often engage ministers who are a part of the work of the whole church and related to the ministry staff but who have a very specific ministry function apart from the central life of the congregation. Examples include ministers to college and university communities, outreach ministers to the special-need populations of city neighborhoods or rural communities, ministers to different ethnic or language communities or to international communities near or related to a congregation. Sometimes such persons are members of an individual church staff, and sometimes they are supported by several churches or a fellowship.

While such ministers may also serve as an associate or assistant, the term *missioner* or *special-program minister* more accurately defines their ministry. (I distinguish a "missioner" as one who remains in contact with a congregation while engaging in a specific ministry, while a "missionary" is one whom the church, perhaps in cooperation with other churches, sends or supports to perform ministry in a distant location.) These are ministers who are gifted and trained for a very specific purpose and who should be encouraged to keep that work as their primary, if not exclusive, focus. Their work is by its nature different from that of the church's pastor or associates and assistants. The pastor should exercise supportive supervision and encourage the congregation to empower their ministry for the purpose they have called them to serve.

Churches with multiple staff members often have rich resources. They often also have special challenges. Ministers are to model Christ, yet they are human. One result is that staff needs can demand a great amount of the pastor's time. Much church conflict and confusion is traced to conflicted or dysfunctional staff relationships. A growing body of literature exists to help guide churches and ministers in developing effective ministry together. It begins, however, in understanding the primacy of the pastoral role and in having a clear understanding of the purposes for which ministers additional to the pastor are engaged.

Selecting Pastors and Ministers

Baptist churches secure their pastors by election. This practice reflects a dedication to the free choice exercised by the people and a confidence that the guidance of the Spirit may be discovered by prayerful searching by the congregation. It is also a reflection of the independence of Baptist congregations. Other ministers of the church may be selected similarly by election, whether by a board or committee with oversight for their particular work or by the whole church. Sometimes associate or assistant ministers are selected by the pastor to serve "at the pastor's pleasure." In such cases, it is still generally wise for the pastor to submit his or her selection for affirmation by the congregation. In this way the spirit of independence may be maintained while allowing for strong pastoral leadership.

The choice of a pastor is one of the most important responsibilities a congregation will exercise. If a church chooses prayerfully and wisely, the church may enjoy effective pastoral leadership and care for many years to come. Therefore, when the pastoral office is vacant, the congregation must respond with good judgment and deliberation. The purpose is not to find a new pastor as quickly as possible but to find, by the grace of God's guidance, a pastor appropriate for envisioning and leading God's work through that particular church. A productive match between pastor and people, like a good marriage, is more the product of persistent good judgment than of happenstance and good fortune.

In preparing to fill the pastoral office, the church must first appoint a pastoral search committee (or pulpit committee) to search for appropriate candidates. That committee should be made up of a selection of church leaders and members who represent the many constituencies and areas of church life. That committee should first meet prayerfully to consider the needs of the congregation and to develop a consensus regarding the kind of pastoral personality, experience, and focus they wish to find.

Many resources are available for a search committee's work, including denominational personnel offices, regional or executive ministers, seminary placement offices, other ministers and laypersons whose knowledge and judgment the committee respects, and others. Ultimately, however, it is the committee members who must recommend to the congregation a candidate whom they believe God has led them to discover. The committee should be unanimous in the choice whenever possible.

Pastoral search committees often place undue emphasis on some particular aspect of the pastoral role. Often they regard preaching as the most important function of ministry. While preaching is the most visible pastoral role, other attributes must also be considered.

In contrast, sometimes committees will overreact to attributes lacking in the previous pastor. The opposite is also sometimes true: a committee may search for the candidate most like the most recent pastor. Either approach may temporarily quench a particular thirst, but neither will provide the leadership the congregation truly needs.

When the pastoral search committee has interviewed several candidates, reviewed the needs of the congregation, and prayerfully considered which one among the candidates seems best suited in gifts, experience, and focus to become their pastor, they should then recommend the candidate to the congregation.

Usually this is done by means of a guest-preaching opportunity for the candidate, followed by a time of fellowship and dialogue with members of the congregation. In a large church, it may be advisable to extend this visit over a weekend or longer, in order to allow personal contact with the candidate by members of key boards and committees or constituencies. Then, at a meeting called for the specific purpose of a vote (no less than a week following the candidate's presentation to the church), a call should be extended by means of a vote. The call should be unanimous. If that is not possible, the call should be by at least 80 percent of the members present and voting. Any lower percentage will either cause division within the congregation or else exhaust the new pastor in trying to "win over" those who opposed him or her.

The selection of other ministers on the staff of the church should proceed along similar lines, unless the responsibility for staff choice is left with the pastor alone. Even if that is the case, the pastor may wish to work with a small advisory committee to assist in assessing the personality and skill of candidates to be considered. If, on the other hand, the choice of candidates is left to a board or committee, it should proceed in a manner similar to calling a pastor, except that its profile and qualification expectations should be determined by the particular ministry he or she is to perform. The pastor should always be a key part of such a search process for staff ministers. His evaluation of personality mixes, staff dynamics, and other considerations are critical. If the choice of candidates is to be made by committee vote, the pastor should clarify his or her preference and reasons for it prior to the vote. Some selection processes give the pastor the privilege of approval or veto. If the committee makes a choice at substantial variance with the pastor's preference, the committee and pastor should discuss their differences straightforwardly, and if agreement cannot be reached, it is preferable to reconsider or start a new search process rather than to insist on a seriously divided selection. There is no more certain path to staff misunderstanding than for a search committee to choose a minister about whom a pastor has serious reservations. Once a selection is made, the committee should keep all prior discussions in confidence and make a unanimous presentation. If, subsequent to a call, a new staff minister is informed that he or she was not the candidate the pastor preferred, or that the committee was not fully supportive, it is unlikely that a relationship with the pastor or the committee members will survive that information. Their respective ministries, and the whole church, will suffer as a result.

Finally, when the choice is made and the pastor (or staff minister) is chosen, it is important that the church devise a welcoming process designed to encourage the pastor and to build the foundation of support for his or her ministry. This is not only a case of hospitality but also a way by which the minister may become aware of the congregation and its needs. It is most important that during the early days of a pastorate or ministry, the minister must be loved, supported, and honored. Bonds of trust and respect must be built. Churches all too quickly discover avenues by which criticism and complaint can surface. Let those things happen in the context of support and love. The present frequent terminations of pastors and ministers among Baptists, whether voluntary or otherwise, is a mark both of great embarrassment and poor judgment. When a minister leaves a congregation under any other than the most joyous and respectful circumstances, it is as often the failure of the church to support the minister as it is the failure of the minister to serve the congregation well.

Critical Ministerial Issues

Ministry has always been challenging. God's purpose in the world is often very different from the world's own agenda. In the modern world ministry has also become complex. Ministers are required to become specialists in many things and yet as a profession are the last of the true "generalists." The issues resulting from this are too numerous for the scope of this book. There is a growing and extensive library related to growth in ministry, skill development, spiritual growth, and the development of ministry staff relationships, not to mention the development of church ministries and programs. Nevertheless, just as Hiscox originally identified several issues that were critical to ministry in churches, similar issues are critical now.

Pastoral Authority

A pastor is placed over the church by the calling of God and by the free and voluntary consent of the congregations. Yet pastors and congregations will find that assent to such an assertion is easier theologically and in the abstract than in practice. All would agree, perhaps, that a pastor should not be a dictator nor regarded with blind devotion. Neither would many claim that he or she should be a slave to the passing agendas or whims of assertive members of the congregation, whether elected to office or self-appointed. Somewhere between these poles is the broad road of proper authority.

Ideally we might agree with Hiscox, who said that "the pastor who maintains a dignified and consistent Christian and ministerial life, commending himself to the confidence of the people, will receive all the deference he desires, and will have accorded to him all that personal respect and official reverence which he needs to claim" (p. 61). We must surely also agree that "his authority will be a moral force, to which those who love and honor him will yield" (p. 61). Yet pastoral authority remains difficult to define and harder to exercise with confidence. There are two issues in present church life that consistently call pastoral authority into question.

The first is a general crisis of leadership present in nearly every aspect of our culture and life. From small community concerns to large and global challenges, people everywhere are searching for leadership. But as soon as it emerges or is identified, leadership is frequently subject to intense scrutiny and attack. The reasons for this phenomenon are not entirely clear. But what is certain is that it affects the pastoral role in churches. One specific consideration is that the pastor is no longer the primary—or even the most important—interpreter of world events and life experiences. Even the most isolated communities of people are exposed to media personalities, experts, opinions, and observations that may challenge pastoral perspectives. Such challenges make leadership in spiritual affairs difficult. Another consideration is that few communities have escaped a debate about fundamental life values. This debate fuels polarization in communities and churches alike, and leaders are often disabled when they are suspected of favoring one side.

The second is the problem of theological diversity. Although it is related to debates about values, it is specific to the church. Not since the Reformation has there been such universal ferment about the authority and role of Scripture, the dimensions of theological truth, and its application to daily life and the purpose of the church. All of these greatly affect pastoral roles and authority. This is especially so because pastors must preside over discussions and debates on these issues, and they are issues about which pastors cannot or should not be neutral. It is, therefore, a rare pastor who is not constantly subjected to severe testing regarding his or her own opinions on such matters as well as on his or her leadership role.

Against these troubling winds, a pastor must steer a certain course by articulating a vision for the church, developing understanding and support for the vision, and providing leadership to the church's leaders to demonstrate effective goals and strategies to accomplish the vision. Pastoral authority is wisely gained from developing trusting, lasting relationships with church members and by personal ministry among them. Conversely, it is rarely exercised simply by assertion. Rather, let the pastor preach with confidence, provide pastoral care with compassion and sensitivity, and challenge the church to follow where he or she proposes to lead. In politics, true authority is derived from the consent of the governed. In churches, pastoral authority is prescribed by the Scriptures, but it is granted by the congregation.

Pastoral authority, then, must constantly be of concern not only to pastors but to the whole congregation. By open dialogue, study of Scripture, prayer, and seeking the guidance of the Spirit, a pastor must rely more than ever on the confidence that comes from God's presence and from the certainty of God's call.

Likewise, congregations must accept responsibility to support and follow a pastor's lead, unless by reason of scriptural understanding or conviction of conscience they are simply unable to do so.

Length of Service

There is no optimal period of time for a pastor to serve a church or for a minister to remain on the staff of a church. In fact, God may intend for differing periods for the use of varied gifts and the changing needs of congregations. Also, community circumstances, the needs and concerns of a minister's family, the ability of the minister to remain vital and growing while in the same position, and the ability for a minister and a church to grow in grace together all impact this question.

A pastor of prophetic vision and fervent preaching may bring a church to a moment of conviction that another pastor of a more nurturing nature may be better able to bring to life. In one circumstance a pastor with marked administrative gifts may renew a church with many institutional accomplishments in ministry and then remain to manage and perfect them. In another circumstance, the same pastor may be called to use those skills with prophetic deliberation and then move on promptly to seek new realms of institutional chaos to organize. Also, persons change and grow, as do congregations. As a general rule, a minister should not remain beyond the time when he or she feels challenged and fulfilled by the particular ministry, nor should a minister leave while still finding great challenge with much to accomplish just because a new opportunity presents itself. And churches should not long tolerate ministers who seem merely to "hold on" or those who have long records of short ministries. Both stifle the work of the gospel.

Nevertheless, short tenures, forced terminations, and a preoccupation with "career development" have wreaked havoc on church life and have worked to disable the productive ministry of many congregations and ministers. Such circumstances bring the judgment of God on the church and human judgment about the effectiveness of God's work through the church. Let churches and ministers beware of sudden and hasty changes brought on by momentary times of frustration or contention with one another. Let both beware, too, of the power of the spiritually sick within a congregation who claim personal authority by the technique of opposing pastors and stirring up constant trouble. It is often the most able and inspired among ministers who are opposed and attacked by those who seem threatened by a healthy ministry. In such cases, the minister must possess patience and confidence and call upon the responsible members of the congregation to share in the concerns of disruption and strife—and they must respond with their support.

A minister may offer the best ministry of which he or she is capable and still find that a significant number within the church believe it might be best for him or her to seek a new field of service. After prayerful consideration and, where provided, the careful counsel of a ministerial relations committee or the diaconate, it may seem the ministerial relationship should end. In such circumstances the minister should depart with dignity, and the church should provide for the support and care of the pastor during a time of his or her transition if a new call has not yet been clarified.

When unplanned departures disrupt careers and family life, ministers should ever remember that Jesus said, "Foxes have holes, and birds of the air have nests; but the Son of man has nowhere to lay his head" (Matthew 8:20). The ministry sometimes calls its servants into times of uncertainty, and the decision to leave a particular ministry may be one such time. Churches should be aware of the quarrels and conflicts that are their own. If a minister has been part of one, or even at the center of one, the pain of his or her parting may be severe. But he or she will ultimately move on to new ministry and new callings. The pain and anguish of broken relationships within the body of the church will require time, prayer, and diligent effort to repair.

Churches at peace are those that accomplish the Lord's work: "So the church throughout all Judea and Galilee and Samaria had peace and was built up; and walking in the fear of the Lord and in the comfort of the Holy Spirit it was multiplied" (Acts 9:31). Let ministers and churches both, therefore, work and pray for such experiences and invest heavily in them. And when pastors and churches sever relationships, may they go in the assurance of mutual prayer.

Ministerial Support

Pastors in particular and ministers in general are worthy of adequate support. They deserve support first in the prayer and undergirding by fellowship of the congregation they serve. Let them feel loved, appreciated, cared for, and valued. Second, they deserve support in the financial and material means by which they and their families might live in the community to which they have been called.

What should a minister be paid? That is the question likely to call forth every opinion as well as every complaint and criticism in the congregation. Churches should dedicate themselves not only to adequate support but to responsible processes by which that support is established and reviewed. Many Baptist churches find a ministerial relations committee helpful in making such determinations, but only if the congregation at large is willing to respond to its leadership and guidance. It is, sadly, often the case that once a minister has been called, his or her salary remains the same or is increased by less than adequate amounts over the years of service. This is an insult not only to the value of the minister in the community but to the priority of God's work in the church.

Appropriate reference points for establishing pastoral pay should be based on community standards so that the pastor may live in dignity among the people he or she serves. In most communities the salaries of school principals, college deans, and managers in industry and other professions may help establish guidelines. A church that wishes to keep a gifted and productive pastor must provide a foundation for its pastor's well-being. And a church that wishes for a pastoral change must have more integrity than to withhold support in an effort to force the pastor to leave.

Expectations of Ministers

Modern ministry is often a "burnout profession." New ministers, fresh from the power of a call and the high expectations of ordination, often find that after a few years they are neutralized by exhaustion, bitterness, and plaguing doubts whether ministry is their proper vocation. Sometimes this is because a minister has not attended to his or her own needs for recreation and spiritual growth. But all too frequently it is because churches are not clear in their expectations about the ordained ministry or are conflicted in their expression of them.

In defining the work of ministers, we have already alluded to the many roles ministers perform. For churches and ministers too, preaching is the primary role. But ministers, especially pastors, are also expected to be teachers and resource leaders, skilled administrators in church affairs, and chief executive officers in leading the institution; they are asked to be visionaries as well as focused on the details necessary in following up plans. A pastor must be a staff leader and supervisor but also a colleague and friend; he or she must be a stern disciplinarian but also a loving shepherd. A minister must command the respect of the laity, but equally, must serve to equip the laity for the ministry and witness that is properly theirs to exercise. It is not surprising, therefore, that expectations can come into conflict and that pastors do not universally meet every expectation with equal satisfaction. Indeed, while all these expectations and more are appropriate in certain circumstances and times, no minister could meet all at once—and never all with equal ability. Let both ministers and churches confess this reality with humility.

In responding to expectations, ministers need first to keep in focus that it is God they serve first and utmost. Service to the church is because God has called them to that service and because the church is truly God's own. Second, each minister must be acutely aware of both gifts and areas in need of growth. Third, pastors must be open and sensitive to the expectations others have for their ministry, but equally they must be confident to express their own priorities as they understand God to have shaped them in their ministry. Churches, likewise, have a responsibility to clarify expectations and to be consistent in expressing them. Over time, formal, mutual evaluations and reviews of both pastoral performance and congregational expectations will enable changing expectations to be negotiated and established.

Related to this problem is the all-too-common dilemma many pastors face in churches of all sizes and traditions: namely, a dysfunction between expectations, responsibility, and authority. For example, sometimes a segment of a congregation expects a pastor to regularly visit in homes of members because that is what they believe he or she should do and that is what they were used to their pastor doing where they came from. A pastor who fails in that expectation will be subject to severe criticism. Yet the church leaders may have assigned a low priority to home visitation or may have delegated it to a minister of visitation as a primary task. For another example, sometimes a church engages a pastor on the strength of his dynamic and inspiring preaching. But after a time some members become frustrated that the pastor prefers to spend time in study and sermon preparation and exhibits less interest and skill in church administration. It is equally important for the pastor to make adjustments where reasonable and for churches to take responsibility to celebrate what the minister does well and productively, while finding ways to support and delegate those things he or she is less able to do. It is most important of all for church and pastor to keep open channels of communication so that a minister's abilities may build up the church and so that the minister's deficiencies do not invite the congregation to tear down the minister and, ultimately, its own ministry.

Conflict is the order of business in our time. Its sources are to be found in personal, cultural, political, and other expressions of diversity. Churches, like every other gathering of persons, are vulnerable to conflict becoming the chief activity of both their fellowship and mission. This must not be allowed to happen, for when conflict takes hold, the church lets go of the mandate of the Great Commission and of its mission, and it becomes an embarrassment rather than a witness to the gospel. It is impossible for churches to avoid conflict entirely. Rather they must attempt to keep it to a minimum and manage it, as good stewards of the church's energies.

The results of conflict in church life are especially burdensome for ministers in general and pastors in particular. Whenever conflict arises, even if it originally had little to do with the pastor or pastoral leadership, the pastor suffers. In the midst of it, the pastor's role is to lift up the truth of the gospel and to be, wherever possible, a peacemaker. Sometimes the pastor's responsibility is simply to endure with patience. Other times it is to affirm a cause or side in the conflict, simply because it is right and of God and he or she can do no other. Sometimes, if conflict cannot be diminished or resolved, it is the pastor's sad responsibility to leave that particular field of ministry and seek a new place of service. To remain forever in a conflicted, combative fellowship is to waste a calling and spiritual gifts and to be diverted from the good work God has called him or her to do.

Churches should regard dissension and strife within the body as anathema. It should be addressed at its very beginning. If it threatens the church's work and health, the nature of the conflict should be exposed quickly and forthrightly. And, if it seems that no resolution can be had, no mutual tolerance and respect in Christian love can be achieved, let the church divide with dignity. The kingdom is better served by fellowships that can each function with its own strength than by one community so divided that it cannot function. If the conflict involves the pastor, directly or indirectly, then the church is responsible to protect the pastor's ministry if possible and reputation if it is subject to the tyranny of gossip, envy, or malice. If the conflict is in part due to the pastor's style of leadership or personal characteristics, then, as Hiscox so aptly said it a century ago, "If he be in fault, let them tell him so, and win him from his mistakes" (p. 64).

The Ministerial Relations Committee

Advocacy for ministry comes from no less a source than God. Yet here, amidst human frailty and imperfect, sinful institutions, ministry needs advocacy among those whom the minister seeks to serve. Many churches have, in recent years, established a ministerial (or pastoral) relations committee to attend to this need. In the best of circumstances, such a committee can ease the process of interpreting priorities perceived within the congregation to the pastor or ministers, and likewise, help members of the congregation understand ministerial concerns more clearly. Also, it can provide leadership in determining salaries, vacation, continuing education needs, and other considerations in support of the pastor or ministers.

A ministerial relations committee can be a special committee of the church, a subcommittee of the diaconate, or a task force of an advisory or executive council. However it is structured, members should be chosen for sensitivity, confidentiality, and dedication to effective leadership. Whenever possible, members should also represent a broad cross section of church life. The committee should be at least five members and no more than nine members.

The committee should meet with the pastor or minister on a regular basis to share concerns and to find supportive ways both to increase the minister's effectiveness and to identify places needing attention in the congregation.

The work of such a committee is defined more specifically in materials produced by ministry councils and personnel departments of many denominations and fellowships. Regional ministers and executives can also often provide guidance and counsel in aiding a church to develop a structure for this important work.

Evaluation and Discipline of Ministers

Ministers follow a divine calling but are still human. Even the most inspired and dedicated ministry can benefit from effective responses and evaluation. All ministers are, from time to time, in need of support and discipline to keep them effectively focused and responsive to their call. Occasionally ministers fail grievously in their tasks, stumble in their moral behavior, or violate professional standards or ethics. The ongoing work of a ministerial relations committee can be effective in developing a process of nurture for a growing ministry. The same group may also be needed to contemplate how to respond to serious lapses in ministerial performance or behavior.

One of the most difficult and threatening experiences in a church's life is when the church, or a significant portion of it, has lost confidence in a minister, or worse, when a minister seems to have lost his or her footing in faith, or worst of all, when a minister is accused of a crime or unethical behavior. Leaders of all kinds are now subjected to intense public scrutiny, and those in ministry perhaps most of all because they occupy a sacred trust in the community of faith. The church, therefore, must be prepared spiritually and practically in order effectively to deal with such unhappy occurrences.

First, it cannot be emphasized strongly enough that the responsibility for responding to charges or accusations against a minister should be clearly delineated within the congregation, and the body or group charged with that responsibility should be allowed to perform its functions in response without interference. Nothing can inflame and ultimately divide a church faster than allowing response to a controversy regarding ministerial performance or behavior to quickly become a matter of ungoverned public debate within the congregation.

Over one hundred years ago Hiscox spoke with feeling when he reminded congregations that great caution should be exercised "even in giving heed to unfavorable reports against a minister of the gospel" (p. 66). Ministers are subjected to constant criticism by the very nature of their calling and work. Criticism, accusations, and gossip are most often groundless, and it is tragic when a ministry is destroyed and a church crippled by giving credence to false claims and accusations. "Never admit any charge against an elder except on the evidence of two or three witnesses," said Paul (1 Timothy 5:19). The work of a minister calls him or her into all sorts of company. Jesus, for example, was criticized because he kept company with "winebibbers and adulterers," and the Pharisees thought him morally unfit because he healed on the sabbath and allowed his disciples to prepare a meal on the same day. While ministers should exercise good judgment and care in their public and private conduct, ministers would violate their calling if they were not at times found in the company of the morally uncertain and in circumstances foreign to respectable society. Most accusations or complaints against ministers are the result of misperceptions, unresolved personal feelings, or other reasons for which the minister cannot be held responsible. Evil knows no boundaries in attempting to disable the church, and disabling the minister's reputation is the most effective strategy to accomplish that goal.

When it seems there may be substance to a charge, however, or when comments and criticism seem to be grounded in evident problems in a minister's spiritual, personal, or professional life, the church must respond for the sake of the gospel, the sake of the church, and the sake of the minister. If it is largely a personal matter, such as a minister struggling with depression, a failing marriage, or a loss of faith or calling, a church is well advised to delegate his or her most trusted friends, if possible, to raise concerns and to urge counseling, support, or spiritual direction.

If it is a matter of professional misconduct or failure, the ministerial relations committee, or some other body properly delegated to the task, should meet formally with the minister to lay open the concerns or charges so that he or she might respond. Based on that response, further consideration may help save the ministry of that person by discovering a means of recompense or reform. Some local minister's councils are equipped to assist in such cases; denominational offices can also often provide advice and counsel.

If the matter is one that involves the civil authorities and has legal implications for the minister or the church, or both, it is wise for the minister to seek legal counsel, and perhaps for the church to do likewise. For example, at present the whole matter of sexual harassment or misconduct has emerged as an area of great sensitivity in many areas of professional relationships and is particularly threatening to the ministry. An accusation of this sort certainly brings questions of personal and professional behavior into focus, but it may also have legal ramifications. Churches that have well-defined denominational connections are always wise to consult the resources available to them, as are pastors and ministers.

It is most helpful for a church to avoid questions of guilt or innocence whenever possible. Churches are not to function as courts of law but as agencies of redemption. Even when charges against a pastor or minister are substantiated, the ultimate purpose of the church is not to condemn but to seek redemption, both for the damaged person or persons and for the offending minister. By exercising a loving discipline, a church may recommend means by which the minister might recover integrity and possibly his or her ministry, even if not in the present position.

However, if a pastor or minister believes he or she has been wrongly charged, Baptist church tradition allows for a council to be called. Such a council functions in a similar way to an ordination council and should include respected ministers or denominational leaders in addition to members of the church. Its purpose is to hear charges and defense, and all other material pertinent to the dilemma, and then to offer an advisory recommendation to the church leadership, and ultimately to the congregation, for action. This may be achieved by means of a vote. Recommendations might range from dismissing a minister for cause on one extreme to exonerating the minister and urging the discipline of a church member on the other. Ultimately, as Hiscox pointed out, "Judicial acts belong to a church, and not to a council; nor can a church transfer its authority for the exercise of judicial functions to any other body" (p. 67). This is at the core of Baptist principles and traditions.

Two mistakes can prove very costly to the work of both the church and the minister and, ultimately, to the gospel. The first is to circumvent church processes in the mistaken belief that it is better to cover up or hide a problem. Sometimes well-meaning leaders might privately suggest that a pastor leave, without first thoroughly examining the truth or objectivity of charges against him or her. If the pastor, even though innocent, leaves the congregation in an attempt to avoid embarrassment, his or her reputation and ministry may be damaged. And a church whose pastor leaves under such circumstances may require a generation or more to repair the mistrust, broken relationships, and bitterness that will surely result between its members. The gospel, the church, and the ministry are all best served if charges against a minister can be dealt with openly and forthrightly.

The second serious mistake is when a church allows issues relating to its ministers to become public matters within the community which surrounds it. The work of ministerial relations committees, church councils, or other means to deal with issues surrounding a minister's performance or behavior should be handled with the greatest of privacy. None but church members should attend such meetings, and members of the media or press should be kept uninformed, at least until a resolution has been made regarding the circumstances. Ministers who are "tried" in the public media are not only badly damaged themselves, but additionally, the church is greatly weakened for the work it is called to do.

Epilogue on the Ministry

Ironically, it is in the consideration of these unhappy eventualities of ministry that, with bright clarity, the significance of the ministry to the church emerges. A church is defined by its ministry, and often by those whose personal ministry is most public. The personal relationships of ministry are, consciously or otherwise, suggestive of relationships with Christ, and the symbolic role of the minister in the church impacts upon individual perceptions of God. Let no mistake be made on this account. Despite the Baptist emphasis on democratic processes and the equality of all men and women in spiritual access, Baptists have a high view of ministry.

Baptists, perhaps because of their high commitment to the priesthood of all believers, have sometimes been tempted to devalue the role of church leaders, ordained or otherwise. But the success of a church in fulfilling its gospel function and responding to Christ's own call for its discipleship, corporately and individually, rests with its ministry as with no other. Let those therefore who respond to the call of ministry do so with the greatest commitment. Let the church claim its highest and best in spirit and in gifts to perform it. And let churches and ministers together work in common calling to do the work of the gospel and to bring honor and glory to Christ, the model for every ministry and the Head of the whole church.

NOTES

1. The role of women as church leaders, particularly as ordained ministers, and especially as pastors and preachers, is a subject of debate and controversy among some Baptists and Baptist churches. The reality is that many Baptists do ordain women to the ministry. In discussions of ministry I have elected to assume that ordained ministers of any vocation or responsibility might be equally male or female. Therefore, I have elected an inclusive style and approach and have mixed pronouns to reflect this simple reality. In so doing I do not presume to suggest resolution to this issue in every church but respect the right of each church to search the Scriptures and the mind of God on this very significant issue.

Chapter IV

Leaders and Officers in the Church

The ordained ministry is vital to a church's well-being and spiritual health. But the continuing vitality and strength of a church depends equally on the development of effective leadership among the laity, a clear understanding of church processes and procedures, and the development of commensurate authority and responsibility to carry out the functions of the church's ministry, programs, and missions. This is especially true among Baptists, whose theology affirms the role of the laity and whose churches are organized along democratic principles.

Contemporary church organizational life, however, has become both complex and highly structured. This is partly because Baptists have been committed to involving as many church participants as possible in the organizational life of the congregation. It is also true, however, that churches have increasingly taken on the organizational style of business and political models of modern institutions. It is possible for an overly complex organization to drain the energy of church life by shifting the focus of the church from its reliance on the Spirit and its true mission to a preoccupation with institutional maintenance. Therefore, churches and church leaders are challenged to create leadership channels that enable the congregation to accomplish its goals without exhausting the spirit of the church.

We turn first to the model of the church in the Scriptures. In the New Testament's record of the apostolic era, we find descriptions of only two offices: pastors and deacons. From the little evidence available, it seems apparent that a proliferation of offices and leadership roles grew up beyond the local congregation more quickly than within it. Baptist churches have generally rejected many of the internal and external developments of older church structures. Nonetheless they have added offices and leadership roles to accomplish a variety of functions all their own. They are thus vulnerable to a certain bureaucratic style. Let us, therefore, first review the scriptural offices. And since we have already discussed the ordained ministry in general and the pastoral office in particular at some length, we shall first review the role of the diaconate. We shall then proceed to review other church offices as they have been commonly created and exercised and finally to review leadership alternatives in Baptist churches.

Deacons

The diaconate is the lone nonpastoral office found in the early church. The term *deacon* comes from the Greek *diakonos*, and, as we recall, literally means "minister" in the specific meaning of servant, as one who "ministers to" or who serves others. In the Scriptures this meaning applied to the apostles and even to Christ. In the language and experience of the church, however, it has most often referred to specific officers in the church.

Origin and Qualifications

Scriptural precedent for the diaconate is most often identified in the election of the seven to help the apostles in carrying out acts of charity, compassion, and practicality (Acts 6:1-6). Following Pentecost, a large ingathering of new believers had stressed the capabilities of the original, tightly knit fellowship of the earliest Christians. Care of the needy and of aspects of fellowship life together had become so burdensome that these responsibilities began to threaten the spiritual duties of prayer and proclamation. And, according to the scriptural reference, care of the needy was apparently not being accomplished with consistency. Therefore, in Acts 6 we learn that "seven men of good repute, full of the Spirit and of wisdom" (v. 3) were chosen to perform these activities, so that the apostles might devote themselves "to prayer and to the ministry of the word" (v. 4). These seven were set apart for this work with prayer and by the laying on of hands, an ancient rite symbolizing investiture and empowerment.

Qualification for the diaconate seemed to rest in three categories: that they were men; that they were of good reputation; that they evidenced the power of the Spirit within. Baptist churches have, for many generations, broadened the definition of "men" to mean "persons" in one of two ways. First, many churches have developed boards of deaconesses, originally to bring ministry and charity to members of their own sex, and then later to specialize in acts of compassion and care. More recently, women have frequently been included as members of integrated diaconate boards. The question of whether gender identity is a qualification for church offices of any kind is currently a matter of varied interpretation in Baptist churches. However, it is interesting that in this most ancient of church offices women have historically offered faithful leadership and ministry. And even the most traditional reader should be aware that scriptural language that is often translated to mean "men" was not as frequently as specific as the translation. In any event, the Christian church developed in a cultural climate in which women had no standing apart from their husband, father, or other male family head. This is not true of our time.

Regarding the other two qualifications, there should be less controversy. That the deacons should be of "good reputation" was especially important because their distribution of charity required them to handle money and to develop equitable standards for the distribution. That they should be Spirit-filled was equally important. First, only those empowered by the Spirit could be expected to be sensitive to the needs of the community, and especially the needs of the weakest in the community. Second, it is evident from the personal history of some of the seven in subsequent events that their duties as deacons took them beyond the confines of the mundane and temporal needs of the church. In fact, several became foremost as counselors and coadministrators with the apostles in some spiritual interests as well. However, it is important to understand that this heightened leadership role most likely developed because they were Spirit-filled and not because of their specific role as deacons.

Selection and Duties

In modern Baptist churches deacons are chosen by vote of the church, often having been proposed by means of a nominating committee or upon recommendation by the pastor. They should ideally represent a cross section of the membership of the church with regard to age, circumstances, economic status, and other considerations of membership constituencies. They should, nevertheless, be faithful, prudent, experienced, and spiritually mature persons.

In some Baptist churches the diaconate still serves to guide the secular functions of the church, especially regarding finances and property concerns. However, in an increasing number of congregations, these concerns have been delegated to other boards and officers, such as trustees, property management committees, finance committees, and others. It is appropriate for the deacons to exercise leadership in these areas, but it is not necessary, especially if it overtaxes their ability to respond in other areas.

The primary duties of deacons should be to exercise ministry and to care for the sick and needy among the membership, and also, when appropriate, to act as counselors and assistants to the pastor and other ministers in advancing the spiritual welfare of the church. In the absence of a pastor, it becomes the duty of the deacons to conduct devotional or prayer gatherings or to arrange for their leadership, to provide for the pulpit responsibilities of the church, and to administer the spiritual concerns of the church in general. By tradition, deacons in many Baptist churches are charged also with the responsibility of preparing the elements for the Lord's Supper (also called Communion or the Eucharist), and assisting the minister in serving the elements to the congregation. There is no scriptural precedent for this practice, however, and churches should not allow deacons to be perceived merely as ritual participants or as jealous guardians of the Lord's table. In addition to Communion preparation and service, deacons are often also delegated responsibility for a broad variety of other worship and devotional needs, including the reading of Scriptures, caring for candidates for baptism, chancel preparations, and the exploration of traditional and other worship programs that enliven and encourage spiritual growth in worship.

There are two problems associated with the service of modern deacons. The first is that in some churches deacons can become little more than honorary, ritual leaders, often chosen only from the most senior members of long standing, and with little official or unofficial purpose. This is a poor understatement of a rich role of leadership provided by the Scripture and tradition. Deacons should be exemplars of servant ministry and models of spiritual leadership in the congregation.

The second problem is that in many Baptist churches the diaconate has developed into the "power center" of the congregation and can exercise an unbiblical tyranny over the church and, in some cases, the pastor. In such cases, diaconal ministry reverses the role established in Acts by making the servants in fact the supervisor. Indeed, many of the short-tenure pastorates and forced terminations that plague Baptist churches and weaken their witness are the result of "power struggles" between pastors and boards of deacons. A century ago Hiscox addressed this problem by saying, "Deacons should be watchful guardians of the purity and good order of the churches, striving to maintain a healthful tone of Christian faith and activity in the body. But they must act only in conjunction with the pastor, not independent of him, except possibly in very rare and urgent cases. Hence, while it is desirable for the pastor to have meetings with his deacons often or statedly for consultation and advice, it is not proper for them to hold meetings as a board of deacons, independent of and without the advice of the pastor" (p. 74, n. 4). A pastor should be accountable for his or her ministry to the congregation. But it is not appropriate for the pastor to work under the supervision of the deacons. Concerns regarding professional evaluation or performance of ministry should be designated to the appropriate, responsible group. And the pastor and deacons should maintain an appropriate biblical relationship.

Number of Deacons and Length of Service

The number of deacons in a church is a discretionary matter and should vary according to the size of the congregation, the intensity of need, and the quantity of qualified candidates available to perform the service. General practice suggests that one deacon for every twenty-five members in smaller churches, or every fifty members in larger churches, should be adequate. In very small or newly established congregations, a minimum of three deacons is suggested.

Although we may imagine there was no limit of service time for deacons in the apostolic era, modern deacons should generally serve a specified term of office. This practice will prevent diaconal burnout and will also encourage others to extend their gifts and abilities in this service. Traditional service length is often a period of three years. Some churches allow for reelection immediately, while others require that after one or two terms of service, a deacon may not be elected until a year's time has elapsed.

A few churches have established a practice of electing a few exceptionally worthy deacons to "life deacon" status. The basis for such a practice is a concern for institutional continuity, a desire to recognize persons of unusual spiritual maturity and good judgment, and other high motives. Stability and good order may result from such a practice, but there are also dangers. For example, relying upon the judgment of a few persons can result in a burden of leadership that may be unfair to the life deacons and may also cause leadership stagnation in the church. Such a practice also seems unavoidably to encourage deference to the most senior members of long standing in the congregation. If a church chooses to designate some as life deacons, it is wiser to make the designation honorific and not authoritative.

Ordination of Deacons

In Acts the seven were set apart to be empowered for their duties by prayer and the laying on of hands by the apostles. This action imparted a sacred trust to them and recognized the importance of their duties. In the past, many churches practiced ordination of deacons, but this ceremony has fallen into disuse. Ordination may invest the office with greater importance and help focus the work of deacons in a spiritually appropriate manner. If this practice is adopted, however, great care should be taken to clarify to the congregation the difference between ordination to the diaconate and ordination to the Christian ministry. Churches that elect to ordain deacons should hold the service of ordination during a

Sunday worship service following the election of deacons. The service should reflect the solemnity of the purpose, the support of the congregation, and the commitment of the deacons being ordained.

An effective, dedicated diaconate with a clear vision of its purpose and work can be a powerful influence for the good witness of a church. A pastor and a diaconate, empowered by the Spirit and working in harmony toward the vision of Christ's kingdom, are a blessing to themselves and to the church.

Other Church Officers

Many other church offices, though not first identified in Scripture, have become necessary or useful as the church has developed throughout history. To a large extent, these other church offices are delegations of functions from what were originally pastoral or diaconal roles. For example, whereas at an ancient date a church might have only a diaconate, now most churches have boards of trustees, Christian education, and missions.

Likewise, whereas a pastor at one time was the exclusive and sole administrator and leader of a congregation, now most churches delegate many specific responsibilities to treasurers, building managers, moderators, and secretaries. Therefore, while many modern church offices do not have a direct biblical precedent, their functions are rooted in scriptural evidence and the practices of church life.

In addition, there are many other individual offices, committees, and leadership roles commonly found in Baptist churches. Individual offices often include a moderator, clerk, treasurer, financial secretary, and a church-school superintendent. Committees are often appointed to provide nominations for church offices, organize ushering, auditing, finance and budget concerns, and sometimes also programmatic issues such as evangelism, music, and special community concerns or denominational programs. Ad hoc committees may also be appointed for short-term or specific subject tasks.

A detailed discussion of all of these functions is not possible here. However, the following descriptions may provide a general guide and may be supplemented by some of the suggested reading in the bibliography and notes to this section. Two works especially, both now almost classics, would be especially useful: *A Baptist Manual of Polity and Practice* by Norman H. Maring and Winthrop S. Hudson and *Church Officers at Work* by Glenn H. Asquith. (See Appendix G.)

Board of Trustees

Churches are treated by government agencies and laws as one category of "nonprofit" institutions. As a rule, state and federal laws establish requirements for reporting of status, filing of reports and fees, and especially for exemption of taxes on property. Most often state laws relating to religious corporations require that there be a specific body that holds legal title to the property of the church and is responsible for its financial and legal affairs. State law may even specify the number, tenure, and method of election of the members of such a body. In churches this body is usually the board of trustees.

In selecting the members for such a board, attention should be given to placing board members with expertise or experience in matters of real estate, insurance, legal liability, and other matters of corporate responsibility. Boards of trustees should be small in number, usually no more than required by law, and should serve limited, rotating terms. They should be constituted so that their actions must be approved by the church. As the legal agents for the church, their powers should be circumscribed so that they do not set policy for the church but rather carry out the will and administer the resources of the church according to priorities established by the congregation.

In some churches, trustees also handle financial matters related to the operating budget. However, it is most often advisable to have this function handled by a separate committee for that purpose or as a specific function of an advisory board.

Board of Christian Education

Modern churches operate a variety of programs of training, Christian nurture, family life, or other spiritual growth opportunities. In addition, many churches operate day-care centers, nursery schools, weekday schools, and adult opportunity programs. For the sake of effective coordination and planning, churches are advised to place responsibility for the whole range of such programs under a board of Christian education (Christian nurture, spiritual growth, or the like). The work of this board may be carried out as a whole or through subcommittees for specific programs, such as children's work, youth work, leadership education, child-care committee, nursery school committee, and so on, depending on the program complexity of the church.

When this model of administration is chosen, the board needs to coordinate closely with the superintendent of the Sunday school, the pastor, and other ministry staff members. As with other boards, members should be selected for their interest as well as expertise in various areas and programs of education and should represent the constituencies in the church. Terms should be limited and rotating.

Board of Missions and Outreach

Leadership and supervision of the church's mission programs is sometimes provided by the diaconate and, in some churches, by special support groups within the church, such as the women's or men's fellowship groups. However, in many Baptist churches general oversight for supporting and encouraging mission projects and programs is vested in a board especially identified for that purpose. Members should be selected on the basis of their commitment to missions programs as a priority of the church—and from as much of a cross section of the church as is possible. Terms should be limited and rotating to encourage broad participation.

Church Clerk

The church clerk is an elected individual officer of the church who is responsible for keeping accurate records of church meetings, writing the official correspondence of the church (regarding reports to denominations, transfers of membership letters, and so on) and maintaining the membership roll in good order. The person selected for this office should be one who is meticulous and accurate in detail and able to participate in the meetings and administrative work of the church. A clerk may not need to be rotated out of office, and, in some larger churches with paid staff members, the clerk may be a member of the administrative staff specifically elected to carry out these functions. Sometimes the work of a clerk will be assisted by two other elected offices: a membership clerk and a church historian.

Treasurer

The church treasurer is an elected officer who works closely with the board of trustees as the custodian of church funds, and, where such responsibilities are separated, with the finance committee for administering the budget of the church. In a large church that employs a church administrator, the treasurer should supervise any activities of the administrator relating to financial affairs. As a general practice the treasurer should be bonded, and the books of the church should be audited annually by outside auditors for the protection of the church. The treasurer may need to be exempted from the rule of term limits, or to have longer term limits, as it is wise to elect a capable treasurer for longer periods. However, as treasurers seem eventually to succumb to the temptation of believing the church's funds are under their direction and prioritization, it is also wise to be sure that the treasurer reports to the congregation and disperses funds as established by the church.

Financial Secretary

The work of the financial secretary is the exacting and important task of maintaining accurate records regarding members' financial contributions. This is important not only for the ability of the church to project and plan for financial needs but also because individual members will expect accurate records for tax purposes. If a system of pledging or annual commitment is followed, the financial secretary must identify payments and contributions as they are received and keep an accurate accounting of them. Likewise, special gifts for designated purposes, memorials, building funds, or special offerings will need similar record keeping. At regular intervals the financial secretary will send each contributor a written status of account, and, at the end of the year, a complete record of the year's contributions in all categories will help contributors in reporting their taxes.

The development of personal computers and inexpensive software for financial programs will greatly assist a financial secretary, as well as a treasurer, in their work. In churches where an administrator is employed, a financial secretary may delegate some of the weekly tasks of record keeping to the administrator. However, the financial secretary should be responsible to verify that the records are accurate.

Church-School Superintendent

In many Baptist churches, the Sunday school developed separately from the development of the church itself. Often it met in conjunction with the church but was entirely independent and had its own officers and finances. In some churches, each class was independent of the church or the other classes. In recent decades, the Sunday morning educational activities have become integrated with general church programming and have become an activity of the church itself, often under the direction of the board of Christian education. In such cases, the superintendent is an officer of the church and a member of the board of Christian education ex officio, while contributions are received as part of the general budget of the church by the financial secretary. Curriculum materials and other resources are then expensed as part of the budget of the church education program. Nevertheless, a superintendent has a significant role to play in providing for teacher recruitment and training, developing new classes and programs, administering the details of the program (such as room assignments and material orders), and other tasks. The person chosen for this office should be one dedicated to the importance of education, nurture, and spiritual growth and who has good administrative skills. Superintendents are hard to find and therefore important to encourage. If term limits are established, they should allow for lengthy service. Church-school programs often assist the work of the superintendent by providing for clerks, secretaries, and assistant superintendents for specific age groups or programs.

Moderator

The moderator, or as the position might alternatively be called, the president, is the person designated to preside over church business meetings and meetings of an advisory council or executive committee. Some churches automatically designate the pastor as moderator, while others view this as an elected lay office of the church. Either way has both advantages and disadvantages. If the pastor serves in this role, his or her authority as leader and chief officer of the church is strengthened. The pastor is most likely to know the items required for agenda consideration and most likely also to exercise balanced judgment. In times of controversy, however, it places the pastor in a difficult position in presiding over debates among members—particularly if the debate involves his or her leadership or program directions.

On the other hand, the existence of a lay moderator may imply an alternative leadership of the church. To avoid this, the moderator's description of duties must be carefully and specifically written in order not to confuse roles between the pastor and the moderator. When this model is used, the pastor must value the moderator as an administrative leader, and the moderator must respect the pastor's long-standing role as the overseer of the church. Particularly in times of controversy or conflict in the congregation, a moderator must avoid providing a tempting alternative leadership for factions or segments of the congregation. Also, if a church chooses to have a moderator, the position description should ensure that the duties of that office do not conflict with the pastor's appropriate role in supervising staff, coordinating the church programs, and providing spiritual leadership.

Committees

Committees differ from boards in several important ways. First, they generally do not set policy but rather give oversight to specific areas of concern or activity or provide for a specific function, such as property management, financial management, or sponsorship of a particular program. Second, committees may either be standing committees, elected or appointed each term to maintain a function or solve a problem, or they may be ad hoc or temporary committees, created for a limited term and for a limited function. They may be elected to their work, if the committee is specified by the church constitution or bylaws, or they may be appointed by the moderator, pastor, or, in the case of subcommittees of boards, by the board chairperson.

Two common examples of short-term, specific committees are

the pulpit or pastoral search committee, appointed for the term required to find a new pastor, and the building committee, appointed for the term required to develop and execute plans to build a new building, add an addition, or renovate church property. Members of such committees should be chosen to ensure the expertise required for the task and to represent constituencies that have a high interest in the area where leadership is required. Unless committees are authorized and held responsible for specific functions, their plans and activities should be approved by the board that sponsors them or by the church as a whole. The exception is an informal committee that may be appointed by the pastor, moderator, or other officer for the purpose of assembling information and perspective on an issue regarding which some other board or office will make a decision or proposal.

Advisory Council or Executive Council

An effective church organizational structure should accomplish its programs and missions in a cooperative manner by providing effective coordination for its officers, boards, and committees. Such coordination should provide effective stewardship of the resources of leadership, energies, and commitments of the church. Such coordination may be accomplished informally by the pastor working in leadership and cooperation with other church leaders. However, many churches find that the creation of an advisory council or executive council greatly enables this task.

An advisory or executive council (also sometimes called a cabinet or leadership council or governing board) should consist of elected church officers and the board and committee chairpersons of all standing committees, including the leaders of such auxiliary organizations as women's groups, men's groups, and youth organizations. Alternatively, the council might be formed by several members elected "at large" from the congregation. The council should assist the pastor by encouraging effective communications between all aspects of church life, coordinating the priorities and work of the groups and organizations represented and developing cooperative arrangements where it may assist the accomplishment of goals. One specific task that is often assigned to an advisory council is that of leading the church to envision and develop long-range plans for the church and then to monitor the progress of such plans.

In general an advisory or executive council does not establish separate programs from those represented by groups in its circle (education, missions, worship, finance, etc.). It should serve, however, as a communications and coordinating center. In some church organizations, such a council functions to review items to come before the congregation for approval and may, if it chooses, make recommendations regarding the effectiveness or priority of such recommendations.

Church Representatives

Churches that have established denominational affiliations or join in partnership with community organizations for the accomplishment of certain tasks will have need of designated representatives to those organizations. Examples include children's homes, retirement or nursing facilities run by denominations or community organizations, schools or child-care facilities operated by the church or with church cooperation or denominational governing boards. If the church wishes to be officially represented (according to the bylaws of the organization with which it is in partnership), it should choose carefully such persons who have an interest in the organization, who will communicate with the church and with the organization in a regular and concise manner, and who will represent the church in a positive way. If there are organizations (such as denominational structures) to which the church should send representatives, these positions should be accounted for in bylaws or operating procedures. Such positions are often of vital importance in allowing the church to carry out its work of mission or outreach with vitality and effectiveness.

Other Leadership Roles

In a church, as in other organizations, often a variety of leadership roles are not determined by election or appointment to an office or committee. Such leaders include church-school teachers and volunteers in a variety of tasks and projects. Such leaders may not be accounted for in bylaws or constitutions but should, of course, function in response to and under the supervision of the constitutionally established leadership of the pastor and church officers. Nevertheless, their roles are vital and in some cases determinative in the church's life. Persons serving in such roles should be frequently consulted and, when it is appropriate, included in the decision-making processes of established boards, committees, or officers.

Managing such leadership is often a challenge precisely because it is empowered by informal or extraconstitutional processes. For example, a faithful, long-term member accumulates a leadership role because of his or her length of tenure. Also, members already perceived to be leaders in the community or assumed to be major financial contributors to the church may be granted an informal leadership role by part or all of the congregation, regardless of whether he or she currently holds a particular office. This can be of great benefit and blessing to the church. More often it can be a challenge to the constituted leadership and, therefore, church stability.

Churches, therefore, should be attentive to the differences between elected leadership, perceived leadership, and voluntary leadership and, as much as possible, respect the differences and encourage a corporate sense of priority and protocol in exercising these roles. They should, for example, be careful to balance the responsibilities of offices with the authority needed to carry out the duties of the office. They should also be vigilant to support the duly described offices of the church. Church conflict can arise when the person currently serving in an office is abandoned by some who, for whatever reason, choose to prioritize the leadership of another. Likewise, church leaders are wise to consult with unofficial leaders in the congregation in making decisions. Whenever possible, those who possess an informal but recognized personal leadership should be frequently among those placed in appropriate leadership roles where their leadership can be made accountable in church processes.

One specific leadership role that has been present in churches since the New Testament era is the leadership based on particular gifts. The church has always perceived some leadership as the work of the Holy Spirit or the risen Christ. Most often such persons achieve leadership by reason of function, not by office or title. Such gifts, such as healing, wisdom, prophecy, tongues, utterance, were real in the New Testament church experience and are often recognized as present in churches today. These gifts, or *charismata*, are addressed specifically in 1 Corinthians 12:4-11,27-31; Romans 12:6-8; Ephesians 4:11; and 1 Peter 4:10-11. The presence of the variety of gifts described in the pastoral letters has always been a challenge for congregations precisely because they are demonstrated in the functions of leadership offered by those who possess the gifts rather than by official expectation or description. Sometimes such leadership can seem impulsive and lacking in accountability. Nevertheless, such gifts may be received and harnessed by a church for the greater good of the whole community if those who possess them and those who follow them are reminded of Paul's admonition that "the same God inspired them all in every one" and that we are to seek the "higher gifts" (1 Corinthians 12:31). The most effective way in which leadership by gift can be harnessed for the good of Christ's church is to encourage such leadership to be servant leadership. All leadership should be focused not on exercising priority over other leaders or over one another but on accomplishing the will of God and the work of the church, as discovered and determined by the whole community in prayer and consultation.

Alternative Styles of Leadership

As churches develop and grow, it is appropriate to review and reevaluate leadership structures, organizational styles, and operating procedures. Such a practice ensures that a church does not become a victim of procedures and forms that no longer function well. It also allows for a church to review how effectively its manner and style of leadership through church offices is enabling it to accomplish its purpose and mission. A growing body of material is available from Baptist and other denominational sources to assist in such periodic review.

In recent decades, several alternatives to traditional Baptist structures have been found effective in some situations. One is the use of a single-board concept of church leadership. In that case, instead of multiple boards and committees (trustees, finance, education, etc.), a single governing board is responsible for the broad range of oversight, decision making, stewardship, and programs of ministry within the congregation. To enable it to carry out its functions, the single board frequently appoints task forces to carry out specific programs or functions. This style of leadership is best suited for a small or moderate-sized congregation because it claims fewer persons for management and oversight and enables a greater number of persons to be involved in missions and programs of the church.

Another alternative found in some Baptist churches is that of government by elders. This style of leadership is preferred by congregations that desire strong, centralized leadership roles. Elders are chosen on the basis of proven leadership consistent with the church's goals and function as the board of initiation and review for the work of all other officers, boards, and committees. In some churches, however, elder rule has exceeded the accepted norms of Baptist church organization by developing a self-perpetuating board. Sometimes boards of elders are appointed directly by the pastor in such churches. Unless the elders are approved by the whole church in some regular way, whether they are nominated or appointed by the pastor, nominating committee, or the board itself, this practice is not Baptist. Baptist churches faithful to their tradition and history should elect leadership that is responsive to the whole congregation, regardless of the particulars of their organizational structure.

Leadership is now, as it was in the days of the apostles, a critical issue in church life. The effective church will devote a significant amount of its energy to developing and encouraging effective leadership and will support the work of its leaders by offering prayer, engaging in helpful dialogue, and understanding the significance as well as the cost of their labors. In Baptist churches, especially, the leadership of the laity will ultimately determine the success of a church as an instrument of God's work and kingdom or, alternatively, its failure as just one more flawed institution of human creation.

Chapter V

Christian Worship

Worship is a universal human response to forces and personalities that give meaning to individual lives. Divine worship is an act of adoration, praise, or sacrifice offered to God. Christian worship is such an act performed in the name of Jesus Christ in response to Christ's own invitation to come into God's presence in his name. In churches that are organized in the name of Jesus Christ and confess Christ to be the head of the church, worship is the central activity that binds the church to Christ and its members one to another.

In its best sense, Christian worship is a response offered by those who have experienced a holy presence in their lives, or who, having witnessed such a presence in others, desire to experience it for themselves. Worship is the joyful activity of those who have experienced God and wish to continue enjoying God's presence. It is the work of God's people who desire to offer a holy service pleasing to God. It is the preparation of those who desire to be obedient and faithful to God, for it opens their hearts and prepares their minds for the greater service God has for them to do. Worship can be offered individually and in private. In the latter case, it is most properly called devotion or meditation. We speak here of public, corporate worship—the act of worshiping God as a church.

Throughout Christian history, many traditions and expressions of faithful people have contributed to a great variety of worship activities. For some, the mode of worship itself has become the defining act of true faith. For others, the principles of right belief have been carefully embedded in the activity of worship. Some

Christian people worship according to strict principles of ceremony and ritual; others worship in spontaneity and simplicity. Among some Christians worship is an activity of the mind, while among others it is principally a matter of the heart. But everywhere worship is the most important activity of the church because it invites men and women to come into God's presence and because by faith the people of God believe that in worship God hovers near.

The worship of many churches is defined by an official, ecclesiastical theology; by the materials of a prescribed prayer book; or by formative historic principles that define their religious community. Creeds, confessions of faith, historic principles of definition, sacraments, rituals, and ceremonies are all examples of the theology and experience of a particular denomination or communion of Christians at worship. As such, these materials are more than resources but are, in fact, defining essentials for the specific worship of a particular people as they worship God according to their understanding and experience.

Baptist churches, as the most free among free churches, are neither defined nor limited by creeds, theological principles, or practices. In worship, Baptists are free to borrow from all the experiences of the whole church, past and present, or to create new experiences. Because Baptists celebrate the priesthood of individual believers—"soul competency" among believers—worship is less concerned with an exact definition of a corporate community and more concerned with leading individuals into an effective and satisfying relationship with God. Nevertheless, worship among Baptists is guided by a theology that shapes its resources for those who engage in it. For Baptists, worship serves to deepen a spiritual awareness of God around and within. It urges participants first to confess Christ as Lord and Savior and subsequently to deepen their commitment to Christ in work and witness. Baptist worship, therefore, most often seeks to assist humankind in confronting the presence of God and experiencing God's grace, in giving praise to the presence of God, in understanding the mind of God through his Word and revelation, and in making a commitment to doing the work of God as God has ordained it.

The independence of Baptist churches serves to create individuality and great variety in worship. Worship in many Baptist churches carries the echoes of nineteenth-century camp meetings and revivals, while in many others, liturgical formality is the norm. Some Baptist worship is preacher- and preaching-dominated. Elsewhere worship is participatory and led by the laity. Baptist worship has been shaped by the diversity of cultures, languages, and ethnic heritage from which local congregations were derived. And, because of the freedom and independence of Baptist congregations, worship frequently responds to the styles, needs, and community concerns of the context in which the church has developed. Nevertheless, worship in Baptist churches everywhere is commonly defined by the reading of the Scriptures, the singing of hymns and spiritual songs, by preaching and prayer, and by opportunities for response and personal commitment.

The theology, experience, and formation of worship is an important focus for rewarding study and reflection. There are extensive resources to assist in comprehending the history of worship among Christian denominations and churches and to help guide the development of worship in general or to understand aspects of its components in particular.[1] Nevertheless, we shall review some of the most common and significant elements of worship here.

Scripture

The careful, effective use of Scripture should be at the heart of every experience of worship. Scripture is the remembered, revealed Word of the God we approach in worship. Therefore, it has the power to guide and shape our approach to God in worship. The words of the ancient Scriptures were always on Jesus' lips: "It is written," he might say in introducing a teaching, or "You have heard it said," in calling to mind a memorized text for interpretation. The use of Scripture for worship among all Christians is important. It is especially so for Baptists, who encourage the interpretation of the Word of God by each believer. Baptists understand the Scriptures to be a significant guide for understanding God, and some Baptists view them as the sole guide. Nevertheless, it is surprising how often Scriptures are casually used or even neglected in Baptist worship. Those who plan worship experiences should first turn to the Scriptures for guidance and direction. Those who participate in worship should strive to understand the significant role they play in enabling them to approach God's presence.

Scripture texts should be consistently used to shape the theme of a service. Scriptures are most appropriate for adaptation in developing invocations and benedictions and, where they are used, responsive or unison congregational prayers. The Psalms and prophetic books often provide resources for such prayers or responsive readings. Many worship resource books, such as the recently revised Hiscox's *Star Book for Ministers* (Valley Forge, Pa.: Judson Press, 1994) or *A Manual of Worship, New Edition* by John E. Skoglund and Nancy E. Hall (Valley Forge, Pa.: Judson Press, 1993), provide direct resources of scriptural prayers and readings, as well as examples of how to create them to meet the needs of specific worship services. The words of ancient Scripture texts were frequently on Jesus' lips as he taught, preached, prayed, and prepared for his death. Those who plan congregational worship will be guided by his example.

Scripture texts should be read publicly during worship. The public reading of Scriptures is both an ancient and important aspect of worship. It is a role that may be contributed with good leadership by the laity as well as the clergy. At the beginning of Jesus' ministry, he was invited to read the Scriptures in the temple in Nazareth (Luke 4:16-21). In doing so, he was following an ancient custom and was invited not as a rabbi but as a member of the faith community of Israel. (We know that his role was a significant one because when he placed a new interpretation upon the ancient text, the congregation rejected him.) When Scriptures are read in public, those who read them should do so with clarity and dignity, so that all who hear them might understand the words. In public worship services, at least two Scripture texts should be selected for public reading: one from the Old Testament (or Old Covenant) and one from the New Testament. If three texts may be chosen, then a text from the Old Testament should be followed by an Epistle reading and a gospel text.

Scripture readings will enrich the themes of worship. During particular seasons of the Christian year, such as Christmas, Easter, or Pentecost, or preparatory seasons leading to them, such as Advent or Lent, Scripture texts can provide an especially heightened sense of expectation and understanding. Services that emphasize groups within the congregation (Men's Day, Women's Day, etc.) should include appropriate texts to undergird the theme. The same is true of thematic emphases, such as Missions Sunday or Christian Education Week. The resources of Scripture will bring to life the present issues and opportunities of church life.[2] The effective use of Scriptures in worship should also include a plan to introduce the great variety of biblical stories and resources in worship, not only for the purpose of teaching but for the purpose of encouraging those at worship to explore the many varieties of experience with God. There are many resources and aids to assist the worship planner in this regard. One resource used by Baptists and others in recent years is the lectionary, a biblical reference resource that organizes Scripture readings for use in worship during a three-year cycle.

Of course, Scripture texts should be carefully chosen to provide the foundation for the sermon or for a series of sermons. Even when the preacher chooses a theme for a sermon rather than an expository or narrative approach, the words of the preacher should be rooted in the Word of God. (Nothing will expose an unprepared preacher like a sermon in belated search for a text!) At least one of the texts chosen for public reading should contain the text or the context for the sermon or meditation in the service. If the preacher is also the primary worship planner, the selection of appropriate texts will assist in developing both the sermon and the service. If others are involved in planning worship, such as a musician or a group of lay or staff participants, the coordination of texts, music, sermon, and other worship resources will greatly enhance the unity of the service.

Scriptures also contain powerful resources for services of special character, such as funerals, memorial services, weddings, dedications, or anniversaries. There are no words of comfort like those of the Psalms, nor words in celebration of human love as an example of God's blessings as the love stories of Scripture, nor words of commitment or remembrance for significant occasions as the recorded remembrances of God's ancient people. In devising such services, a worship leader who turns first to the texts that define our faith will not be disappointed.

Prayer

Scriptures provide those at worship with the resources to search the mind of God by using remembered moments of God's revelation. Prayer provides those at worship with an opportunity to communicate themselves into the presence of God and to prepare for God's response. In worship, prayer is a vital and important component.

Jesus taught more about prayer and its use in coming into God's presence than any other act of worship. It would be difficult, therefore, to overestimate its importance in the modern church. We have from Jesus an invitation to engage in prayer: "Ask, and it will be given you; seek, and you will find," Jesus promised his disciples (Matthew 7:7). In the act of prayer, Jesus emphasized the significance of corporate worship: "If two of you agree on earth about anything they ask, it will be done for them by my Father in heaven" (Matthew 18:19). He taught that prayer was an intimate communication with God: When Jesus prayed he said, "Abba, Father"—which means, literally, "Daddy" (Mark 14:36). Paul affirmed that we are to pray in a similar manner (Romans 8:15). Equally, Jesus taught that private prayer was essential to developing spiritual integrity and maturity: "When you pray, go into your room and shut the door" (Matthew 6:6). Jesus gave us an example of prayer that all Christians have adopted in some way: "Our Father who art in heaven . . ." (Matthew 6:8-15). And he also gave us the example of his personal devotion to prayer in the garden prior to his arrest (Matthew 26:36-46, John 17). If Jesus is the example, then prayer is at the heart of the experience of both private and corporate worship.

The practice of prayer must be varied to shape and guide the variety of worship experiences. A prayer offered with the choir and other worship leaders before a service might differ from the private prayer the leader might offer in the privacy of the study or chapel or from the prayer offered in the worship service itself. Prayer offered in an intimate act of worship in a hospital room or in a home following a death will differ in tone and content from a public prayer offered at the memorial service of a well-known member of the congregation. Prayer offered in a counseling context, calling for penitence and renewal, might be more personally specific than a prayer offered for a similar purpose for the entire congregation at a Sunday service.

Yet, as Hiscox reminded us, "in spirit all prayer is essentially the same" (p. 99). In prayer, we may come to God with the cares of personal lives or with the concerns of the whole world, but in coming to God in prayer, we must temporarily exclude the surrounding noise of our lives and the continuing chaos of the world so that God may hear us and so that we may hear God. In prayer we may include adoration and praise, confession, repentance, and penitence; we may offer thanksgiving for blessings, pour out our hearts in supplication for our needs and the needs of others, and plead for the intercession of Christ in our lives and in the experiences of others. All of this is in the spirit of assurance Christ gave to us by saying, "If you ask anything of the Father, he will give it to you in my name" (John 16:23). Still, this core unity of prayer must be expressed in different ways as required by corporate worship.

Prayer in Public, Corporate Worship

Those who pray in public worship offer prayer in one of two ways. First, they may *lead* others in prayer. Second, they may pray *on behalf* of others, inviting others to unite in spirit in the prayer they offer. A third kind of prayer in public worship, the *benediction or blessing*, is most often offered by the pastor or worship leader. This prayer is in the form of assurance, of opening the means of grace to the participants: "May the Lord bless you and keep you . . ."; "May the Lord make his face to shine upon you . . ."; "Go in peace, in the name of the Father, and of the Son, and of the Holy Spirit." In this role, the worship leader acts as intercessor to bring God's blessing and grace into focus for the worship participants.

In leading others in prayer during worship, the worship leader has a very specific and significant role. In order to fulfill it, he or she must be adequately prepared. Some of the preparation may have been accomplished by others prior to the service if a written or responsive prayer is provided for an invocation, for example. Here the job of the prayer leader is to invite by word and example the whole gathering of people to unite in spirit and in words to call upon

God's presence for the experience of worship. If the prayer is not written, then the words offered in prayer by the leader should not only offer the prayer of the leader's making but also invite the prayers for a similar purpose from the participants' hearts.

Public prayer leadership must not be taken for granted. "Whoever would draw near to God must believe that he exists and that he rewards those who seek him," says Hebrews 11:6. "Let him ask in faith, with no doubting" (James 1:6). The prayer leader must lead by being convinced that God is able to respond and by inspiring others to that same conviction. A worship service that begins or continues with prayer that seems unconvinced that God is present or able to be found has a long way to go to find God. Unconvinced prayer is unconvincing! The prayer leader who reads a prepared prayer as mere words on a page does not lead worship; neither does the worship leader whose prayers from worship to worship are the same, whether written down or spoken from an uninspired ritual in the mind. One who leads worship with prayer needs first to identify the need for prayer in himself or herself and then to be convinced of the need for prayer by others. Only someone in this spirit—fervent in the belief of prayer—can usher a congregation into both the majesty and intimacy of God.

Much of corporate prayer can become monotonous and stereotyped if those responsible for leading in prayer are not diligent in seeking new resources. It is sometimes argued that prayer that is not spontaneous is not valid. However, very few are able to depend upon spontaneity in leading public prayer without lapsing into unwritten rituals of their own. Therefore, those who devise prayers for worship should be familiar with the prayers of the Scriptures— the Psalms, the prayers of the prophets, the prayers of Jesus and of the apostles. There are also great prayer resources from our ancestors in faith in the church.[3] The spiritually alive prayer leader will use these resources not only to enliven his or her own prayer life but also to devise effective prayer leadership for worship.

The prayer leader should also be sensitive to the current state of the congregation's concerns, well-being, and spiritual needs. Prayers of invocation or intercession that help to identify areas of personal pain, trouble, or doubt will help release the congregation to join in prayer to overcome these concerns. In leading prayer for others, there should be linkage to the theme of the day or to the text and sermon. It should be long enough to be a serious communication with God—but still relatively brief. Long prayers in public contexts tire the human spirit and invite the mind to wander away from God.

Prayer leaders should also speak distinctly. This is particularly important if lay members of the community are asked to lead in prayer. Those unused to speaking in public should be given training and encouragement so that they inspire confidence and give clarity to those being led. The language of prayer should also be clear and concise. There are some who are convinced that a peculiar "holy language" or tone of voice should be used in giving leadership to prayer. Such habits divert the listening ears from their proper focus on God and focus them instead on the peculiar tones and words of the prayer. Jesus was impatient with those who adopted "airs" in praying, and so are most members of worshiping congregations: ". . . do not heap up empty phrases as the Gentiles do, for they think that they will be heard for their many words" (Matthew 6:7).

In a service of worship, prayer is appropriately used at the beginning (invocation); at the end (benediction); at the beginning and/or conclusion of the sermon; at the dedication of the offering; during specific ritual or "life-passage" moments in the service, such as baptism or the Lord's Supper; and to conclude an infant dedication, a Sunday school commencement recognition, anniversary, dedication, or the commendation of a particular event or circumstance, such as the beginning of a new program or ministry. There should be a reason for each prayer in a service, and each prayer should stay focused on its own purpose. Let an invocation be an invocation—that is, seeking the presence of God. Let it not be a prayer for every circumstance remembered or imagined. Let a benediction be a benediction—a brief moment of blessing and assurance of God's continued presence for the congregation—and not a recapitulation of the entire service, or the sermon, or the events of the week in the news.

The place for the broad concerns of prayer is in the pastoral prayer—the prayer offered in behalf of the congregation and not strictly in leadership of it. The pastor is in a unique role in the life of the worshiping community. The prayer to which his or her attention must most be offered is often entitled the pastoral prayer but may also be offered in several parts, such as "prayers for the congregation," "prayers for the community," and "prayers for the world," or in some other set of subdivisions. Often such a prayer is offered following a time of announcements, expressions of concern in the congregation or community, or a welcome to the people. In some churches, a pastoral prayer might follow a time in which members of the congregation are invited personally to share their concerns, celebrations, or requests for intercession.

How or when such prayer is listed is not nearly as important as how it is offered. Such prayers should not be lengthy—few congregations can stay together in a prayerful mode for more than about three minutes. But they should be comprehensive. Here, from a pastor's knowledge and oversight, the congregation can be inspired to offer true confession; here, from a pastor's anguish of heart, he or she can pour out the need for healing, for renewal, for restoration of spirit. Here, from a pastor's perspective on the community, a plea for justice, mercy, or hope can be offered. Here, from a pastor's intimate knowledge of his or her people, the barren and dry experiences of individual lives and the corporate life of a congregation may be brought before the Lord for refreshment and redemption. Pastors often most highly value their role as preacher and, commendably, spend great amounts of time on their sermons. But pastors who can pray with effectiveness will be most remembered for their prayer.

Just as significant moments bring great opportunities, they bring great temptations. All varieties of public prayer can become pedantic, trivial, or offensive to both God and congregations. In his original comments on prayer, Hiscox observed that "certain defects into which the pious sometimes unconsciously fall . . . deserve attention and correction" (p. 101). In agreement with his principle, these are some of the most common faults:

Preaching Prayers: Prayers in which Scripture is explained, doctrine expounded, and instruction offered to the audience. (These are properly functions of the pulpit and the classroom.)

Exhorting Prayers: Prayers of warning, rebuke, and exhortation directed to groups or even individuals in the congregations, presumably calling them to righteousness; sometimes their personal sins are pointed out. (These are properly functions of personal counseling, confrontation, or dialogue.)

Historical Prayer: Prayers that recount lengthy histories and stories from the Bible, the congregation's experience, or personal lives, and from which lessons or conclusions are derived. There may be some exceptions for anniversaries or special occasions— but use with caution. (David, Solomon, and Ezra indulged in them only on very special occasions.)

Oratorical Prayers: Prayers seemingly devised for competition in an oratorical contest, with greater attention to language than to content. (Jesus was especially critical of them in Matthew 6:6.)

Complimentary Prayers: Designed to extol the virtues of guests, prominent congregation members, or others. The net result is to flatter the persons rather than to worship God. (Both God and the congregation will know the difference.)

Fault-finding Prayers: Prayers focused to make prominent the real or fancied faults of the congregation, individuals, leaders in the community, and where the difficulties are deplored, advice is given, remedies are suggested to God, or guidance for divine rebuke offered. Sometimes names are mentioned. (These are hard to resist, but prayer leaders should be mindful that God is able to see within every heart and will deal accordingly.)

Whether prayer is offered as leadership so that others might join, or whether it is offered on behalf of others, prayer is vital to effective worship. Preparation and planning of worship should allow for great attention to prayer if worship is to be effective. Preachers have been commended to spend an hour in preparation for every minute in the pulpit. Those responsible for the public prayer of worship might adopt a similar standard of an hour of private prayer and preparation for every minute in public prayer.

Prayer in Prayer Meetings, Small Groups, or Home Gatherings

Many Baptist churches sponsor midweek prayer services in addition to Sunday morning worship. Sometimes they have been associated with a meal or other programs. And, in an attempt at stewardship of time, sometimes such meetings coincide with the meetings of boards and committees of churches. Sadly, in many churches, the midweek program has been abandoned, having fallen victim to the complexity of modern schedules and family life.

Nevertheless, the development of prayer outside of the Sunday worship experience is critically important for the growing maturity of a congregation. Whether a church determines to maintain a midweek prayer program or to develop instead small groups and home meetings for the encouragement of prayer, it is an important function for strengthening the church. Midweek programs have often been mistakenly abandoned due to "low numbers"—and the same reason is often given for the failure to develop alternatives in homes or small groups meeting at varied times to accommodate busy professional or vocational schedules. But numbers are not the significant factor. Those most eager for spiritual growth will attend prayer services or exercises if they are well developed. And even those who come as guests will be nourished and developed in their eventual desire to grow in faith. Therefore, a church that commits itself to prayer in contexts of worship other than Sunday services will prosper.

A midweek program offers the same predictability of time and familiarity as a Sunday service. In that context, perhaps following a light supper or other refreshment, those present may be invited to a time of singing, brief meditation, and prayer. But prayer should be the center. This is the time to encourage participation by even the least articulate. This is the moment when, among small numbers and amidst supportive friends, deep troubles can be faced, great hopes can be outlined, and the most urgent hope for God's grace can be expressed. A wise pastor or leader of these services will offer an opening prayer at the beginning of the service and then invite others to participate, and as well offer effective closing prayer at the end. But in between he or she will encourage participants to exercise their gifts of prayer or will seek to develop those abilities where they are absent. In developing the program:

1. The pastor needs to give priority to the prayer meeting as one place where prayer can become vital. Give preparation to a brief but well-planned meditation leading to prayer and to a focus for prayer itself.

2. Take advantage of small numbers to focus on the needs of individuals. Don't worry that crowds are not present. Lavish prayer attention on individuals.

3. Do not presume to make it a "teaching experience." Instead, assume the posture of learning. In prayer meetings many pastors have come to learn the power of prayer for themselves.

4. Be sure to allow for singing and provide for accompaniment. Emphasize the old and familiar hymns, for it will probably be the older and traditional members who come to these services. But occasionally they will be glad to learn new hymns to teach the congregation. (If the church is a new church—this advice is reversed! Now is the time to teach new hymns and old—and to spend some time acquainting participants with certain church "basics" of both theology and church practices.)

5. Begin and end the meeting on time, but remain with those who linger. A midweek program is often a time when much intensive pastoral work can be accomplished if a sensitive pastor is available and listening.

Many midweek services have died because ambitious pastors or staff members have sought to translate them into educational opportunities, Bible study sessions or more formalized worship experiences. All of these have value and are sorely needed. They might even be offered on a different evening or the same evening at a different time. But none of them take the place of an opportunity for prayer for those who hunger for it.

In addition to traditional midweek prayer meetings, small group experiences in prayer in homes or places of work can be effective. Small groups and prayer are a fruitful combination, and many churches have experienced both numerical as well as spiritual growth by encouraging them. The small group phenomenon has generated a large amount of good literature that we cannot duplicate here. However, there are some common dynamics that will support a small-group approach to prayer: a hunger for community and intimacy; a desire to find a trusted place where openness can be shared; a belief that small, intimate settings encourage personal growth; familiarity with small-group contexts through professional-development events, self-help groups, and twelve-step programs such as Alcoholics Anonymous and others.

In developing prayer life through small groups, leaders should develop resources for prayer, including materials on types of prayer, historical personalities who helped shaped the discipline of prayer, and biblical resources for prayer. Also, group prayer leaders should be selected for training and development in their own knowledge and understanding of prayer and should meet regularly for their own growth. While small-group prayer life is not part of the traditional worship experience of the church, it may well help develop the spiritual resources of the church in the future and better enable it to be vital and energized in its corporate spiritual life.

Finally, many churches are experiencing renewal by experimenting with alternate forms of prayer in worship. Some forms are shaped by so-called contemporary styles (contemporary being defined by whatever present tastes and styles might dictate) or by the exploration of prayer and worship experiences common to other historic traditions and expressions of faith. Many Baptist churches have experienced significant spiritual growth by becoming familiar with the daily services of confessional churches, particularly services such as evensong or compline in the Episcopal Church or the services of healing developed by several denominations. Many church members also report great personal growth in their exploration of the historic spiritual writers of prayer discipline, such as John of the Cross, Teresa of Avila, or, in the present century, Thomas Merton. Baptist churches who are secure in their principles and traditions may discover many resources in traditions apart from their own and are free to do so as a result of their independence and spiritual freedom. As long as it is brought openly and honestly and with the humility that comes from recognizing the omnipotence of God, any prayer appropriate for worship is likely to be helpful for personal or congregational use also.

Preaching

Among Baptists, preaching is often nearly synonymous with worship. This confusion should be avoided. Preaching can be accomplished outside a traditional form of worship, and worship can be experienced without preaching. Nevertheless, preaching is most effective when it inspires and assists worship and worship provides the most productive context for effective preaching.

Preaching is the proclamation of truth—God's truth, the Good News, the message of salvation, the promise of eternal life.

Preaching is therefore the shaping of God's Word through the experience of the preacher to be communicated to the lives and experiences of the audience. The preacher is the herald (*kerux*), the proclaimer, and his or her address (*kerygma*) is the message proclaimed to the audience. The primary object of preaching is to bring people to Christ so that in Christ they might experience the presence of God and grow in spiritual maturity and Christian discipleship.

Preaching takes on different character and tone depending on the audience and purpose of the moment:

Evangelistic preaching is preaching directed toward those who have yet to encounter Christ or who have yet to accept Christ as God's unique expression as Lord and Savior. Its purpose is to confront an audience with the reality of Christ and to gain their acceptance of him.

Educational preaching is preaching devoted to increasing the biblical or spiritual understanding of those who may have accepted Christ but are now in need of further commitment and growth. Educational preaching may be thematic, expository, or narrative in style. It may be strictly biblical, or it may draw on examples from the history and experiences of Christian people in different times. Its purpose is to expand knowledge and experience in faith.

Ethical preaching is preaching devoted to enabling an audience to use faith experience and the presence of Christ to make important personal decisions and to live effective Christian lives. Such preaching may be strictly biblical but may also draw on the insights and lessons of theologians, historical figures, or personal experiences.

Confessional preaching is preaching in which the preacher shares aspects of his or her own faith pilgrimage. Its purpose is to invite others to join with him or her in spiritual pilgrimage or to encourage others by the reassuring example of Christ's presence in his or her own life and experience.

Pastoral preaching is preaching in which the preacher brings the gospel to bear upon significant life issues such as death, despair, broken relationships, aspirations, values, personal choices, or specific concerns within the congregation.

Doctrinal preaching is preaching focused primarily upon explaining particular Christian doctrines, demonstrating their truth, and attempting to convince the audience of the importance of belief in that doctrine.

Liturgical preaching serves to enhance the worship of a particular theme or day, such as Good Friday or Maundy Thursday, or a season, such as Lent or Advent, or to heighten the effectiveness of a specific aspect of worship, such as the Lord's Supper, a dedication, or a memorial.

Interpretive preaching is preaching devoted to enhancing understanding of significant events in the life of the world and community in which the congregation lives. Its ultimate purpose is to reveal the direction of Christian discipleship in the midst of those events.

Preachers and students of preaching may categorize preaching in a variety of ways. However, all effective preaching is characterized by a common purpose to bring people to Christ and to enhance their discipleship. Preachers should strive to balance their preaching styles and purposes in response to the needs of the congregation or context to which they have been called. It is natural that preachers may be more gifted in some styles of preaching or more comfortable in the use of particular approaches. Two principles should be observed. First, preachers should preach to their gift, that is, use with great effectiveness what they are most gifted to do. Second, they should not be limited only to what they do well. Developing alternate preaching styles will result in growth for both the preacher and the congregation and will prevent stagnation in both.

Preaching in our time requires particular perseverance and faithfulness. For example, even for the most devout Christians, a preacher is often the least credible among the interpreters of personal meaning and the significance of world events available. Preachers have strong competition from views being presented on television, in newspapers, magazines, books, and through computer information networks. Nor do most persons hear the message of Christ first or primarily from their preacher, but again through radio and television preachers and teachers and in a variety of other places. Nor is Christianity the only faith experience available to them. Media sources, friendship networks, and other sources provide alternative religious doctrines, mystical experiences, and spiritual realities. These and many other challenges of an increasingly secular age require that preachers be dedicated to their task and not lose heart.

Modern pressures on churches and church life bring great demands for growth, success in worldly terms, decisive and successful leadership in pastoral offices, and many other strong expectations. Preaching, as the church's most visible form of communication, is frequently called upon to accomplish tasks for which it was not scripturally intended and for which it is ill suited. Preaching is often expected to promote programs, increase attendance, develop support for building plans, or build consensus for community activities. Such expectations are, at best, secondary expectations of preaching—and are always a dangerous diversion from its primary task. Although we might imagine that pressures on preaching were less vigorous a century ago, Hiscox's direction on this subject is still quite to the point; he said that preaching "is not to entertain an audience, nor to crowd the house with hearers, nor to build up wealthy and fashionable congregations, nor to replenish the treasury, nor to teach literature, science or art, but to save and nurture souls by an exhibition of Christ crucified. For this purpose our Lord designated 'some, pastors and teachers, for the perfecting of the saints, for the work of the ministry, for the edifying of the body of Christ'" (Ephesians 4:11,12).

Although it is claimed that there are relatively few great preachers in our time, we are blessed with a great many helpful resources on preaching. Those who would be effective in preaching will gain from them what they can. But in summary, good preaching will be focused always and inevitably upon Christ, even if the topic or text begins elsewhere; it will be plain and simple in style, remembering that the purpose is to be effective, not highly embellished; it will be instructional, allowing the hearer to retain two or three significant insights or points when it is finished; it will have a clear structure, in order to avoid confusion; it should be delivered with clarity, using the best speaking and presenting skills the preacher can develop; it will be interesting, using effective examples that serve to highlight the points and to make them memorable; it will be colloquial—that is, respectful of the education, experience, and culture of the audience to whom it is delivered; and it will be brief. Even if the sermons of great preachers of past ages required an hour or more to deliver, modern audiences are conditioned to receive information and even inspiration in smaller doses. The wise preacher will make fifteen minutes the goal—and never exceed twenty-five minutes. Sermons requiring greater length should be subdivided for a series.

Finally, when preaching is part of a worship service, it should be integrated with the Scripture texts, hymns, and theme of the service whenever possible. Preparation for preaching should be coincident with preparation for worship, and each should influence the other. On some occasions the sudden and late presence of the Holy Spirit may require a change in direction for a sermon, and when such a moment occurs, the preacher must follow the Spirit. But the effectiveness and drama of such a moment will be increased if it is in contrast to a consistent practice of careful planning and coordination.

Music

With rare exception, music is a vital part of worship. Hymns and spiritual songs have been part of Christian worship since the New Testament churches. Music to prepare for worship, to enhance portions of worship, and to conclude worship has a long and ancient history. And entire services of worship are often framed in music. Among the ancient Hebrews, music, combined with sacrifices and offerings, constituted almost the entirety of worship. More recently, requiems, the sung "evensong" service of the Episcopal traditions, hymn festivals among Baptists and others, and the adaptation of some larger choral works for worship use, to name a few, have become effective means for worship experiences. Music and worship are inseparable perhaps because music gives best expression to the combination of our deepest feelings and our highest thoughts.

Nevertheless, there is often misunderstanding evident in the use of music in worship. Therefore planning for its use in worship should demand great attention from those who plan worship and clear communication with those who provide music, including the congregation. One place of confusion is the distinction between music as a component of worship and music as art. As Hiscox once said, "Music may become high art in the house of God, but that does not make it worship" (p. 104). Music that draws attention only to itself or glorifies human accomplishment rather than leading toward the glory and presence of God defeats the fundamental purpose of worship. Those who plan and prepare music for worship are wise to follow in the spirit of J. S. Bach who wrote on most of his compositions, "For the glory of God alone."

Another place of confusion is the function of music as part of the culture of a particular people. When music is accepted or rejected on the basis of cultural consistency, it serves to emphasize disunity in human experience rather than unity in the Spirit of God. Both worship and fellowship in churches can be destroyed by making the type or style of music the standard rather than its effectiveness in worship. For example, some well-educated and culturally refined congregations affirm only traditional hymns and the music of Bach, Beethoven, and Buxtehude as worthy of worship, while rejecting folk hymns, praise songs, or the more current popular music of the young as "uncivilized" or "uncultured." Likewise, in African American churches enormous disagreement is frequently sponsored in debates over whether chants and drum-dominant music of Africa or spirituals from early American experience will be included, or whether European and traditional American hymns and music will exclude all others.

Like all other aspects of worship, music should serve to prepare and lead the congregation into the presence of God, and provide, like prayer, a vehicle to express our yearnings and concerns to God. In unpretentious Christian services, singing is often the only corporate act that can be called worship in the most accurate sense. A song can express adoration, confession, supplication, and praise. And it can be done in unison or in harmony—all of which underlines the unity and common experience together of God's people. For this reason, the ancient Hebrew pilgrims approached the Holy City by singing songs we now have received as the Psalms. For the same reason, worship in the primitive Christian church was commended "in psalms and hymns and spiritual songs, singing and making melody to the Lord with all your heart" (Ephesians 5:19).

The music of worship, therefore, should begin with hymns and songs. They should be simple, lyrical, and either familiar or made familiar to the congregation. The combined hymnody resources of the church are enormous, far surpassing the pages of any one hymnal. And they grow by the creativity of the young in age and the young in spirit who create new music in the tones and rhythms of popular music, as well as in the rediscovery of ancient music. Let those who plan congregational music for worship be eager to increase their knowledge of hymns and spiritual songs, and let them encourage both familiarity and diversity in the life of the congregation.

The music of worship may well include prelude and postlude music provided by an organ or instrumentalists, choral anthems and responses, and other presentations within the resources and capability of the congregation. Such music can add immeasurably to our approach to God, for it helps to soothe our spirits, focus our minds, and approach a prayerful attitude. Because music is a universal language, it can attract the unbelieving, encourage the doubting, and calm the troubled. It is one act, other than common prayer, that can unite a whole congregation in one voice or in one ear. It is no accident, therefore, that music—and its particular subset, sacred music, has a strong place in the history of worship.

Nonetheless, in developing worship, greater attention should be devoted to including the congregation in developing music than in providing music for their passive entertainment. "Let all the peoples praise thee, O God: let all the people praise thee!" (Psalm 67:5). That is not to say that a choir should not sing or that an organ or ensemble not play. But it is to say that congregations should occasionally be taught to sing responses with a choir. The music should lead into community expression rather than entertainment, and whenever possible, musically gifted members of the congregation should be included in offering the music of worship. God is not as pleased by the perfection of our music in worship as by our passion and our participation in it.

Music, perhaps more than any other aspect of worship, has become a symbol of our cultural, theological, and personal diversity. As such, it often becomes the focus of great debate and the source of expressions of distaste. Since the 1960s, when "folk services" gained popularity, music in worship has often seemed to define perceived differences in appropriateness, worthiness, and effectiveness in worship. One challenge for worship leaders is to promote sensitivity and tolerance in the use of varied musical styles. Baptists, perhaps more than any other group of Christians, have the opportunity to explore the musical resources available in the whole church and from many cultures. Baptists themselves have originated or used many of the musical forms of the present, from African American spirituals to gospel to adaptations of highly developed classical forms. Folk music, rock music, the music of immigrants, and the music of cultures indigenous to mission fields in the past have also become part of Baptist worshiping congregations. Sadly, they do not always rest easy together and without careful leadership may become signs and symbols of disunity.[4]

Offerings and Commitments in Worship

Nearly every service of worship should offer an opportunity for congregational and personal response. One such occasion is usually the reception of an offering. The offering as a part of worship is often misunderstood. It is not, as is generally supposed, simply a means for receiving financial support for the church's needs—though that is a worthy reason.

An offering, especially in more ancient rituals of worship, is a more broadly defined occasion for offering an obedient response to God's presence. As such, it offers creative opportunities to enhance worship. For example, at seasonal times of worship such as Thanksgiving, an act of blessing the harvest may be combined with the offering—a recognition of the receipt of abundance now returned to God. Likewise, the dedication of church officers, leaders, or teachers might be incorporated into an offering segment of worship—in recognition of their personal gifts being offered for use in the church. When offering is so understood, it needs to have more than a perfunctory place in the order of worship and should serve to highlight a human response to divine presence.

The offering as a moment for the receipt of tithes and financial contributions should be sponsored with great dignity and seriousness. It should be perceived not only by the worship leaders, but by the congregation as well, as a very sacred moment when they respond to the presence of God with something of appropriate value from their own lives and means. The offering can be situated at several points in the service. Two places in particular are following the reading of Scripture, especially the gospel, or toward the end of the service, following prayers, sermon, and even a last hymn. If the Doxology is used in presenting the offering, it may well serve as the last sung words of the service prior to the benediction. Wherever the offering is placed, it should flow naturally as a part of the logic and liturgy of the service, whether formal or informal. And it should never be introduced with apology or with a sense of inappropriateness. The popular notion that churches and money should be kept separate is one result of such a negative attitude. It also contributes to the notion that some "mundane" aspects of life, such as money, do not deserve the interest of God. Quite the contrary is true. Whatever offering is invited should be given and received in a spirit of sanctification.

Invitations and Personal Responses

A second type of personal response in Baptist worship is the moment of personal commitment. This may come as part of the offertory section, or, as in some traditions, in response to the concluding hymn of the service, usually following the sermon. A moment of dedication—whether a first-time acceptance of Christ or as an act of rededication and renewal—is always an inspiring and encouraging result of worship. Regrettably, many churches have abandoned this practice and leave questions of membership to a private matter of committee procedures. Churches may be guided by their own traditions and taste in these matters, but if acts of dedication, commitment, or renewal are desired, the following may prove helpful:

First, not every worship experience will have—or should have— such a response as a result. If no one is moved to such response, the service should not be prolonged to encourage it. This practice often demeans the primary purpose of the service to worship God and instead redefines it to have primary function to elicit individual response.

Second, opportunities for personal response should not be directly linked to the sermon. An "altar call" linked to the morning's preaching forces every sermon to be evangelistic. It also forces preachers and others to believe there is no other value to preaching than to achieve personal responses.

Third, when one does respond as a new believer, it should occasion celebration and an introduction that is sensitive to the person who has just made a response. It is often tempting to a pastor to tell too much about a person's recent spiritual struggles or life issues when their privacy should be respected.

Finally, there should be follow-up to those who make a first confession of faith or an act of rededication. Such moments usually indicate a time of significant spiritual growth that will allow a pastor or trained layperson an opportunity to share it and to build a strong bond with the church.

There are many other aspects of worship that may be included in regularly scheduled services or provide the occasion for services specifically designed for their inclusion. These components include the ordinances, such as the Lord's Supper and baptism; worship focuses that relate to significant life-passage moments, such as birth, death, marriage, or life development; and worship opportunities that focus on special opportunities in the church or programs of the church. These are worthy of separate consideration.

NOTES

1. Hiscox first published the *Star Book* for just this purpose of assisting Baptist churches to develop meaningful worship experiences, as well as to provide pastoral aids for special services and rites. Judson Press has also published a number of works to assist in worship development. One recent publication is *A Manual of Worship, New Edition* by John E. Skoglund and Nancy E. Hall (Valley Forge, Pa.: Judson Press, 1993).

2. In developing Scripture texts and readings for such services, a Bible concordance may be helpful. Also, denominational materials are often available to suggest worship resources. In addition, many denominations publish worship resource books and manuals that will enrich and expand available Baptist resources.

3. The *Book of Common Prayer* of the Anglican or American Episcopal tradition is a classic in the use of language to articulate spiritual, moving prayers. Another resource that contains a variety of prayers from the church in many ages, as well as prayers from other spiritual traditions, is the *Oxford Book of Prayer.* Both are cited in the bibliographical resources section.

4. It cannot be frequently enough affirmed that tastes in music, as in many other expressions of worship, are linked to the perspectives of one's genera-

tion, life experience, and personality. Frequently, "good old hymns" and preferred preaching styles and methods of communication are linked to cherished memories or meaningful stages of life. In choosing music, particularly, the worship leader must strive to be inclusive. Music expresses the theology, faith, and feelings of a congregation as nothing else does. Arrogance in suggesting "correctness" of form or taste should be avoided. The congregation's preferences (as seen by their enthusiastic participation in hymn singing), rather than adherence to a specific standard, should be the criterion for choosing hymns. At the same time, worship leaders should strive to develop tolerance and appreciation among generations and segments of the congregation for tastes other than their own. Finally, all should be led to an openness of spirit in experiencing new music and new forms of worship.

Chapter VI

Christian Ordinances, Rituals, and Ceremonies

The worship and fellowship life of a church is defined, enriched, and expanded by its attention to ordinances, rituals, and ceremonies that recall its origin, shape its purpose, and connect its experiences to God and the people who, in covenant together, constitute the church. These are more than mere traditions or significant creations of the moment. These are the participatory moments that bring focus to grace in Christian life, invite the Holy Spirit to be specifically present, and define the significant moments of both personal and community experience.

Christian Ordinances

Hiscox originally defined Christian ordinances as "institutions of divine authority relating to the worship of God, under the Christian dispensation" (p. 82). In the previous chapter we have, in fact, considered a variety of ordinances because the reading of Scripture, preaching, singing, and praying might all be defined in such terms. Nevertheless, in a more precise and distinctive sense, Baptists have commonly called baptism and the Lord's Supper (also called Communion or the Eucharist) ordinances and have asserted that they are the only Christian ordinances specifically committed to the church for perpetual observance.

Some Christians call these two observances, as well as several others, *sacraments*. In churches of highly developed ritual and creedal definition, sacraments are considered to be outward and visible signs of the work of an inward and invisible grace. Baptists have been suspicious of such definitions, however, because instead of being merely *signs* of grace, it has at times seemed tempting to view them as the *means* of grace. Since the Reformation, therefore, many Protestants in general and Baptists in particular have rejected a sacramental view of baptism and the Lord's Supper.

Baptists have, however, established these two events at the heart of Christian worship and discipleship. They have also defined them as the two uniquely authorized functions of the church, as the only sacred rites demonstrated by Christ to be continued by his church. In doing so they have recognized that these two ordinances are scriptural in precedent and that Christ himself was a participant in them. Baptists also believe that Christ explicitly commended them to be observed by his church. As Baptists approach these two observances, they are not only visible signs perceived by the senses but places of individual participation understood by the heart. They are therefore both teaching principles and defining moments of Christian experience.

Baptism[1]

Baptism is a symbolic act of ritual cleansing, practiced among Baptists by immersion in a pool of water. It is sometimes viewed as a "rite of initiation" since baptism precedes membership in a Baptist church. This is an incomplete description, however, because baptism in and of itself does not admit persons into the membership of a church. Likewise, its first significance is not to qualify a person for specific church membership. It is, instead, a "seal of the new covenant," as some have described it, or a "testimony to the covenant" because it is prescribed as the first Christian act of a new believer after the experience of saving faith. For the one who experiences it, baptism should indicate an acceptance of Christ, a desire to be united in Spirit and in fellowship with Christ, and should function as a sign of discipleship in the times to come. Membership in a church is one opportunity and expression of that discipleship.

The Institution of Baptism

Baptists, like most other Christians, believe that baptism was instituted by Christ when he first submitted to baptism for himself at the hand of John the Baptist. John came preaching repentance and offered baptism as an act of repentance and of faith in the redemptive Messiah he believed was to come. Jesus' disciples later baptized in Jesus' name as the Messiah who had come, and as a sign of the kingdom he had established in his name in the hearts of those who received him.

It has been argued by some that baptism was intended as a new sign or "seal" of the old covenant—one in place of circumcision by which Gentiles might enter the faith of Israel.

It is generally agreed, and especially claimed by Baptists, that baptism was instead ordained as a sign of a *new* covenant. This confidence is based on the statement that John preached a baptism "for the forgiveness of sins" (Mark 1:4) and upon his own confession that "I baptize you with water; but he who is mightier than I is coming, the thong of whose sandals I am not worthy to untie; he will baptize you with the Holy Spirit and with fire" (Luke 3:16). This latter confession implies an initiation into a new experience with God and a new activity of redemption.

Even more, however, baptism has been adopted as a universal Christian experience because Jesus' own participation in it signified a transforming and transcendent experience. Matthew tells us that after Jesus was baptized, he came out of the water and "the heavens were opened and he saw the Spirit of God descending like a dove, and alighting on him: and lo, a voice from heaven saying, 'This is my beloved Son, with whom I am well pleased' " (3:13-17). And if the example of Jesus' own experience were not sufficient, Jesus at the end of his ministry also gave the instructions to "go therefore and make disciples of all nations, baptizing them in the name of the Father and of the Son and of the Holy Spirit, teaching them to observe all that I have commanded you: and lo, I am with you always, to the close of the age" (Matthew 28:19-20).

These are powerful examples and instructions. It is therefore easy to understand why Christians in general and Baptists in particular have instituted baptism as a rite of great spiritual power and impressive form. It is designed to have a sacred influence on both those who receive it and those who witness it.

The Administration of Baptism

The word for *baptism* comes from the Greek *baptizo*, which means "to immerse" or "to dip." Theologians from different perspectives have argued that "to sprinkle" or "to pour" also fulfills the meaning of that word. Baptists have always been convinced of the more literal and complete definition. And, as archaeologists and other scholars have added to our understanding of early Christian practices, Baptists have been affirmed in their belief that immersion was the method of baptism used by the earliest Christians.

In addition to the specific meaning of the word, the description of Jesus' own experience where he "went up immediately from the water" (Matthew 3:16, Mark 1:10) suggests that he had gone down into the water and rose up out of it. Similarly, the symbolism attached to baptism by the earliest Christian church also supports an immersion theory. When Philip baptized the Ethiopian eunuch, it says in Acts that "they both went down into the water" (Acts 8:38). And in Romans, Paul says of this ritual, "We were buried therefore with him by baptism into death" (Romans 6:4). It is this understanding that in baptism the subject dies to sin and is raised up in hope of new life that retains for baptism its powerful impact as an ordinance in the church.

It is a matter of historical interest for Baptists to note that the administration of baptism—namely by immersion—is the source of the name "Baptist" for our denominations. It was at first a derogatory title intended to ridicule reformers who believed in adult baptism by immersion. Nevertheless, early Baptists did not universally agree in all things regarding baptism. In the American colonies, for example, many Baptist churches emerged from those who "separated" from the standing churches of the Congregational order in New England. Among them, vigorous debates took place regarding the efficacy of baptizing infants as well as the requirement of immersion as the mode of administration. "Pedobaptists" (those who advocated infant baptism) were vigorously opposed by "anti-pedobaptists" (those who recognized only adult baptism). This mid-eighteenth-century debate was settled in favor of the "anti-pedobaptists" as the Baptist conviction and was carried into new churches as Baptists moved west and south.

In Baptist churches, therefore, baptism is administered by immersion. (However, some Baptist churches have allowed for sprinkling or pouring for the extreme elderly, those for whom immersion would present a problem of health, or when an opportunity for immersion was not available.) In an earlier era, or until now among rural churches, baptism often took place in a lake or a river. Among some groups of Baptists, baptism was often especially anticipated during summer "camp meetings" during warm weather.

On the other hand, my own grandmother distinctly remembered her baptism in a frozen creek in the extremes of winter. Such services were often attended by the power of the symbols of nature. In more modern times, most Baptist churches have provided for baptismal pools in designing their church buildings. Baptism can therefore take place in all seasons. Often it is administered in a special service, or as part of the Easter celebrations, or on other specially chosen days.

Baptism itself should be administered with dignity and a calm spirit. Usually the ordinance is performed by an ordained minister, but in churches where such are not present or available, it can be administered by a deacon or any private member selected for the task. The validity of baptism is not dependent on the administrator but on the profession of faith in the candidate. Regardless of the circumstances of the administration of baptism, preparations should be made to ensure the greatest dignity possible for the service. Those assisting the candidates should provide practical necessities of clothing (robes or gowns) as well as the means of drying and redressing in privacy following the ceremony. Likewise, the one performing the baptism should have practiced the physical aspects of the ritual so as to avoid an accident in the water, causing danger or embarrassment to the candidate or discomfort to those witnessing its administration.

The Subjects of Baptism

It is at the core of Baptist conviction that baptism is to be administered to those, and only to those, who have exercised and professed a saving faith in Christ. That is, baptism is administered as a sign of belief, and not as a condition to belief or as a means to belief. This saving faith presupposes repentance for sin; a turning to Christ as Lord and Savior; and a commitment to a continued, maturing experience as a disciple.[2]

Baptists believe that baptism can only be experienced by individuals old enough and sufficiently developed in conscience to confess individual belief: "He who believes and is baptized will be saved; but he who does not believe will be condemned" (Mark 16:16). And from the testimony of the earliest church we read, "So those who received his word were baptized" (Acts 2:41). Those who baptize infants say that baptism is to be given to believers *and to their children*. Although the Scriptures occasionally recount households being baptized, the Scriptures give no specific examples of the baptism of infants, nor do they teach anywhere that children can be participants in grace simply because of the faith of their parents.

In modern times especially, Baptists have encouraged baptism among an increasing number of very young adults or even children who have expressed a desire to be baptized. It is admittedly difficult in such cases to determine whether such a desire is formed as the result of a genuine spiritual encounter with Christ, or as the result of parental or social expectation, or as a yet immature response to the idea of faith, perhaps encouraged by a pastor, Sunday school teacher, or others. In working with such a young person, parents, teachers, and ministers should exercise loving caution and care, and delay baptism if it seems uninformed or the result of an immature decision. Baptism is robbed of its significance and power if it becomes mere ritual and associated with childhood sentiment. On the other hand, some very young persons have achieved a remarkable expression of faith. And if this is the case, they should not be prevented from baptism.

A different circumstance is presented by the increasing phenomenon of adults who have been previously baptized in another Christian church or tradition, whether as infants or as adults. Such persons, desiring to become members of a Baptist congregation, may request baptism by immersion as a part of their initiatory experience in their new church. Sometimes they also desire not to be baptized by immersion, believing that their original baptism was valid and that to engage in another would be either a pointless "rebaptism" or an act offensive to their previous church or denomination. In assisting such persons in their choice, prayerful sensitivity should be exercised. The following principles may be helpful:

First, if a person has been baptized in another Christian church, either as a child or as an adult, but the first baptism was not by immersion, then the Baptist congregation should rightfully encourage baptism by immersion. To do so is simply to be consistent with Baptist belief and tradition that immersion is the valid form of baptism. No comment or judgment need further to be made either by the candidate or the minister regarding the validity or efficacy of the earlier baptism experience.

Second, if a person has been baptized in another Christian church and now desires to be a member of a Baptist church, but does not wish to be baptized by immersion, the candidate may be encouraged to experience a new baptism as an act of reaffirmation of original Christian experience, which also affirms the scriptural example of immersion. Sometimes, however, such a person may resist this invitation and desire to be made a member of the Baptist fellowship by recognizing an earlier baptism. In this case a church may elect to receive him or her by "Christian experience" and thereby recognize the spiritual validity of the earlier baptism. As we have noted, in some churches a category of "associate membership" has been established if the church is unwilling to receive as full members those who have not been immersed. Of course, a church is free to require baptism by immersion of all members and therefore to refuse membership in any category to one who elects not to be immersed. In such a case, the church should exercise the greatest degree of love and compassion in outlining its belief and decision.

Third, if a person has been baptized by immersion, but in another denomination that practices immersion or in a Baptist church of another fellowship or denomination, the previous baptism should be recognized. While there may be significant theological or ecclesiastical divisions between Baptist denominations, baptism itself is scriptural and of the manner and experience of Christ. The validity of an earlier baptism should not therefore be questioned, even though other differences of faith or practice may exist.

In considering candidates of any background or circumstance, for baptism, let churches remember that baptism, as sacred a rite as it is, is nevertheless "an outward sign of an inward grace." It can have no significance to those who have not received the inward cleansing of the Spirit. On the other hand, withholding baptism from any who have experienced inward grace is an attempt to deny what God has already accomplished. Therefore, consideration of all candidates should be approached with the greatest of humility and supplication for God's guidance.

The Obligation to Be Baptized

Baptism is the most significant single act by which a new Christian believer states his or her faith and desire to continue in Christian discipleship. Yet it might still fairly be asked, "Is one obligated to be baptized?" On the one hand, the answer must be no. The grace of God is not limited by the waters of baptism, and God may encounter, save, and restore any whom God chooses. And it would be arrogant to claim that those who experience saving grace but, for whatever reason, are unable to be baptized, are kept from the eternal presence of God.

Nevertheless, all persons are called to repent of sin, to accept Christ as the means of salvation, and to continue in this life in obedience to their Lord's commandment. Baptism is the visible means by which repentance is confessed, the acceptance of Christ is verified, and the intention to obedience is symbolized. It seems contradictory that one who trusts in Christ for salvation would then desire to disregard either his commandment to be baptized or to withdraw from public profession of faith.

While one can be saved without baptism, it is doubtful that one can truly claim to be a disciple and neglect it. "Repent, and be baptized every one of you in the name of Jesus Christ," said Peter at Pentecost (Acts 2:38). Baptism is not essential to salvation. But it is a necessary sign of obedience. This is a particularly important understanding in an era of great and growing diversity in belief and standards. There is a temptation for some to live unrecognized as a Christian, "spiritually incognito," so to speak. In succumbing to such a temptation, one preserves the option to claim Christ personally but to avoid sharing in the public responsibilities of Christian witness or in the duties of Christian community. Indeed, one who expresses a desire to be a Christian but is reluctant to be baptized may provide the best evidence not to be baptized, for a desire for blessings and rewards without contribution and commitment is ultimately a selfish and mercenary attitude. It most likely indicates that new birth has not yet transpired.

The Significance of Baptism

Just as one might ask whether one is obliged to be baptized, another might ask, "What does baptism do for me?" That is, in what respect is the believer personally different after baptism? In reply it must be stated that baptism does not produce the faith of a new heart, nor does it possess magical power to convert or cure the soul. Regeneration is by the Holy Spirit alone and should precede baptism.

Yet as an act of obedience, the reception of baptism brings joy, hope, and a profound sense of belonging to spiritual community with others who have experienced the same joy. In baptism the believer feels that he or she has come out into the world and made a public commitment to Christ, thus giving triumph to his or her spirit. Baptism often brings great personal peace.

In addition to the personal benefit the baptized believer receives, there is a public significance to baptism as well. It is a powerful symbol of renewal for the whole community of believers. It projects a sense of history and a vision of the future. It points back to Christ in suffering and death, to burial and humiliation, and then reminds us of resurrection. It points forward to the continued presence of Christ in the time to come and reaffirms that what he accomplished once in his resurrection, he accomplishes again and again in our justification and redemption.

Baptism is a continuing example of God's work of redemption in Christ. That is what gives to this ordinance its great power and significance and what makes it at once an intensely personal experience and a profoundly public act of renewal. "And you were buried with him in baptism, in which you were also raised with him through faith in the working of God, who raised him from the dead" (Colossians 2:12). The community of faith is empowered anew each time it confronts this thrilling reality. It also underlines the unity of

God's people, for there is "one Lord, one faith, one baptism" (Ephesians 4:5). Baptism speaks with the reassuring certainty only faith can bring to our vulnerable and fragile human experience. It speaks of life in the face of death: "We were buried therefore with him by baptism into death, so that as Christ was raised from the dead by the glory of the Father, we too might walk in newness of life," said Paul to the Romans (6:4).

Baptism predicts the future of the faithful. It is rooted in the belief of resurrection to come, whether in human physical bodies or in bodies, as Paul conjectured, "of some other grain" (1 Corinthians 15:37). In baptism those who rise from the baptismal waters achieve hope that, like Christ, they shall also rise from death.

But most of all, baptism is a confession of faith. Its symbolism teaches the great, central doctrines of the gospel. It symbolizes, for example, Christ's death and burial for our sins and his resurrection from the dead for our justification (Luke 12:50 and Acts 2:32-36); and it demonstrates our death to sin and rising to a new spiritual life in Christ, with fellowship with Christ in both our dying and in our living (Galatians 3:27).

It demonstrates promise for the resurrection of the saints, of which the resurrection of Christ is but the prophecy and promise: "For if we have been united with him in a death like his, we shall certainly be united with him in a resurrection like his," said Paul (Romans 6:5). And it speaks to the promise of life everlasting: "But if we have died with Christ, we believe that we shall also live with him" (Romans 6:8). Finally, it expresses the hope of our eternal life in unity with God forever: "For by one Spirit we were all baptized into one body—Jews or Greeks, slaves or free—and all were made to drink of one Spirit" (1 Corinthians 12:13).

The Lord's Supper

The Lord's Supper, also called Communion or the Eucharist, is the second ordinance (or sacrament) that Baptists believe Christ established and is therefore to be observed by churches until the end of time. Like baptism, it is a ritual of simple but deep symbolism. Perhaps even more than baptism, it has a powerful and shaping effect on its participants. Because of its central significance in the theology and practice of church life, it has historically been the focus of heated and bitter controversy among Christians. Indeed, definitions regarding the nature and practice of the Lord's Supper have been at the center of most divisions in the church, even among Baptists.

The Institution of the Lord's Supper

Communion is based on the celebration of a Passover meal among Jesus and his disciples on the night before his betrayal and arrest (Matthew 26:26-30; Mark 14:22-26; Luke 22:14-20). Of it Paul wrote to the Corinthians: "For I received from the Lord what I also delivered to you, that the Lord Jesus on the night when he was betrayed took bread, and when he had given thanks, he broke it, and said, 'This is my body which is for you. Do this in remembrance of me.' In the same way also the cup, after supper, saying, 'This cup is the new covenant in my blood. Do this, as often as you drink it, in remembrance of me.' For as often as you eat this bread and drink the cup, you proclaim the Lord's death until he comes" (1 Corinthians 11:23-26).

The Lord's Supper is so situated in the scriptural narrative of the passion and death of Jesus as to be a point of transition. At the meal, Jesus shared in fellowship and worship with his disciples; following the meal, Jesus was arrested and began his anguish as the Paschal Lamb "being led to the slaughter." Because of this, Baptists have generally believed that Jesus established the meal as a symbolic reminder of his role in salvation and as a communal event by which first his disciples and later believers could be bound with him forever. For example, Hiscox originally viewed it specifically as a "seal of the new covenant" in belief in Jesus as "the Lamb of God, who taketh away the sins of the world" (p. 91). However individual Christians view the Lord's Supper, it has served as a sacred moment of dwelling in the presence of Christ and of sharing in the common spirit of discipleship.

Other churches and groups of Christians have placed different or more specific interpretations on the observance of this ritual. Some have believed that the bread and wine of Communion are to be received as the literal body and blood of Christ. This is not a view held by Baptists, who believe that the elements are not physically changed (transubstantiated) but that they are symbolically representative now, as they were on the night of the original supper, of Christ's body and blood. Nevertheless, the pathos of the events that surrounded the historical event after which Communion is patterned have served to encourage Christians to sense a holy presence as they participate in it themselves.

The Administration of the Lord's Supper

The Lord's Supper is observed in a variety of ways among Baptists: in the structured formality of a worship service; informally as an aspect of a church "spiritual retreat" or other gatherings; as part of a service or ordination or installation of a pastor; as a ministry to the sick to remind them of the healing power of Christ and of the strength of the fellowship to which they belong, or to the dying as a reminder of their continued participation in the fellowship of Christ, whether here or in a life to come.[3] In all circumstances the symbols are the same: memorials of Christ's body and blood, shared by believers to commemorate his sufferings and death and to show their continued faith, participation in sacrifice, and hope in Christ's continued life and presence.

Generally it is the pastor who presides at this symbolic meal, serving the bread and the cup to others.[4] After some form of the words of institution have been spoken, a single prayer or separate prayers of thanksgiving are offered for the bread and the cup. When deacons are present, the pastor passes the plates and cups to them to be served, in turn, to the congregation. In a symbolic gesture of service, the pastor may also serve the deacons when they have finished serving the congregation. Then, when all have been served, the pastor leads the congregation in receiving first the bread, then the cup, by speaking an appropriate word of invitation. Guidance for appropriate words and prayers to be used, as well as orders of service for Communion, can be found in many service books, including *A Manual of Worship, New Edition* by John E. Skoglund and Nancy E. Hall.[5]

Whether the Lord's Supper is served in great formality or in an informal circumstance, it should be conducted with dignity and reverence. In many Baptist churches a special offering is received following the Lord's Supper—one usually dedicated to the service of the needy in the community or for a specific mission or outreach purpose. The service is then closed with a familiar fellowship hymn, following the precedent of Jesus and the disciples in Matthew 26:30: "And when they had sung a hymn, they went out to the Mount of Olives." The hymn "Blest Be the Tie That Binds" has become a tradition for many congregations.

In many churches it has become the practice to extend the "hand of fellowship" to new members on the occasion of the Lord's Supper. Likewise, some churches especially recognize those who have been recently baptized by seating them where the deacons can serve them first. These are appropriate gestures by which the expanding fellowship of Christ may be recognized. However, any words of recognition or introduction should be spoken before the meal is shared.

Similarly, churches that have a custom of remembering those who have recently died may choose to remember their names in conjunction with the Lord's Supper, particularly at the new year, or on a particular Sunday during the liturgical year, for example, near the day of All Saints observed in other traditions. If this custom is followed, a memorial prayer may be offered prior to the serving of the meal or at the conclusion of it, before the singing of the last hymn. The purpose of the memorial prayer ought not to be to extol the virtues of the deceased. Instead it should recognize the loss of the deceased to the present fellowship and confirm hope of their continued presence in the eternal fellowship of Christ.

The Obligation of the Lord's Supper

It is a sacred privilege for every Christian to participate in Communion. Jesus, in his observance of the meal, said, "Take, eat ... drink of it, all of you" (Matthew 26:26-27). To fail to participate is to be disobedient to his commandment, "Do this in remembrance of me" (Luke 22:19). It is unthinkable that a Christian would desire to neglect participation in this meal, except for unavoidable, extreme circumstances. Likewise, no person should approach the table of the Lord's Supper casually, for to do so is to diminish and disrespect its significance.

Participants in the Lord's Supper

Almost universally, Baptists encourage only those who are Christian believers to participate in the Lord's Supper. Few churches, however, make any clear effort to prevent its participation among those who are seeking clarification of their faith but who are not yet baptized or members of the church. Most churches do not encourage children to participate, believing that until a child has grown to a maturity sufficient to deliberately regard baptism and church membership, sharing in Communion might diminish its ultimate value for them.

There is, however, a larger issue concerning participation at the table. Among Baptist churches there has historically been a division between those who practice "open Communion" and those who practice "closed Communion." Open Communion is practiced by churches that permit anyone who desires to share in the meal and who believes himself or herself to be qualified to come to the Lord's Table without question or condition. In such churches, those present who are members of other Baptist churches, other Christian churches or communities, and even those who belong to no specific denomination are welcome to participate. Behind this practice is the belief that the desire to participate in the fellowship of the Lord's Table is itself a confession of faith and that only Christ and the participant are able to determine whether it is effective for their spiritual well-being.

In churches that practice closed Communion, on the other hand, the Lord's Supper is restricted to immersed believers who are members in good standing of a Baptist church. In some cases it is restricted at least to those who have been baptized by some means, if not immersion, in a Christian church, while in others only those who have been baptized by immersion as adults are invited. The most strict form of closed Communion is practiced in churches where the Lord's Supper is offered only to those who have been baptized by immersion in that particular church. This most strict observance is associated most often with the Landmark Movement in the South and lower Midwest, but has other adherents as well. In general, however, the practice of the most restrictive forms of closed Communion has diminished in recent decades.

In considering whether to practice open or closed Communion, churches should carefully consider the degree to which a closed Communion enhances the significance of church membership and the intensity of fellowship. This benefit must be balanced against the degree to which it separates the church from fellow Christians of other churches or isolates some who are seeking the presence of Christ and prevents them from drawing near.

The Frequency of the Lord's Supper

There is no scriptural evidence for establishing the schedule of sharing in the Lord's Supper or for particular times or seasons of it. There is some evidence that early Christians participated in this observance daily. Later, for some, it became a weekly ritual, and for many Christians, it is still practiced on one of these schedules.

Among Baptists, there are several traditions. Some practice it quarterly, others monthly, and others on some other seasonal basis. The great majority of Baptist churches share in Communion once a month, usually on the first Sunday of the month. In addition, many Baptists have adopted the custom of sharing in Communion on the Thursday preceding Easter (Maundy Thursday) as a part of an observance of repentance and preparation. Other churches also schedule the Lord's Supper for anniversary observances, services related to the new year, or other special days. This sacred meal should be scheduled when it has spiritual significance and never when it has no meaning or value to those participating.

Although the Lord's Supper is based on a specific, historic moment leading to sadness, and is thus properly a memorial meal, its true significance is as a sign pointing to the ultimate hope and glory of Christ. It thus functions as a mediating ritual, an activity that enables the church to remember with thanksgiving the salvation made possible in Christ and to look forward with rejoicing to the joyous hope of a radiant future in Christ's control. For many Baptists and other Christians, Communion points to nothing less than the return of Christ on earth: He who was dead is alive again and shall come to reign in glory. This is a position that shares the eschatology of the New Testament church, which believed that Jesus would return in their time, or at least that he would return physically before the end of time. It is a view scripturally based on

Jesus' promise, "I tell you I shall not drink again of this fruit of the vine until that day when I drink it new with you in my Father's kingdom" (Matthew 26:29). It is a view consistent with Paul's remembrance of the event: "For as often as you eat this bread and drink the cup, you proclaim the Lord's death until he comes" (1 Corinthians 11:26).

Other Baptists believe that the consummation of Christ and his church will take place in a spiritual dimension beyond present human understanding. Their interpretation does not require that the Lord's Supper point to a specific, physical return of Christ on earth. All Baptists can be united, however, in the belief that Christ is proof that God rules history and that our time, as all times, is in God's hands. It is of this unity of common expectation of Christ in future glory, whether here or there, that the Lord's Supper speaks most powerfully. It is a powerful witness of Christ's redeeming activity and our Christian faith.

Communion is, by example, also the source and example of several vital gospel doctrines:

It testifies to the love of Christ, of his grace, and of his faithfulness to all who trust in him. By its very fellowship it becomes a symbol of unbreakable unity in Christ in a fragmented and broken world: "The cup of blessing which we bless, is it not a participation in the blood of Christ? The bread which we break, is it not a participation in the body of Christ?" (1 Corinthians 10:16). Christians, divided and broken as we are, are called to fundamental unity in faith by Paul's word: "Because there is one bread, we who are many are one body, for we all partake of the one bread" (1 Corinthians 10:17).

The Lord's Supper also provides a physical and real example of the image of spiritual empowerment and nourishment we receive in Christ. Its bread is the symbolic source of the bread of new life: "Cleanse out the old leaven that you may be a new lump, as you really are unleavened. For Christ, our paschal lamb, has been sacrificed. Let us, therefore, celebrate the festival, not with the old leaven, the leaven of malice and evil, but with the unleavened bread of sincerity and truth" (1 Corinthians 5:7-8). "I am the living bread which came down from heaven: if any one eats of this bread, he will live forever; and the bread which I shall give for the life of the

world is my flesh" (John 6:51). Its wine is the living source for those
who thirst and who would be satisfied.

Rituals and Ceremonies

Baptist churches have developed out of reform impulses and
movements that frequently rejected rituals, ceremonies, or practices
that did not have a clear scriptural basis. In doing so, they have
practiced simplicity in worship and ministry. Increasingly, however, many churches have rediscovered beauty and value in rituals
that help to open the meaning of Christian spiritual growth and in
ceremonies that enable the significant moments of individual or
church-life changes and circumstances to be interpreted in the light
of the gospel. We have already discussed two clear examples of
major rituals of great importance in the life of the church: ordination
ceremonies for ministers and services of constitution for new
churches. There is a sense, too, in which both baptism and the
Lord's Supper must be considered essential sacred ceremonies in
the life of the congregation.

There are, of course, many more significant moments that are
common in Baptist churches, and there is now a new interest in
creating rituals and ceremonies that are effective in teaching and
interpreting the gospel. These are minor events in the sense that
they do not carry the central significance of ordinances, but they
may nonetheless represent significant opportunities for faith to be
given specific expression. Some might be encompassed as part of
a Sunday worship service, while others might more properly be
conducted in homes, as part of festive events, or as special services
particularly for the persons involved. The following represent a few
examples. They are discussed without necessarily prescribing their
use but to raise their possible use for consideration among Baptists.

A great many potential rituals within the faith experience of a
church are derived from the need to recognize, celebrate, bless, or
participate in significant life moments. These are "rites of passage"
that are common to human experience. Within Baptist theology and
experience, there is no basis for granting a specific sacramental
standing to such moments, nor can the purpose be to bring assurance of God's specific approval of them. However, some significant

moments seem to cry out for God's participation. In this regard, the church as a community of people has the opportunity to enhance the bonds of human relationships and, as a community of faith, to strengthen the bonds of Christian commitment.

Birth and death are fundamental life experiences common to everyone. Churches, therefore, have almost universally discovered ways to celebrate the newness of life or to focus Christian hope against the finality and grief of death. In addition, marriage, though not a universal experience, is such a profound moment of commitment that, as one traditional marriage ceremony notes, Jesus' first miracle took place at the celebration of a wedding in Cana. And, we know, the image of the church as the bride and Christ as the Bridegroom is one used by Christ, the writers of the Epistles, and the Revelation of John. Let us, then, reflect on ways rituals and ceremonies of faith might enhance these experiences.

Wedding Ceremonies

The earliest Baptists, like some of their Puritan predecessors, believed marriage was a strictly human institution and did not provide for religious rituals to recognize them. Nevertheless, the hunger for a marriage to be a spiritual union as well as a physical and legal one has demanded that the church be a participant. Some churches restrict their building use, or the pastor's participation, only to couples who have been baptized and who are members of the church. Others extend the use of the building and the pastor's presence to any who sincerely desire a Christian marriage. Either approach has justifiable merit. However, one cost of a restrictive policy is to lose an opportunity to present the witness of the gospel and the loving fellowship of the church to individuals who may be especially open to their influence and who ultimately might be open to the saving grace of Christ as the result of their marriage.

Regardless of policy, it is the wise pastor who understands that a couple desiring to be married in the church, or with the participation of a pastor, is searching for spiritual direction. This is true even among those who have shown no previous interest in the church. In addition to the ceremony itself, a pastor may wish to arrange opportunities for personal and practical counseling that may encourage or even establish bonds with the church. He or she may be in a position to provide spiritual guidance that may help the marriage survive the challenges that may otherwise prevail against it. In planning the ceremony, the pastor has a nearly unequaled opportunity to open the gospel to the couple as they seek to comprehend the nature of the commitment they are making to one another. The ceremony may be the culmination of an early life experience within the church, or it may be the beginning of a sense of worship in the presence of God. In both cases, it is an opportunity to ask for God's guidance and presence in one of life's most significant changes.

Infant Dedications

When Baptists rejected infant baptism, they did so in the belief that baptism was an act that required a maturity of understanding properly to choose. Nevertheless, the momentous experience of birth seems naturally to bring new parents a desire to share both their joy and, even more perhaps, their new sense of responsibility. Even those who have previously neglected spiritual things may be led, when a child is born, to reconsider the purpose and meaning of life.

A church, therefore, is able to extend its fellowship to young families in an inviting and powerful way by means of a ritual of infant or family dedication. In such a ceremony, whether performed as part of a regular worship service or as a special service for the purpose, it is the parents and extended family (and friends) who are asked to make a commitment to effective parenting, to raising their child in the knowledge of Christ, and to encouraging their child to receive Christian training and guidance. If the ceremony is shared with the congregation in worship, an added benefit is to invite the congregation to share in commitment and support of the process of raising a new and spiritually unformed life into a life in which the presence of Christ might be seen.

There are strong scriptural examples to validate this ceremony, including Jesus' own presentation in the temple after the customary eight days (Luke 2:22-35) and, much later, Jesus' own blessing of children. In order to prevent confusion regarding the ceremony's possible similarity to an infant baptism, it should be made clear that this is an act of *dedication* for parents (and congregation). It is also a reminder of an ancient tradition of presenting the infant to God and dedicating themselves to shaping his or her life to God's service (1 Samuel 2:24-28). As part of the ceremony, Scripture passages appropriate to the reception of life and Jesus' own response to children might be read, the child's name might be spoken as a first act of public presentation, and symbolic gifts of life may be presented, such as a flower, a certificate of dedication, and a children's Bible or book of Bible stories for his or her early use. Dedication services are included in many manuals of worship.

Funerals and Memorial Services

Death is the natural end of human life. But it does not come easily, nor with a sense of hope, without the hope of the gospel. Therefore, a Christian funeral is often an important part of the grief process for those close to the deceased person and an important part of spiritual growth in coming to terms in a personal way with the promise of eternal life.[6] Whenever possible, such a service should take place in the church in which the deceased person has participated and should include the participation of the congregation. If the church location is not suitable by reason of distance or because the family prefers it, a funeral-home chapel or parlor is also acceptable. A more private service at the graveside should also be included as a final act of parting and expression of hope.[7]

A funeral service should not neglect the need to mourn; a premature call to triumphal faith may fall on deaf ears or even damage the faith of those who grieve. Nevertheless, such a service should be permeated with the reassuring words of the Psalms ("Whither shall I go from thy Spirit? . . . even the darkness is not dark to thee, the night is bright as the day; for darkness is as light with thee" [Psalm 139:7,12]), the great and hopeful words of Jesus ("In my Father's house are many rooms; if it were not so, would I have told you that I go to prepare a place for you?" [John 14:2]), the guiding thoughts of Paul in the Epistles ("But if we have died with Christ, we believe that we shall live with him" [Romans 6:8]), and the great images of life to come in Revelation. The manner of the service may not be as important, however, as the symbolism of the community of believers gathering in strength and faith to be in support of those left behind.

The purpose of the service is not to exalt the deceased but to glorify the God who creates us and receives us. In that regard, the personality of the deceased should be remembered as a gift from God. If his or her life was exemplary, then it may be remembered as an effective example. If it was a troubled life, then without any embarrassment it may be seen as a life in struggle to find the center of God's presence and which now awaits transformation. Baptists believe in the transforming power of Christ in the Resurrection. Therefore, the primary purpose of such a service is to reaffirm faith at life's most difficult moment of loss. "For I am sure that neither death, nor life, nor angels, nor principalities, nor things present, nor things to come, nor powers, nor height, nor depth, nor anything else in all creation, will be able to separate us from the love of God in Christ Jesus our Lord" (Romans 8:38-39).

Other Life Passages

Life passages offer Christians a physical parallel to passages of our spiritual growth and transformation. Therefore, churches may have many additional opportunities to enable their members and participants to understand God's blessings and God's claims as they experience change, both for good or ill. For example, rituals might be developed to recognize wedding anniversaries and birthdays, especially the "significant" ones (such as tenth, twenty-fifth, and fiftieth wedding anniversaries, and twenty-first, fiftieth, and eighti-eth birthdays). A congregation might sponsor a celebrative dinner at which such anniversaries could be recognized and prayers of thanksgiving and blessing included. Alternatively, a ritual of thanksgiving and celebration could be developed for use in a home context or as part of a regular worship service.

Similarly, a recognition of major life transitions, such as when young adults depart for college or training experiences, can assist in developing a pathway for the future. Graduations, leaving home to live independently, and job changes or advancements might respond to a moment of blessing or dedication. Services to repeat and reaffirm wedding vows can help to strengthen marriages; such a service might follow a series on marriage growth or renewal. A ritual of engagement might well help establish an anticipated wed-ding as a Christian and spiritual experience. In short, life brings many opportunities for moments when events can be connected to

God's grace, blessing, and guidance.

It is easier by far to celebrate the ritual of a joyous and positive experience than an unhappy one. Nevertheless, seasons of uncertainty, sadness, or tragedy most need the presence of a Christian community and redemptive faith. In recent years many churches have discovered rituals that enable outreach to persons experiencing such times. For example, some churches have developed rituals to address work transitions such as unemployment, job changes, or a move to a new community. (In the case of a move, such a ceremony may also help both the congregation and the persons moving to deal with parting and grief in spiritually meaningful ways.) A significant promotion or the acceptance of new professional responsibility may provide an opportunity for a church to share with the person accepting new responsibility in a ritual of dedication and in the assurance of support by the congregation in prayer. Retirement can bring joy—but it can also bring anxiety. Therefore, a ritual to "refocus" life in new and possibly more rewarding ways can bring grace to such a time.

A high divorce rate in many communities has seriously eroded family life. It also affects church communities where all too often church members are devastated by a separated family and feel as if they have to support one or the other of the former couple. Yet both persons are likely to need the ministry of the church more than ever in order to rebuild their lives. Rituals of repentance and forgiveness can assist some former couples to recognize the broken places of their lives and to ask for God's renewing grace, even if reunion in the marriage cannot take place. Rituals that enable separated parents to renew and reaffirm their continuing role as parents for children, despite their own broken marriage, can help assure a continued sense of family responsibility and care for children, even when the parents go in separate directions.[8]

Faith rituals dealing with less formal relationships within the church community may also prove helpful. For example, churches within communities that have experienced a disaster or traumatic experience may be assisted in recovering by a ritual of renewal and spiritual refreshment. Just as new members are often greeted with a hand of fellowship, members returning from an absence, especially if it is an absence motivated by anger or misunderstanding, might be received in a ritual of renewing the church covenant. Rituals of forgiveness and reconciliation may be a significant help to individuals or groups within a church who have experienced significant conflict and desire to be healed from it.

These are but some examples—neither limited nor prescribed— of ways by which the structure of faith experience and the presence of God's guidance and grace may be developed in church life to assist and enlarge spiritual vitality among individuals and groups within the congregation. There are also powerful ritual possibilities for the whole congregation that may enhance spiritual aspects of community life.

Ceremonies for the Church

Corporate rites and rituals within the congregation have been rejected by many Baptists in principle but practiced as a matter of habit. In fact, as long as they do not become obstacles to the presence of the Spirit but instead function to heighten and focus its power, they can be very empowering for the church and its mission. For example, many churches have celebrated the church anniversary with a special service or social function, and many have assimilated the essentially secular Mother's Day and Father's Day occasions for special emphasis. There are, however, a great many other possibilities.

The first Sunday of September in many communities might be a "back to school" celebration, in addition to a commencement for a new Sunday school year. Likewise, special worship days may be established and rituals developed to commend and bless the elderly, those in the congregation from distant or foreign countries, or those who are students temporarily in the community by reason of their current education. Services of renewal for baptismal vows help to keep commitments fresh, a service of covenant for the new year may help break old spiritual (or ecclesiastical) habits and make room for new directions, and, as previously suggested, a day for remembering the dead, whether as part of an All Saints Day cycle or simply by choice of date, can be a powerful bond of remembrance, as well as an opportunity for hope and thanksgiving.

Baptist churches, which are not bound by any specific rituals or ceremonies, are free to create and adapt special opportunities for worship as opportunity or need develops. If such rituals and ceremonies are performed with the purpose of enhancing the spiritual presence of Christ in this life, and with the motive of bringing grace to bear on the experiences by which individual lives are bound with churches in community, the benefit is great.[9]

NOTES

1. A comprehensive treatise on baptism written by Hiscox is included as appendix C in this volume.

2. Baptism, strictly speaking, should be administered once and not successively as a repeated sign of spiritual growth. However, there are often cases in which candidates believe that an original baptism had taken place when they had not yet experienced a saving faith or had been urged upon the candidate for other reasons than spiritual awakening. In such cases the outward form may seem to be repeated, but the spiritual fact of baptism is occurring for the first time. The decision to engage in such a baptism should rest with the candidate and the minister. In any case, Baptists should remember that external signs are always secondary to heartfelt, internal experiences. Another special case often relates to those who travel to the biblical lands of Palestine where, in a desire to experience a physical connection with Christ, some desire to be "baptized" in the Jordan River. Such moments may be permissible as acts of fellowship with Christ and personal rededication, to be viewed as entering the waters of the Jordan and not as another baptism, strictly speaking.

3. I diverge from Hiscox in one aspect of his view of the Lord's Supper. Hiscox advocated the view that the Lord's Supper was distinctively a church ordinance and therefore could only be observed by the whole church and not by individuals (even if church members), nor in private places, including sickrooms, hospitals, or other places of need. He did allow, however, that the church might "by appointment, meet in a private house, a sickroom, or wherever it may elect, and there observe the ordinance. Therefore, in such instances, the pastor is accompanied at least by one or more deacons representing the congregation as a whole" (p. 95, n. 6). It is my belief that the whole church is represented when the pastor, or even one or more deacons, preside at a Lord's Supper for the sick, isolated, or dying. In such moments the few present are symbolically extending the fellowship of the whole church to the isolated member. Likewise, groups of church members meeting for spiritually significant reasons might well conduct a service of Communion. In that case, they should be understood to be symbolically including the whole church

fellowship. However, the church should be aware of such specific services and in no case should any such observance of the Lord's Supper be allowed where it implies a division within the congregation or a suggestion of spiritual or moral privilege among a few.

4. In many Christian churches, unleavened bread is used for the bread and wine for the cup. Baptists, who are convinced that the meal is symbolic and not literal, have never insisted on unleavened bread but have used several varieties. Because Baptists have often been at the forefront of temperance or against alcohol usage, grape juice has been almost universally substituted for wine. With modern concerns about substance abuse, the use of a substitute for wine is, in fact, a prudent health consideration. Those churches that desire to be biblically accurate and to use fermented wine often provide both wine and juice, to be selected at the preference of the individual.

5. John E. Skoglund and Nancy E. Hall, eds., *A Manual of Worship, New Edition* (Valley Forge, Pa.: Judson Press, 1993). Hiscox himself originally published materials to guide worship leaders and pastors in his *Star Book for Ministers* (Valley Forge, Pa.: Judson Press, 1994).

6. The difference between a funeral and a memorial service is generally defined by whether the remains of the deceased are present at the service. If a casket or urn is displayed, generally the term *funeral* is used. If the service does not include the remains, and especially if it takes place following the burial, it is called a *memorial service.*

7. There has been a tendency to neglect graveside services in some areas in recent years or to conduct them in a chapel near the grave rather that at the grave. I believe this is a mistake. Those closest to the deceased need an opportunity to see and to understand that the one who has died has returned to the earth or the sea and that what lived here is no more. This allows grief to be confronted, and ultimately, for life to go on. Only when the finality of death in this life is accepted can the spiritual hope of resurrection unto eternal life also be accepted.

8. In a few cases Baptist pastors have reported the use of unofficial rituals of divorce to follow the culmination of legal proceedings and separation. The purpose of such rituals is to confront the spiritual separation represented in a divorce in much the same way that legal and economic separation is confronted. Baptists believe marriage should be a lifetime commitment and, therefore, many would not believe a service recognizing a divorce is appropriate. However, since statistics indicate that broken marriages are as common among Baptists as any other group, an opportunity for ministry is clearly present in many churches. At the heart of such a ministry and any rituals associated with it is the recognition of the grief and anguish that accompanies broken relationships. Any ritual that can assist in restoring the relationship, or, if that is not possible, encourage former family members to exercise forgiveness and discover an effective, new Christian life, may be worth exploring.

9. A variety of helpful resources on the significance of life passages and

the role of the church in ministering to them are available. They include Philip Sheldrake, *Befriending Our Desires* (London: Darton, Longman and Todd, 1994); A. Wayne Price, *The Church and the Rites of Passage* (Nashville: Broadman Press, 1989); and Robin Green, *Only Connect: Worship and Liturgy from the Perspective of Pastoral Care* (London: Darton, Longman and Todd, 1987).

Loren Mead has said that "each life crisis . . . is also an opportunity for the community of faith to help a person go deeper into faith and into a new stage of ministry" (*The Once and Future Church* [Washington, D.C.: The Alban Institute, 1991], 52.) Rituals and ceremonies in the church have occasionally been assumed to be at least irrelevant and possibly counterproductive to evangelism. It is worth calling attention to two surveys taken in England that were designed to determine the means by which new Christians came to active faith. Both revealed that the largest group—in each case over 50 percent—had come to such faith at a major turning point in life, such as the birth of a child, bereavement, divorce, or change in professional circumstances. In comparison, events like evangelistic services or crusades were insignificant. (See Robin Green, *Only Connect*, 65, n. 9.) I wish also to acknowledge with appreciation an unpublished paper on the subject of church rituals and ceremony presented to the Worship Commission of the Baptist World Alliance meeting in Uppsala, Sweden, July 1994, entitled "Wanted: New Rites of Passage" by Paul Beasley-Murray.)

Chapter VII

The Witness of the Church

Churches are God's appointed instruments for the salvation of humankind and for demonstrating God's work in the world. As instruments of salvation, churches seek to follow Jesus' instruction to go among all the world's people ". . . baptizing them in the name of the Father and of the Son and of the Holy Spirit" (Matthew 28:19). Churches are called to guide Christian people, as agents of God's work, to minister to the naked and the sick, to the imprisoned, the lonely, and the lost, that they might, in the last day, receive the commendation of Christ (Matthew 25:31-46). It is possible for men and women to be saved outside the church, but that does not excuse the church from its task. It is evident that God provides ministry beyond the church, but that does not release the church from its appointed work.

When Hiscox first wrote to define the mission of the church, he said it was to a "world lying in wickedness," to those "dead in trespasses and sins," and that it should function as the bearer of glad tidings to "prisoners of hope" and as "herald of the great salvation to [the] lost" (p. 106). He took for his text the great passage from Ephesians in which Paul said it was for this purpose Christ gave himself for the church: "that he might present the church to himself in splendor, without spot or wrinkle or any such thing, that she might be holy and without blemish" (Ephesians 5:27). In this regard, nothing has changed since Hiscox's day, and the purpose of the church is still focused on this high calling. In order to fulfill this high purpose, a church must turn from self-centered or narrowly institutional purposes, take on the mind and spirit of Christ, and discipline itself to the guidance and direction of Christ.

To meet this goal, a church must witness in both a corporate and a personal sense. As a *body* the church should develop a program to proclaim the gospel and to extend its influence. Individual members of the church should strive to be and to do what the entire church ought to be and to do as "the light of the world," as "the salt of the earth," as a "city set on a hill, that cannot be hid." And, it is obvious, one task of the whole church is to prepare individuals for their witness beyond the church.

In a healthy church there is work and witness for everyone, adapted and focused for the ability and capacity of each one: old and young, great and small, male and female. The very effectiveness of the church will depend on each member doing his or her own work, not duplicating the work of others or standing idly by while others serve. Toward this end the wisdom, skill, and considerable energies of the pastor, ministers, and officers of a church will be required.

It is often a sad reflection that many churches exert a small, or even negligible, influence in their communities. And that small result may reflect a greater judgment that many church members seem unaffected by their regular experience of prayer, worship, and study in the church. The moral influence of Christian institutions to suppress evil and to increase righteousness, and the personal inspiration of Christian individuals to inspire others to goodness and compassion, should be the first order of any church's business.[1] In general, the witness of churches may be categorized in three major areas: witness as a whole community of faith (such as worship, support of missions, and other corporate commitments); witness through programs of the church (education, community outreach programs, youth work, and other programs for specific groups or needs); personal witness (workplace ministry, counseling, visitation, and other personal activities). The following categories should provide an overview and a sample rather than a comprehensive list of witness possibilities.

Proclamation of the Gospel

The proclamation of the gospel through preaching, personal witness, and the use of a variety of media should be at the heart of every church's witness. Its purpose is the effective communication of the need for repentance, the opportunity for pardon, and the hope of eternal life through faith in Jesus Christ, carried forward into the redeemed lives of believers. It is focused on the salvation of individuals and on the salvation of the whole world. Its authority is found in the words of Christ: "Go into all the world and preach the gospel to the whole creation" (Mark 16:15). It is a work that Scripture promises will be fruitful: "My word . . . shall not return to me empty, but it shall accomplish that which I purpose" (Isaiah 55:11). Traditionally churches have supported the proclamation of the gospel in the following ways:

1. Every church should prayerfully and personally support its own evangelical preaching ministry. The purpose of this ministry is for the conversion, instruction, and growing spiritual maturity of all who may be attracted to it. Its goal is the creation of effective disciples. This is usually accomplished through the pastor and augmented by guest preachers and, where possible, by recognizing the preaching gifts among the laity. The role of the whole congregation in developing a vital preaching ministry cannot be overemphasized. Congregations that support their pastor (and other preachers) through prayer, encouragement, responsiveness, and helpful evaluation will be rewarded by increased spiritual vitality for themselves and effective, evangelical proclamation for everyone. This ministry should be vital and faithful in its task and should be generously sustained. Every means should be used to invite others to experience it.

2. Many churches find special preaching missions, revivals, or preaching programs effective in providing added support for proclamation. Guest preachers and scholars of the Bible, church history, theology, and others can bring added measure to the pastor's own preaching. These events should be carefully planned so that the Spirit will claim them for the best result for both members of the church and others invited to participate.

3. It is a rare church that does not have opportunity to take the gospel's proclamation to places where there is great need to hear it and an uncommon willingness to receive it. Examples include prisons, nursing homes, hospitals, and programs of community outreach, but there are many others. A church seeking to determine

a focus for proclamation must only discover for itself where the wisdom of the world has proved insufficient and where the gospel may bring hope.

4. Some churches have developed lay preaching as an effective extension of proclamation. Often church members have the gift for interpreting the Scriptures in light of their life experiences and, by this means, are able to bring the gospel to circumstances and experiences otherwise closed to the church. This preaching should not be considered as an alternative to that of ordained ministers but as a supplement and extension of it.

5. The church is called to proclaim the gospel to the whole world. Some churches may be able to call missionaries from their own memberships to distant places and to draw from their resources to support them in their work. But all churches have both the opportunity and the obligation to aid in sending the gospel to people the world over. This may be done by cooperating with other churches, by financially supporting the mission programs of denominations, and by other collegial means.

The proclamation of the gospel is limited only by imagination. In our time, technology has made the use of live television broadcasts, videotapes, audiotapes, broadly distributed printed sermons, and other materials available to churches even of modest means. Let every church imagine how it may increase its proclamation by these means and by others just now being introduced. But regardless of the means of proclamation, it begins in the commitment to the task of sharing the Christ of the Gospels with everyone and is only effective when it is the personal, shared experience and perspective of one to another.

Pastoral Care

Pastoral care is the special opportunity for personal witness through care, support, and guidance by pastors and ministers. But it is also a responsibility of the members of the church who, because Baptists believe in the priesthood of all believers, are pastors one to another. The pastoral care of a church may effectively be expressed in many ways, the following three being common among many churches.

Visitation

A program of visiting church members not only demonstrates the care a church has for its members but also helps to develop a sense of community and commitment among them. Visitation was easier when church members all lived near one another in small towns or city neighborhoods. But it is even more important when members are scattered over a large area. Visitation is effective in members' homes but may also be accomplished by arranging for visits to their places of employment, sharing meals together, phone calls, and other means.

A minister is often presumed to be the chief visitor. And an effective pastor will maintain a regular, personal program of visitation among the members of the church. However, a pastor's opportunities of time are limited because of the many responsibilities he or she must exercise. This often effectively limits time for visits to those who are new to the church or considering church membership, to those in hospitals or nursing homes, and to individuals or families in crisis. No matter how much a pastor may attempt to visit members, it will not be enough.

Therefore, a church, under the leadership of the pastor, should adopt a plan for systematic visitation to be carried on by lay members. In developing such a program, there are many resources to train and sensitize lay visitors to be helpful in having a positive and productive experience and to report concerns and considerations back to the pastor and others for assistance. An effective lay visitation program can accomplish many things: it can discover special needs that the church can meet, such as children for Sunday school and elderly persons in need of friendship; if there is sickness or trauma, a visit can facilitate a response from the church to ease the suffering or guide them to assistance; a visit can encounter persons in grief or unhappiness and demonstrate the love of God in a personal way; a visit provides an opportunity to invite unbelievers to meet Christ or believers without a church to participate in the church; a visit can also reclaim inactive members and help unhappy members determine whether they might return to the church or need to consider another.

Clearly, a visitation program requires time and commitment and must rely on organization, training, and growing expertise among its participants. Nevertheless, in no other way can Christians effectively imitate their Lord who "went about doing good." Jesus' ministry was enacted in the context of relieving suffering, befriending the lonely, freeing the oppressed, and lifting up the fallen. His purpose was always to provide spiritual food, but he began with simple personal contact.

Visitation has suffered in many churches as a result of social change and growing complexity in our modern world. Unpredictable work schedules and the scarcity of time in individual and family lives make scheduling visits hard both for the visitor and the recipient. Also, many persons prefer not to be visited at home, and especially without advance warning. Visitation must adapt to these changed circumstances. Traditional home visitation can be augmented with phone chains, church newsletters, and many other means of contact. For some, a visit to a professional office, over lunch or in some other context, may be the best way to make contact. And because the elderly, the sick, or the abandoned often live in an institutional context, special training or skills may be recommended for those who visit in such specialized circumstances. But nothing replaces Spirit-filled human contact. "Religion that is pure and undefiled before God and the Father is this: to visit orphans and widows in their affliction, and to keep oneself unstained from the world" (James 1:27).

Fellowship Support Groups

In many churches, the only frequent opportunity for gathering together is on Sunday morning or such other times as the church is in worship. This circumstance is socially and spiritually unsatisfactory, especially in churches that have large memberships or whose members are scattered over a large geographical area. Pastoral care must focus priorities to increase the times persons have to share in friendship and Christian fellowship and by which they may experience a heightened sense of Christian community. Combined with programs of personal visitation, a program of fellowship support can greatly strengthen a church and its witness. There are essentially two ways by which the development of such opportunities may be facilitated:

1. In many churches, effective fellowship and community is developed by dividing the membership into small groups based on *geographic districts* or some other arbitrary but easily comprehended plan. The purpose is to encourage a "small-town feeling" among those who participate. Often such groupings of persons meet on a regular basis for conversation, Bible study, prayer, or projects, with the joy of fellowship being one important goal. Such districts may have informal leaders chosen from within their number, or, alternatively, sometimes one or more deacons may be assigned to a group. In the latter case, members of that subgroup of the church may be the specific focus for visitation and care by those deacons. In the most structured approaches, deacons or district leaders may issue annual reports of programs within groups and may give periodic reports to the pastor regarding concerns of individuals within the groups.

2. Other churches reject geographic or district organization as being unnecessary or artificial and develop instead a variety of small gatherings among members based on *common interest*, for example, through sharing in hobbies, recreation, mission projects, study, or prayer.[2] In such cases, a broad imagination works best, developing enough small-group opportunities to interest every and all members. Organizational leadership should work diligently to make certain every member has an opportunity to participate in a group that interests him or her. As with geographic distribution, organization within the groups may be structured or informal, and reports may be given.

The rapid and often chaotic pace of modern life, especially in urban areas, makes regular maintenance of such groups difficult. Nevertheless, the same context of life makes them very important, both to the persons who participate and to the church, as a means of providing support and care to its members. No plan will be perfect, and not all members will participate. Nevertheless, those who do will receive the blessing of support in community and become closer in bonds to one another and to Christ. The Lord has a way of magnifying the work of a few.

Pastoral Counseling

The forces of late-twentieth-century life in nearly every culture have encouraged isolation, loneliness, stress on families, personal moral crises, professional uncertainty, the hunger for life direction, and many other points of confusion. In many churches, the hunger for pastoral care will need the response of pastoral counseling.

Nearly every pastor is also a counselor, even if the role is not approached in a structured manner. Many Christians will trust a pastor only with their most vulnerable concerns, and many others will receive only pastoral advice as worthy of acceptance. Pastoral counseling, therefore, is a vital part of a church's pastoral care. Every pastor should attempt to improve his or her counseling ability and make available an adequate amount of time to offer it to those in need who are receptive to it. However, unless a pastor is specifically trained and skilled in counseling, and unless the church has identified counseling as a primary area of responsibility, pastors should establish limits on the number of persons receiving counseling and the length of time given to any particular individual. Often the best pastoral counseling offers support and encouragement, as well as such practical advice as may seem appropriate, and then assists the person in finding a professionally qualified counselor with whom to continue for long-term counseling if it is needed.

In the last generation, pastoral counseling has also become a specific vocation, often practiced on a fee basis by ministers who have been specifically trained for it. Churches that believe this is a vital need for their ministry may desire to offer counseling services as a part of a program of ministry and call a counseling minister to direct this program. Sometimes several churches unite to support a counseling center to serve their memberships, as well as to provide an outreach to the community.

Likewise, many churches have explored "peer counseling" as an effective use of gifts among the laity. Although such programs must be approached with care and caution and must arrange for training, review, and supervision, the counseling given by one Christian to another can be life-transforming and powerful. Peer counseling can be especially effective in coping with career issues and family concerns and in nuturing personal spiritual growth. The use of laity in such programs also combines very well with small groups.

Many churches, as effective stewards of their buildings and facilities, have also determined that their counseling and care can be magnified by allowing their facilities to be used by self-help groups based on the twelve-step program model, such as Alcoholics Anonymous, Narcotics Anonymous, and others. Although such organizations are not specifically Christian, they can be effective partners for Christian church programs of care.

Spiritual Growth

Encouraging the acceptance of Christ as Lord and Savior and receiving the inward joy of redemption is the first work of the church, but the second, enabling growth leading to spiritual maturity, is nearly equal to it. Every church, therefore, should offer as many opportunities and programs as possible that lead to this result. There are a great many effective ways to accomplish this. A few are outlined here.

Christian Literature

One practical and effective method of bringing believers into contact with the spiritual opportunities and experiences of others is through the use of printed materials, audiotapes and videotapes, and other media. Particularly in churches with well-educated memberships, this is often a means second only to preaching by which individuals are able to explore new spiritual insights and to meditate on Christian possibilities for their lives. Good books, periodicals, journals, and tapes can greatly enhance a congregation's understanding of the Bible, assist its members in defining God's work in their present context, and equip them with the resources for accomplishing it. Several means are especially useful in promoting the use of such literature by every member:

1. A church library, in addition to providing resources for ministers, church leaders, and Sunday school leaders, can also have a lending capability for church members who might not otherwise encounter either Christian classics or recent publications. An annual budget allotment to build a collection, and encouragement for its

use, will be a significant investment in increased spiritual maturity.

2. A regular review and recommendation of religious books and periodicals by the pastor (or other ministers), or by others who have the ability to summarize and critique their contents, can help guide members to new resources and help them evaluate what they read. Such reviews may be published alone and distributed on Sundays or may be a regular part of a church newsletter. Reviews should cover both "classics" from the early church until now and recent contributions in biblical studies, church history, theology, ethics, and personal growth.

3. The publication of sermons and prayers offered by the pastor, guests, or others in the church also encourages greater understanding. Sermons are constructed to be heard, and prayers are offered for the context of the moment. Nevertheless, a sermon once heard and then later read will reveal insights missed in the first encounter and may encourage discussion and reflection. Likewise, prayers distributed after original use may inspire and help others in the development of their personal prayer lives. Most churches have the means by which sermons, prayers, and other public offerings can be transcribed and informally printed.

Christian Education[3]

For several generations churches have used the general term *Christian education* to describe a variety of programs designed to instruct, challenge, guide, or encourage participants in the development of their knowledge of the Bible, the history of the church, Christian morality and ethics, and personal spiritual resources. The Sunday church school has been an important part of such programs. Increasingly, however, churches must look to a variety of means by which the goals of Christian knowledge and spiritual development may be enhanced. Some of the most successful and useful are:

Sunday church school
Sunday evening fellowship/worship/youth programming
Vacation church school
Weekday religious education for children/youth
Midweek or weekend study groups for adults
Leadership education classes
School of missions

Discipleship classes
Retreats
Family life programs
Denominational or other conferences
Renewal weekends
Educational travel

We shall discuss each of these opportunities in varying degree but with the understanding that this area, particularly, requires prayer and reflection to ensure vitality in developing spiritual growth. Of course, each church is also encouraged to consult publications and programs available from the fellowship, convention, or denomination of which it is a member.

Sunday Church School

The present Sunday church school grew out of the church's response to the changed social circumstances occasioned by the Industrial Revolution in the eighteenth century. It recognized that the church's only real opportunity to teach was on Sundays and that children, in particular, were in need of basic literacy education as well as biblical instruction. In recent generations this program has probably reached more people than any other, including worship, in many churches. It provides an opportunity for students to learn and for their homes to be influenced by what they learn; it offers an opportunity for growth on the part of teachers and officers who prepare lessons and work with classes; and it offers a natural context in which lay members, as well as ordained ministers, can share their faith and spiritual understanding. Most often the Sunday church school meets preceding or following the worship of the whole church.

The success of the Sunday church school has enabled it to be considered the teaching arm of the institutional church and should ideally provide opportunities for children, youth, and adults alike.[4] As such, it is often integrated as a part of the total church program, budget, and planning, most often under the supervision of the board of Christian education. The curriculum and activities are planned to carry out the purposes of the whole church. Church school materials should be adopted and coordinated by the church's board of Christian education or other body charged with assuring the quality of its program. In considering this responsibility, it should be the goal of the board and the Sunday school superintendent to develop a comprehensive and cohesive curriculum and program. It should establish and occasionally review its goals and expectations for the accomplishment of each grade level, not only for knowledge to be acquired but for the formation of faith experience appropriate for each level of development.

In approaching this task the board of Christian education or others charged with organizing classes and selecting materials should consider the following critical decisions:

1. A consistent curriculum should be developed for the entire school, and not a scattered approach where every class has a curriculum chosen solely by the teacher. For children and youth especially, each year's material should build on previous accomplishments, with goals for each year to be reviewed.

2. If the school includes adults, a policy decision should be established encouraging age-graded classes or classes determined by common interest or experience. There is much to favor both decisions for different reasons. If an age-graded approach is determined, clear definitions of the classes and a proper means for advancing persons from one group to the next must be explained and encouraged among participants.

3. In choosing curriculum materials, there are essentially two options of kind: the use of a uniform lesson series for all ages or the use of graded lessons. In the first, a uniform plan, lessons are produced according to a plan of study (these are often interdenominational and with a multiyear cycle) by which all age groups are studying the same Bible passages on a particular day. This has the advantage that family members and friends can share aspects of their study discussions. In the second, a graded plan, there is often no regard to uniformity but instead, subject matter is selected according to the interest and needs of the age group. Here life experience is heightened, but at the cost of discouraging common discussion of the day's lesson.

4. In addition, the choice of curriculum material should follow a decision whether the church will follow the curriculum developed or approved by its own denomination or whether it will use materials offered by independent publishers or the publishers of another

denomination. If the church's own denomination is chosen, the particular history of that denomination and the programs of its mission activities may be highlighted. However, a church may prefer the materials offered by another publisher because of theological perspective, attractiveness of presentation, or consistency with the church's educational goals for its program. If a curriculum developed by an independent or other denominational press is chosen, the church must realize its own customs and rituals may be neglected, as well as its history, and it may wish to investigate or develop supplemental materials to address these issues. (Examples for Baptists include baptism by immersion, the principle of the priesthood of believers, the independence of the local church, and other significant Baptist issues.)

Sunday church school sessions are still most often scheduled prior to worship on Sundays or in "extended-session" models that allow children to use all or part of the worship hour for worship or continued study suitable for their age. Some churches, however, are experimenting with different times, such as following a midday Sunday meal or on Saturdays. Other churches have abandoned age-graded approaches and are using intergenerational curriculum materials and experiences for at least some classes.

The major challenge for Sunday church school programs seems to come from changing social patterns, including changing family lives, the pressure on Sunday morning times for the accomplishment of many church programs, and the simple fact of declining Sunday morning participation in many communities. If traditional times and places of education are not effective, churches may prayerfully consider alternatives of time, place, and structure. However, abandonment of church schools in some form is unwise and will eventually result in a biblically illiterate laity and a withering of spiritual life and purpose in the church.

Sunday Evening Fellowship

Until a generation ago, nearly every Baptist church offered a Sunday evening program, including a worship service, opportunities for fellowship or training for adults, and fellowship and training for young persons. In recent years many such programs have been abandoned for a variety of reasons, mostly changing social values and pressure for time. In many cases, only a youth fellowship program remains, and in central urban churches even those programs have often been abandoned.

Nevertheless, Sunday evening remains a time when alternative styles of worship may be explored, perhaps focusing on the needs of persons not able to worship on Sunday mornings or connecting with different tastes and expectations than the traditional service. It is also an appropriate time for family-life programs such as parenting classes, intergenerational programs, or programs built around a particular interest or theme, such as music or recreation. Sunday evening may also be a good time for visitation programs, leadership training, or adult study groups focused on a particular subject for a defined number of weeks. Whenever possible, a Sunday evening program should begin or end with a brief worship service. Most important, the educational programs should have a clear purpose and not be merely a ritual gathering for gathering's sake.

Vacation Church School

Many churches find an intensive opportunity for recreation, Bible study, and fellowship to be a good way to enrich the Christian experience of children and youth during summer vacations. A few churches have successfully developed programs for all ages and have scheduled some events for evenings, when parents and other adults are more commonly able to participate. Such occasions are especially suitable for reaching new families. Such programs have often been called vacation church school, vacation Bible school, or topical names designed to appeal to the interest of children or youth, like "Summer Explorers" or "Christian Adventure." Vacation schools are often scheduled to run for one or two weeks from two to five hours per day. Classroom activities may be mixed with recreation, dramatics, music, and worship to sustain interest and enthusiasm.

Vacation church schools are effective evangelism opportunities, are useful training grounds for new teachers for the regular Sunday church school, and provide many occasions for intergenerational and informal exploration of the Bible, questions of faith, and life direction. Often, if a church does not have sufficient numbers of children or leadership resources, a vacation school may be sponsored by several churches of the same or different denomination, drawing on the skills and resources of each church to build an effective program and staff. In scheduling such a program, the board of Christian education will be wise to consider traditional vacation weeks and school summer activities in order not to compete for the children's time and to have the maximum available staff.

Weekday Religious Education

In many communities churches offer religious education opportunities for students following their release from public school programs. In some communities, children are released from school specifically to attend the program of their own faith. Also, as a result of the 1993 Religious Freedom Restoration Act, it is possible for space in school facilities to be arranged so that religious education programs can be offered for persons of all ages under certain conditions. When churches offer educational opportunities in the public arena or open them to the community, special preparation in selecting qualified teachers and materials will help assure a quality program. Often resources and advice are available from denominational sources.

Midweek and Weekend Study Groups

It is often observed that modern Christians, and certainly non-Christians, are much less aware of the Bible and its resources and of traditional doctrines of faith and practice than their predecessors. This is due to the proliferation of interests, diversity in culture, and growing secularity of society. One result is a hunger for knowledge and spiritual insight among adult church members. Many churches find that regular study opportunities meet this need. Sometimes using a standard curriculum is useful. In other circumstances a topical book, a book of the Bible, a study theme, or some other focus, such as family communicatons, marriage growth, or some other plan is an attractive educational opportunity for adults during the week or on Saturdays or Sunday evenings. There is no limit to the description of possibilities for study and discussion.

It is often effective to plan such group meetings for a specific period, such as six or eight weeks. Or if they continue, the study plan might schedule periodic breaks to enable new persons to join and continuing participants to regather enthusiasm.

Leadership Education Classes

Modern churches require effective leadership more than ever. Especially in an era when leadership faces increasing challenges, Christian leaders need training and encouragement. Church leaders need to have knowledge of the Bible and how its direction relates to the church's work and to their leadership, practical training in organization, conducting meetings, delegating responsibility, methods of development, and the specific skills required for such programs as Sunday school teaching, music leadership, and recreation. Leadership training can be provided by a single congregation or as a combined program of several churches. It is also often offered as a program of the state or regional association of the denomination with which the church is affiliated.

School of Missions

A heart for missions and outreach should be at the center of church life. A school of missions should serve to acquaint church members with mission and outreach programs the church is engaged in or supports, as well as opportunities for new mission programs. A school of missions also provides a forum for learning more intensively about the cultures and needs of communities for which missions are supported. For young persons, a school of missions often provides an early introduction to the great variety of cultures and people in God's great human family. A school of missions can be a highlight of a church year, scheduled for a week when children, youth, and adults may all receive information. If time or resources are limited, a school may be offered on a weekend or on a Sunday or series of Sundays, perhaps in conjunction with existing Sunday schedules.

Discipleship Classes

A unique occasion of education is available when persons have accepted Christ and are eager to move forward in discipleship.

Young persons who have decided to be baptized or are considering that decision may be especially open to a review of the Bible's great message, to learning more about the purpose of the church, and to reflecting on God's purpose for their own unique lives. Adults who have not previously accepted Christ, and especially if they have not yet maintained a significant church membership experience, are likewise receptive to learning more about Christ and about the Baptist tradition. Discipleship classes should ideally be conducted by the pastor, or at least with the pastor's participation, and should be scheduled whenever possible prior to baptism or immediately thereafter. For adults, either those who have recently joined the church or those who are presently "inquirers," discipleship classes may be scheduled on several occasions during the year or as needed. Resources are available from denominations to guide the pastor's preparation. In general, such classes should provide an overview of basic Christian doctrines, denominational and church practices and traditions, and an opportunity to reflect on the personal implications of faith and belief.

Retreats

A retreat is a time of withdrawal from normal activities in order to better reflect on the work of the Spirit within and to recapture a vision for effective Christian living beyond daily requirements. Retreats are loosely modeled after the example of Christ, who often drew apart from the crowds and the disciples for prayer, reflection, and rededication. Retreats sponsored by churches, whether for youth or adults, should be faithful to this purpose. Retreats are often effective ways to present biblical teaching or life-issue training (such as marriage growth, stress reduction by meditation, or family communication development). Retreats may also be effective in providing greater bonding for groups within the church and for leaders in training, committees, boards, teachers, or ministers. Some churches, especially small congregations, have found an "all-church retreat" an effective experience for renewal and church planning exercises.

Family-Life Programs

The church is a family. But the church is also made up of the specific families to which it ministers. Reinforcing the family of the church and undergirding relationships within the families of the church is an important part of a spiritual growth ministry. Churchwide family-life programs are frequently offered effectively at seasonal times, such as Christmas, Thanksgiving, or the new year, or on a seasonal theme, such as harvest in the fall, renewal in the spring, or recreation in the summer. In such programming, activities and interests should be developed to encourage the whole church family to participate and to value one another as members of the family of Christ.

Specific family-life programs may also be effectively offered to families in particular circumstances or stages. Child-raising families, for example, benefit from parenting skills, communication, and marriage growth opportunities. Recently divorced and recently bereaved persons may grow from programs focused on their unique and changing circumstances. Merged families (from remarriages), single persons, retired persons, and many other categories of families have special needs and present the church with opportunities to respond to those needs for new understanding, growth, and spiritual enrichment in ways that provide educational enhancement for the individuals as well as for the whole church. In developing family-life programs, a church should be sensitive to define a category of family to include everyone.

Camps, Conferences, and Denominational Events

Summer Christian camps for children and youth have a traditional place in church educational programming and have often served an evangelical as well as an educational purpose. Now, camps and conferences are offered at many seasons of the year in addition to summer. Some churches are able to sponsor their own camps or conferences. Most churches will find it advantageous to send church members to camps and conferences sponsored by denominational structures and agencies. Many denominations offer seasonal camp opportunities within states and regions in which churches participate. Some denominations also operate national conference centers that offer high-quality conference and retreat programs and that make accommodations available for programs designed by others. In addition, there are many high-quality non-denominational or ecumenical conference centers that will design programs for individual churches or groups or that offer programs with open registration to persons from a variety of Christian backgrounds. Like retreats, camps and conferences, whether for young persons or for mature adults, offer intensive opportunities for reflection, education, training, and renewal. Effective church programming will encourage many members to take advantage of such offerings each year and will provide budget funding to help offset a portion of the expense of attending.

Renewal Weekends

Many churches have developed one or more weekend educational opportunities during the church year. Often these weekends consist of an opening session on Friday evening, a full day of educational events on Saturday, and a specially focused worship theme and possibly a fellowship meal following worship on Sunday. Sometimes such programs begin on Sunday with worship, extend to Sunday afternoon or evening, and then continue on weekday evenings. This format is a highly efficient way to use the special knowledge or expertise of a visiting lecturer or educator. The effectiveness of such a weekend experience is often increased if it follows a single thematic design, such as the study of a book of the Bible, a classic or recent theological work, or a book of Christian literature, or if it addresses a particular challenge to the church. Weekend experiences have also been effectively used for family-life and marriage-enrichment programs. The key to the success of such a weekend is effective planning and delegation of leadership roles to provide for fellowship, meals, materials, and organizational needs.

Educational Travel

Where the interest and financial means are available, travel opportunities often greatly advance the understanding of church members in faith, mission, or life experience. Examples include mission tours to places near or far, where the church is supporting a mission program; faith "heritage" tours to the Bible lands (Israel, Jordan, Lebanon, Egypt, and Syria) or to Europe or Britain (where Baptist or Christian roots in church life may be explored); or, in some cases, tours to locations where mission programs may be viewed firsthand.

In our time, many persons like to travel for recreation and renewal, and church programming may often unite this strong interest with educational programs that enhance spiritual and faith understanding. Many churches have discovered that travel is a particularly effective educational program for young persons (who can travel inexpensively) as well as for retired persons. In developing such programs, a church may wish to unite with other churches, explore travel opportunities offered by denominational agencies, or design their own. Because of the special skills required in such programs, churches are advised to identify qualified travel consultants and to deal only with reputable agencies. Likewise, insurance needs for health, accident, and liability should be investigated.

Christian education may be advanced in a great variety of circumstances. The possibilities are, in fact, limited only by the imagination. The example of Jesus was to meet people where they were, encounter them in the circumstances of their daily lives, and frequently minister to them by teaching. Whether in a city street or on a hillside, people responded because he found them and engaged them. Let all churches use his model as the example, and there will be no end to the programs they might establish.

Church Missions and Outreach

The Christian church was originally commissioned with a mission: "Go into all the world" (Mark 16:15). It was because some of the apostles responded to that charge that the church expanded beyond Jerusalem. Indeed, it has been truly spoken that all Christians are, strictly speaking, the result of the disciples in mission. In response to that challenge, the church has often been a vital missionary force in the world and has accomplished great change in the hearts of men and women and effected great good in the societies and cultures in which they live. It is therefore the high purpose of every church to follow in that tradition and to be a supportive community for the work of missions. We have the joy and the privilege of the gospel because of a missionary, ancient or modern. All Christians therefore have the obligation to ensure that others may receive the gospel.

Mission Support

In fulfilling that obligation, many churches send missionaries from their own congregations or join with other churches in sending missionaries. However, it is often not practicable for an individual church to call missionaries from its own midst and individually to support them in their work. Therefore, it has become customary among Baptists to contribute financially to the support of missions through denominational and independent mission societies. Baptists have often preferred to work together in denominational missions. The reasons are simple: greater work can be accomplished together, and by uniting with others of like mind and spirit, the sense of fellowship among Baptists is increased. In supporting denominational missions, churches are supporting mission programs and agencies that they have helped create by their own representation as well as support.

It is often argued in local congregations that there is much work to be done in the local community and that "charity begins at home." While the essential truth of such a position must be affirmed, it is not appropriate logic for declining to offer mission support over greater distance. Such an attitude is a subtle foundation for not supporting missions at home or abroad. It is the experience of Baptist churches, in fact, that mission support for distant concerns helps to create a greater sensitivity to concerns at home and that support for one encourages support for the other. Conversely, churches that withhold support from those in need often dry up their own spirit of benevolence and end up having even fewer resources for their own work.

Each Baptist church should carefully investigate the opportunities for mission through its own denomination, association, or fellowship. Through denominational mission programs, churches become part of a strong fellowship and often benefit locally by experiencing the faith and commitment of others. Many modern Baptists, though organized separately today, nevertheless recognize

a common, proud tradition of mission commitment that began in
the work of Adoniram and Ann Judson and Luther Rice. In addition,
today Baptists from many denominational backgrounds unite
through the work of the Baptist World Alliance, which helps to
network the varieties of missions established by member denominations. Many Baptist churches are also supportive of independent
mission programs or benevolent programs sponsored by nonreligious agencies, especially in the areas of disaster relief, medical
assistance, and hunger concerns. These are often worthy programs
but should be carefully reviewed for priorities and effectiveness.
Such support should be in addition to basic commitment to the
advance of Christian mission in response to the gospel.

In developing support for missions, a large responsibility rests
with the pastor and other leaders of the church. It is the pastor's role
to help a church lift its vision beyond its own boundaries and to
inspire others to do so as well. Few churches will be mission
churches if the pastor is not committed to missions and to inspiring
others to respond to the privilege of mission support.

Community Outreach

Every church has an opportunity to become involved in concern
and outreach in its own community. The same commission by
which the mission to all the world is established also calls the church
to witness in its own community. This means to proclaim and
uphold the gospel in many of the ways already mentioned. It also
means to address the needs of the hungry, the sick, the lonely, the
imprisoned, and others in need of compassion, justice, or restoration. Churches in the twentieth century have often been pioneers in
providing effective responses to hunger, homelessness, unemployment, child care, care of the elderly, housing for senior citizens, and
other critical human concerns.

Each congregation must consider prayerfully how its resources
and opportunities might be activated to accomplish its own share
of God's work in its community. Programs of social concern and
outreach are an integral part of the mission of the church.

In virtually every community, whether a small village or a large
urban area, organizations and movements dedicated to some form
of civic progress, economic justice, or social improvement are

present. Each church must determine the degree to which it wishes to ally its own commitments and resources to lead or to help accomplish one or more of these ends and to what extent it intends to exercise its outreach alone.

Many churches are able to extend their outreach and, at the same time, to become partners with others in the community who are attempting to strengthen and build community well-being by the simple act of sharing building space. For example, some churches are able to provide space for child care, elder care, or recreational activities for young persons after school. In other cases church buildings are suitable for use by Alcoholics Anonymous groups and similar recovery organizations, for language classes for recent immigrants, or for self-improvement courses of many varieties for people in varying ages, conditions, and circumstances. Sometimes these programs are actively sponsored by a church, or a group of churches. Other times the programs are sponsored by another organization, but the church becomes a supportive partner by offering space for use. In determining this method of outreach, the church will be guided by the compatibility of the program and whether it will prevent the smooth operation of church programs already in progress or planned for operation soon.

Likewise, if the church makes space available, it should engage in straightforward discussions regarding costs involved and whether the guest program has an obligation to assist the church financially in return for the space being used. Many churches develop such relationships quite successfully and are therefore able to magnify their outreach to the community.[5]

Christian churches in general, and Baptist churches in particular, have helped to initiate and nurture a great many community agencies and programs that later became independent and developed a structure of their own. Examples include temperance (or anti-alcohol-abuse) movements, recreational programs, outreach to immigrants and socially displaced persons, youth organizations, schools, colleges, health organizations (including many hospitals, nursing homes, and treatment facilities), and many others. Some have become national organizations and networks of great distinction and effectiveness. Churches are often able to help breathe life into such work and then pray for its success and effectiveness as it grows in maturity. Churches should avoid the temptation to control such work, and instead, should discern new opportunities and needs.

Baptist Churches in Connection and Fellowship

The church is a universal fellowship in Christ. We know that Baptists are divided into many different denominations and organize separately from Christians of other denominations. This seems to be a contradiction to the spirit of the creation of the church as one in Christ. Regrettably, in describing the organizational structures of churches, the New Testament focused only on the individual church congregation. Perhaps the individual congregation is the only church unit that is essential. It is a certainty that Baptists have traditionally been reluctant to grant theological and biblical legitimacy to corporate structures beyond the church because the Scriptures do not present a clear precedent. Nevertheless, it has been the experience of many Baptist churches that by cooperation and fellowship with one another, they are able to fulfill the work of the gospel and the mission of the church more effectively. The means by which Baptists unite with other Baptists, and with other Christians, are many.

Associations

Almost since the beginnings of the Baptist movement, churches of like belief and practice have voluntarily yoked themselves in fellowship with one another. Such relationships have been called "associations." By means of regular communication, meetings, and conventions, associations have encouraged a more effective ordering of church affairs and congregational life and have enabled the publication of literature and the support of missions to be accomplished. Associations have also been an important part of the inspiration, encouragement, and shared vision of churches through preaching, worship, and deliberation together.

As associations developed, they initiated regular quarterly and annual meetings; sponsored rallies and revivals; raised funds for the establishment of schools and colleges; approved standards for ordination; encouraged the work of men's, women's, and youth organizations; and conducted business related to these and other common works. The development of organized mission programs both at home and abroad granted additional importance to associations, for they often became the unit by which churches were acquainted with the mission work and where goals for financial support were established.

By the early twentieth century, the work of many associations had become so vital and complex that in many cases, particularly in populous urban areas, they incorporated and called professional leadership to direct their work on a full-time or part-time basis.

Their leaders, variously called general secretary, executive secretary, mission director, and similar titles, functioned to coordinate the work of the association and to facilitate the work of individual churches. Their staffs often included specialists in Christian education, mission awareness, pastoral leadership, and urban missions. They became especially important in encouraging the financial support of missions; providing training for Christian education within churches; and sponsoring and developing local mission and outreach programs, such as schools for children in poor urban areas, hospitals for those not otherwise able to receive medical care, nursing homes, and other responses to the displacements and needs created by urbanization. Likewise, they became an important link in the process of church selection of pastors and pastoral settlement in new areas of service. Some of the largest and most well developed of these associations continue until now in several Baptist denominations, particularly in large urban areas.

Elsewhere, however, the work of associations began to decline by midcentury. Increased transportation, communication, and access to centrally produced information and literature may have broadened the fellowship of churches and made associations less important. As this development took place, the work of associations was superseded by the development of state or regional "conventions" of churches. In many cases, these larger expressions of fellowship life maintained the representative structure of associations. In other cases, associations were abandoned in favor of some other organizational division.

State and Regional Conventions

Where associations continue, they are most often a part of a larger regional structure; where they have been abandoned, the connectional work of churches has become more specifically focused through the work of state or regional organizations that are, in fact, a further development of associations.[6] These agencies focus on the encouragement of churches, with the strong helping the weak and with staff members of the state or region possessing the expertise to assist churches in program development. Pastoral placement among churches and the development of mission awareness and support remain, however, central to their purpose. Increasingly, the chief professional representative of state or regional structures is entitled "executive" and functions as a "pastor to pastors" and as a resource to churches within the region. Often he or she is the chief administrator for the work and missions of the state or region and serves formally or informally as a regional staff member of the national body.

Most state and regional structures among Baptists function as independent and autonomous organizations. They hold annual meetings for the conducting of business, for inspiration, and for the formation of a common vision of the work and mission they seek to accomplish. Most often their policy-making and administrative decisions are governed by an official board or council that is elected by the convention in annual meeting and approves their work. State and regional structures often share many programs in common and are united by common vision. Nevertheless, state or regional structures are also often shaped by the regional distinctive in theology, worship, mission, and tradition for which Baptists are known.

National Denominational Structures

Because of the different traditions among Baptists and because of regional distinctives, the fellowship of Baptists at a national level is less than fully unified. Racial, cultural, regional, theological, and other differences have thus far prevented Baptists from forming a common family or union that encompasses all. However, most Baptist churches belong, however informally, to a fellowship that has a national connection. This is especially true in North America, but is increasingly true in Britain, Europe, and even in the developing regions and nations of the world. In the United States, for example, six denominations comprise a great majority of Baptists:

the American Baptist Churches in the U.S.A.; the Southern Baptist Convention; the National Baptist Convention of America, Inc.; the National Baptist Convention, U.S.A., Inc.; the National Missionary Baptist Convention of America; and the Progressive National Baptist Convention, Inc. The combined membership of these bodies is over 33.5 million.[7]

Smaller denominational structures include groups who have separated themselves from the larger bodies because of theological differences or other reasons. Others represent groups that have their origins in their national heritage and who have desired to maintain the link between their heritage and their church fellowship, such as German, Swedish, and Romanian Baptists. Operating budgets range from $1 million to well over $100 million per year, often in addition to equal or greater amounts specifically designated for particular mission projects or institutional support.

National denominational bodies have become the most visible expression of programs, mission, and policy for Baptist church life. It is through the national bodies that most mission projects are defined and funded; educational and inspiration materials are published; and standards for ministry, programming, and other vital concerns within church life are established and monitored.[8]

National denominations are governed by representative boards and often are additionally subdivided into boards for missions, education, publication, annuity and insurance, and other functions. Often the boards for these subdivisions exercise considerable power over the specific work of their division.

The rapid pace of change and ferment of the latter part of this century has witnessed the development of additional categories of national Baptist expression. Two such organizations have emerged from theological controversies within the Southern Baptist Convention. The Alliance of Baptists (originally the Southern Baptist Alliance), with an office in Washington, D.C., represents about one hundred churches that were among the earliest to redefine theological, mission, and education priorities separate from the emerging conservative agenda of the Southern Baptist Convention after 1979. The alliance is a fellowship of both churches and individuals. A second example is the Cooperative Baptist Fellowship (CBF), headquartered in Atlanta, Georgia. The CBF is a larger grouping of churches that have been reluctant to break ties with the Southern Baptist Convention but have desired to direct their mission funding by means of their own established priorities.

In addition, several national Baptist groups are loosely organized around particular issues or causes. These groups, most often organizations of individuals rather than churches, focus their attention on concerns that they believe do not receive enough attention from denominational structures or that need particular nurture. One example is the Baptist Peace Fellowship of North America, which focuses on issues of peace, reconciliation, and mediation. Such groups maintain small administrative structures, sponsor annual meetings or conventions, and publish materials specific to their concern. Most often, their constituencies are members of churches related to one or more of the national Baptist denominational bodies.

Of all expressions of Baptist church life, national denominational structures and programs are at present most subject to change. It is too early to comprehend either causes or new directions. However, funding for national structures and programs is declining, and division and diversity within the fellowship among every denominational structure seems destined to change priorities and directions in coming years. These changes are consistent with dynamics in other Christian church bodies and may reflect profound changes taking place within our culture, especially in North America. It is an indication that Baptists need to reaffirm the strength of the individual church and find continuing ways to unite in common vision and purpose in the name of Jesus Christ.

The following is a listing of national Baptist groups claiming memberships of 50,000 or more, as reported in the 1994 edition of the *Yearbook of American and Canadian Churches*:[9]

The American Baptist Association (1905), Texarkana, Ark./Tex.—a group of independent missionary Baptist churches, mainly in the South. Membership is 250,000.

American Baptist Churches in the U.S.A. (1907), Valley Forge, Pa.—formerly the Northern Baptist Convention, with churches throughout the United States but mainly in the northeastern, north central, and western states and Puerto Rico. Membership is 1,527,840.

Baptist General Conference (1879), Arlington Heights, Ill.

—formerly the Swedish Baptist General Conference. Membership is 134,658.

Baptist Missionary Association of America (1950), Little Rock, Ark.—formerly the North American Baptist Association, with churches in the South and West. Membership is 230,127.

Conservative Baptist Association of America (1947), Wheaton, Ill.—churches mainly in the northern and western states. Membership is 210,000.

General Association of Regular Baptist Churches (1932), Schaumburg, Ill.—a fellowship of churches that withdrew from the American Baptist Churches over doctrinal differences. Membership is 160,123.

General Association of General Baptists (1907), Poplar Bluff, Mo.—an Arminian group of Baptists first organized by John Smyth and Thomas Helwys in England. It was transplanted to the colonies in 1714 but died out along the seaboard. It was later revived in the Midwest in 1823 by Rev. Benoni Stinson. Membership is 74,156.

National Association of Free Will Baptists (1935), Antioch, Tenn.—an Arminian Baptist group tracing its lineage to a group organized in 1727 and found primarily in the Old South and border states. Membership is 209,223.

National Baptist Convention, U.S.A., Inc., Nashville, Tenn.—the older and parent organization of African American Baptists. Membership is 8,000,000.

National Baptist Convention of America, Inc. (1880), Dallas, Tex.—a largely African American Baptist body. Membership is 3,500,000.

National Missionary Baptist Convention of America (1988), San Diego, Calif.—was organized following a dispute over control of convention publishing efforts within the National Baptist Convention of America, Inc. Its primary purpose is to extend Christian education, church extension, and missionary efforts. Membership is 2,500,000.

Progressive National Baptist Convention, Inc. (1961), Washington, D.C.—withdrew from the National Baptist Convention, U.S.A., Inc. over issues of ecclesiastical leadership and style. It is predominantly African American but has dialogue and open relationships with non-African American churches, especially the American Baptist Churches in the U.S.A. Membership is 2,500,000.

Southern Baptist Convention (1845), Nashville, Tenn.—the largest of Baptist bodies, having first been strictly a Southern fellowship but now having spread into the North and West. It grew out of historic debates regarding the stance of Baptists toward slavery and emphasizes evangelical style, personal salvation, and a strong mission program. Membership is 15,300,000.

The Baptist World Alliance

Baptists are now to be found throughout the world, although the overwhelming number are still residents of the United States. The growth of Baptist churches in many cultures is testimony to the power and presence of the Holy Spirit, the effectiveness of Baptist missions, and the flexibility of Baptist organizational life that places its trust in the independence of the local congregation. In recognition of the increasing reality of a world fellowship of Baptists, the Baptist World Alliance (BWA) was established in 1905. Its original headquarters was in London, but more recently it is administered from McLean, Virginia, a suburb of Washington, D.C.

The Baptist World Alliance holds a world congress every five years and meets in smaller numbers for executive council and commission meetings each year in a different country or location. The business of the alliance is conducted by its executive council and subcommittees for a variety of purposes. Its primary purpose is to enhance Baptist fellowship, but increasingly it plays a strong role in providing crisis relief through its Baptist World Aid and works to develop international cooperation, particularly through its divisions for men, women, and youth. Commissions are appointed for a five-year period between congresses to study, address, or form resolutions regarding a variety of issues in Baptist church life or in the cultural life in which churches express their witness.

The BWA is structured to be an organization made up of national or regional conventions or denominations. Representation on its boards and committees is by convention or denomination election or designation. Increasingly, however, its financial support is derived from individuals and churches. As with the future of national denominational structures, current social, economic, and political change will determine the future shape of this still relatively young fellowship of Baptists in witness.

Relationships with Other Churches

Some Baptist churches, confessing their limitation as only part of a great assembly of the churches that make up the universal church, choose to maintain formal or informal relationships with churches of different historic creeds or development. Individual churches or local conventions often express this connection through community councils of churches or other interchurch or ecumenical organizations. At the national and international level, some denominations and churches relate to the National Council of the Churches of Christ in the United States, to the World Council of Churches, the National Association of Evangelicals, and others. Many other churches participate in loose affiliations of regional expression. In addition, in recent years there have emerged a number of "parachurch" organizations, which are churchlike organizations devoted to a unique style of proclaiming the gospel and engaging in mission and that invite church support and participation from churches of many denominational identities.

Relationships between Baptist churches and churches of other traditions has always been controversial among some Baptists. Therefore, some churches do not associate as churches in any way with non-Baptist churches or groups that include non-Baptist churches. Of these, some do not preclude their members or pastors from participation in interchurch activities. Others are quite strict in separation and do not allow any interchurch or interdenominational fellowship at all.

In the last generation, however, there has been a shift in lines of identity from making the Baptist identity the single most important reference to making adherence to particular theological or ethical positions an equally important focus. Participation of Baptist churches with other churches is now often determined by whether the point of participation with others is congruent regarding theological belief relating to certain controversial issues, such as abortion and other issues of human sexuality, the role of religion in public life (prayer in the schools, for example), or the role of women in the church. At times Baptist individuals and churches find it more congenial to associate with others who are not Baptist but whose fundamental beliefs are similar than to be in fellowship with

Baptists whose history and church heritage are the same but who follow a different understanding on these or other issues.

Regardless of the official, denominational, and theological positions concerning some of these matters, Baptist churches, like churches of many other denominations and traditions, are experiencing profound change and reorientation as the result of popular, grassroots movements among people, which displace traditional priorities and processes within church and denominational life. Baptists now, as always, can often exhibit profoundly different perspectives as they seek the mind and will of Christ in offering their witness. Baptists are now, as always, encouraged to seek the guidance of the Spirit as they struggle to determine their associations, interrelationships, and directions in providing witness in the future. We are assured, however, that in Christ we are one, that in Christ there is "neither Jew nor Greek, neither slave nor free" (Galatians 3:28), and that "Christ Jesus himself being the cornerstone" (Ephesians 2:20), Baptists should seek to be part of him "in whom the whole structure is joined together and grows into a holy temple in the Lord; in whom you also are built into it for a dwelling place of God in the Spirit" (Ephesians 2:21-22).

NOTES

1. Hiscox observed that "the results of church life and action are often more apparent in the lands of the younger churches overseas than in our own country" (p. 107). Now, even more than in Hiscox's time, we are aware that historic, "mature" churches are not necessarily the most vital and active churches, regardless of the country or culture in which they are located. With the passage of time, churches in every land and culture must stay focused on their mission and ministry and, through prayer and commitment, strive to maintain the vitality and focus of faith and purpose.

2. One strong example of a small-group approach to fellowship combined with mission and service is the traditional model of organization common to women's groups. Often such groups divide women into "circles," which meet regularly for fellowship, prayer, and the accomplishment of activities in support of mission concerns. Women's organizational work in churches is undergoing great change because of the changing roles and expectations of women, and particularly women's more frequent employment outside the home. However, this model is still highly effective and is worthy of

emulation more broadly in other areas of church life.

3. The area of Christian education was not well developed when Hiscox first wrote. A section dedicated to this subject was added as a revision to the 1964 edition of *The Hiscox Guide* because it had become central to the spiritual growth ministry of most churches. Ironically, traditional Christian education programs are presently in a period of great change. In many churches, they have been retitled as programs of spiritual growth, discipleship, church leadership, or other experimental titles. I have retained the Christian education title here because it is the term most familiar to many churches. In doing so the word *education* is perhaps the most vulnerable to change in the future. *Experience* or *growth* are both words that seem to challenge the past use of *education* to describe programming to encourage spiritual maturity.

4. Many churches, however, began as Sunday schools, meeting in school-houses, town halls, and other available buildings. Often, formal churches grew out of these early instructional programs focused primarily on the needs of children and youth. For example, pioneers among American Baptists included missionary evangelists and educators who traveled on "chapel cars" and cooperated with colporters. Colporters traveled from settlement to settlement in the developing U.S. frontier, delivering literature and Bibles and aided in establishing Sunday schools and prayer meetings. Out of many of these there developed many Baptist churches now affiliated with a variety of Baptist denominations. The American Baptist Historical Society, Valley Forge, Pennsylvania, can provide additional information on the early development of these schools and chapels.

5. Churches that encourage the use of their facility space should develop a process of review, both for initial screening of programs and for evaluation and resolution of any problems that might arise. Usually problems focus around issues of maintenance and janitorial service or security procedures. Churches also must resist the temptation to become passive as the result of the programs it helps make possible. Shared use of buildings and facilities should represent effective stewardship and not become an excuse for abandoning a church's own opportunities for outreach and mission.

6. As with most things in Baptist life, this development of fellowship in associations and structures of connection has not progressed with complete logic or uniformity. For example, several of the larger, historic associations in American Baptist churches, such as the Philadelphia Association, the Los Angeles City Mission Society, and several others, have become independent, parallel organizations functioning like state or larger regional structures. Likewise, as a result of major denominational reorganization in several Baptist denominations, states in some cases are combined with others into regions. Sometimes a region will include only part of a state while the other part of the state will be in a different region. These organizational determinations are normally the result of geographic barriers, historic traditions, or political realities.

7. Kenneth Bedeel, ed., *Yearbook of American & Canadian Churches,*

1993 (Nashville: Abingdon Press, 1993). See the listings for the individual Baptist organizations by title. It should be noted that there is some overlap of membership caused by churches in fellowship with more than one national body. It should be further noted that these figures are dependent on the accuracy of membership reports from local churches. Some church membership reports are accurate and up-to-date, while others retain many inactive memberships. Some churches do not report.

8. One major exception to national denominational domination of program and mission life is to be noted in colleges, universities, and seminaries, as well as many hospitals, nursing homes, and retirement facilities. In many cases, these institutions, having been established by Baptist churches, agencies, or individuals, have developed support structures and visions of their own. Historic relationships with the denomination are maintained, but independent boards of trustees set their policies and oversee their operations. Where direct ties are still maintained, they are most often at the state or regional level. One strong exception is represented, however, in the seminaries of the Southern Baptist Convention, which are, by reason of the appointment of trustees by national committee, essentially linked to the national convention structure.

9. Several other Baptist bodies previously listed in *The Hiscox Guide*, but having fallen below 50,000 in membership (or not reporting) are nevertheless worthy of mention because of their unique cultural significance: the North American Baptist General Conference (Forest Park, Ill.), mainly churches of German background; the National Primitive Baptist Convention of the U.S.A. (1907), Huntsville, Ala., mainly in the Southern states; and the Primitive Baptists, who are opposed to all centralization and to modern missionary societies. And, as noted in the text, the Alliance of Baptists and the Cooperative Baptist Fellowship are organizations that do not fit the reporting categories of the *Yearbook* but merit attention as part of emerging Baptist life and institutions.

Chapter VIII

Church Order, Process, and Discipline

For a church to function well over time, it must have an established pattern of order, a process for conducting its affairs to which all members consent and in which they all participate. It must also have the ability to maintain and preserve the discipline necessary to effect its purposes. In defining the nature of the church, we noted previously that the biblical word that identifies the church, *ekklesia*, implies an organized company with laws, officers, and ordinances. We understood it to mean an orderly group distinguished from an unruly gathering. By implication, much of what we have discussed since that consideration has focused on the nature of that order. Still, a church must have a "shell" that encompasses the whole—the standing order by which it operates. It must observe a process by which activity is consistently guided. And through its discipline, it must exhibit an identity and a spirit that is consistent with its purpose as a creation of its Lord, Jesus Christ, and worthy of those who are his disciples.

In the broad range of human affairs, maintaining civilization is always a challenge of sustaining order against the constant inclination toward chaos. In culture at large, a balance must be maintained between rigidity that leads to stagnation and creativity that leads to change. Likewise, in a family there must be order in family affairs, tempered with tenderness and discretion, otherwise the family becomes a mere collection of biologically related, cohabiting individuals. It is even more the case with the church. Hiscox said that "the church is the organic representative of the kingdom of Christ; unless law prevails in the kingdom and order is maintained, how shall the King be honored, the kingdom be advanced, or the world be blessed by its coming and triumph?" (p. 132). Still, the Lord of the church is the Lord of grace, not law. Therefore, the church must set an orderly course in the direction toward which Christ commissioned it and yet be receptive to the wind of the Spirit that "blows where it wills" (John 3:8).

Church Order

Three kinds of order give shape to church life. The first is what the laws of society may expect of it. The second is what the covenants and traditions of the church may determine for it. And the third is what Christ calls it to be.

Most churches are incorporated organizations according the laws of the state or region in which they are established. The need for this legal expression is defined by the complexity of contemporary life. It is a response to the need for the church to have an identity that allows it to function responsibly within cultures that have a variety of institutions and structures. Such incorporation defines both responsibility and opportunity. Responsibilities include filing appropriate reports with appropriate civil authorities regarding the ownership of property, the function of the religious institution as part of the legal community, and the identification of the responsible individuals who represent the organization. Incorporation also brings important protection for church leaders and offices in matters of litigation. In addition, incorporated churches are often exempt from certain local, state, and federal taxes, especially in the United States. Good order in the church will result when legal matters relating to certifying appropriate tax status with regard to church income, the contributions of members, the designation of property owned by the church as nontaxable property when appropriate, and the keeping of valid records comply with such legal requirements.

Churches are also required to arrange for proper and legal relationships with employees and to comply with at least minimal expectations regarding insurance, unemployment, health care, and other responsibilities that are customary for any institutional operation and employer. Churches with multiple staff members should have established personnel policies and manuals to explain them. Pastors who perform marriages or offer regulated professional services should meet expectations for legal certification, when required. The ministers of the church should be expected to perform according to professional standards in interpersonal relationships, administrative actions, and public participation. Churches that operate child-care programs, schools, and other programs usually subject to state or local supervision may not be subject to the same level of intervention as nonreligious institutions. However, the good order evident in a church will desire always to meet and exceed the minimum standards that apply. Manuals of procedure, rules, and regulations pertaining to whole church programs and specialized programs for children are advisable.

As these considerations are essentially legal and professional, a church is wise to maintain a legal counsel not for the purpose of seeking litigation or of avoiding compliance with the laws of the jurisdiction but precisely because it desires to avoid litigation and to live in harmony with the laws, unless a matter of conscience dictates otherwise. Likewise, a church may not be financially liable to the same scrutiny as a public corporation, but it should frequently seek the services of a qualified accountant to assure its membership and others that its financial affairs are in order.

The second kind of order is the internal order the church has established for itself. Normally a church will be guided by a constitution, bylaws, and a covenant. These are the tools of definition and process by which everyone in the congregation can be equipped to be effective participants in the life of the church. A well-ordered church will not fail to hold meetings when they are prescribed nor to observe the procedures established by these documents. And if, as often is the case, the documents are out-of-date, deficient, or in need of revision, good order demands that these be reviewed and revised. It is ultimately the path to chaos simply to ignore standing procedures or to create informal variations on procedure that have not been reviewed and assented to by the church. Respect for good order in church life is even more important than meeting standards that matter to the world outside the church. It is evidence of the total stewardship of a church both to members and to the world around it.

The third kind of order is the order of Christ. Laws can preserve a church's property and defend against unreasonable attack or accusation, but they cannot preserve its spirit. Constitutions and covenants can describe what a church intends to be, but they cannot transform the church into that creation. The church is the bride of Christ. Assigning specific roles to a bride is not a universally agreeable practice in our time of changing role expectations for men and women. This is, nevertheless, a powerful metaphor. In Jesus' time, being a bride carried clear expectations: A bride was first and foremost a well-chosen woman who was expected to order the household. She organized the resources of the household to support and maintain her husband's role in the community; she exercised love and care for her whole family; she extended gracious hospitality to strangers; she served as her husband's agent in distributing benevolence and charity to the poor in the community; and she defended the weakest in the household against injustice and abuse. However much we have experienced changes regarding the arrangements of human family responsibilities in our own time, in Christ's time the role of ordering a household was a bride's task. As the bride of Christ, the church is called to that good spiritual order, and fulfilling that calling is necessarily a spiritual process by which order becomes evident.

Church Process

Laws, constitutions, and principles of operation, even aspirations to spiritual health, only establish the foundations of order. They are enacted by the dynamic process by which church life is carried out in its planning, interaction, operation, mission, ministry, and fulfillment of purpose. By *process* we mean those established methods of conducting business, effecting programs, communicating, meeting, deciding, determining, leading, following, consulting, cooperating, and other procedures by which the ministers, leaders, and members of the church interrelate.

In some times and places churches were governed by established hierarchy. This is not the Baptist way because it fails to appreciate the contributions and collegial participation of all members. In other times and places, churches have been guided by strict adherence to laws and principles. This is sometimes effective but often fails because laws are imperfect and Christians, like other persons, often forget principles or fail to uphold them. In Baptist churches, the best processes are those that recognize common goals and the direction of the Spirit and that devise means by which cooperation leading to consensus within the body can develop.

In a business, a profitable or successful result often justifies the process that led to it. In a church, however, the end result may not be as important as the spiritual journey that leads to it. For example, church leaders may build new buildings, establish programs, or hire and terminate staff members by an effective use of power. But they may destroy or weaken the church in doing so. In establishing processes that build and strengthen the church while leading to effective results, the following principles may be helpful:

1. Communicate effectively with the congregation so that the church's stated goals, needs, and programs are understood; create processes by which the congregation, individually and corporately, may communicate with church leaders and ministers and make those processes well known.

2. Establish church meetings on a regular and well-publicized schedule, and schedule them at times when the greatest representation of the whole church might attend and participate.

3. Agree upon principles of debate and decision making that guarantee that every opinion may be stated and considered and that encourage decisions to be the result, not further debate.[1]

4. Plan for the use of prayer in business sessions and discussions when at appropriate times. Often difficult decisions become clearer and entrenched, polarized spirits within the congregation become more flexible when concerns are approached in prayer.

5. Establish an alternative style of meeting when decision making is not the first priority or when a decision cannot be reached until greater clarity in the body has emerged. Such meetings, often called "forums" or "gatherings," are usually run by the presiding officer but might be conducted by any church member so appointed. Their sole purpose is to encourage clarity and consensus. They should begin with the establishment of simple rules of discussion and information sharing that encourage all to participate. No motions or official proposals should be entertained or allowed at this

point; instead, the sole purpose is to seek clarity and understanding about a program, idea, consideration, or controversy.

6. Monitor the work of boards and committees to make certain their responsibilities are being carried out. Often the failure of one committee or board leads to frustration elsewhere and can lead to a breakdown of process in the church.

7. Make a strict separation between conducting the business of the church and the worship of the church. But recognize that business that is preceded by worship will more frequently accomplish Christ's work, and that business that accomplishes Christ's work leads to more authentic and joyful worship.

8. Establish a clear vision for the church program and ministry and articulate that vision frequently through established channels of communication, such as a newsletter, announcements, sermons, business meetings, and other communication channels. Encourage church members to understand how aspects of church life and ministry are prioritized in relation to the vision and goals of the church.

A church must necessarily be sensitive to changes of expectations regarding institutional organization and leadership in the world beyond the church. That is not to say that the world should transform the church—quite the opposite! But it is to suggest that in order to minister to the world, and with people who live in the world, the church must understand the forms and structures of the world's business. For example, the popular institutional words of the present generation are "consensus" and "community." Such words, and the theories of leadership and organization that accompany them, exercise a powerful impact on church members who become influenced by them. Many church members, in fact, derive their organizational expectations from training and practices in their places of employment and in community activity. Expectations change from generation to generation.[2] These changing emphases will cause church members to view church processes and procedures differently. Church leaders should, therefore, occasionally examine how prevailing attitudes of institutional organization and management will affect life in the church where they are called or elected to serve.[3]

Despite this observation, however, the church is called to serve the timeless purpose of Christ. In doing so, it must evaluate its programs, purposes, and fellowship by the standards that only Christ has established. In no circumstance is this task more challenging than in maintaining the focus necessary for the church to be the church. Like an athlete, a church must be fit for its task. Fitness requires discipline.

Discipline

Discipline is the way by which fundamental assumptions, laws, covenants, or agreements are implemented to define and preserve the purpose of the church. It is, in some respects, a foreign concept for much of the church in the last several generations. Many church records reveal incidents in the past in which members were censored for lapses in personal behavior and church leaders and officers were rebuked for judgments, decisions, or behavior determined to be detrimental to the work of the church. And on more than a few occasions, churches severed relationships with members who were determined to be destructive to fellowship, faith, or witness in the church. Such moments are rare in recent times.

Few, perhaps, long for the reestablishment of such painful procedures in church life. On the other hand, the church is often weakened by its inability to define its character and purpose against the un-Christian behavior, neurotic impulses, or determined disruptions by members. Much disabling church conflict could be avoided if proper discipline were administered when members of churches engage in controversy and then extend their estrangements in ways that result in polarized, dysfunctional congregations. In addition, church membership has become a nearly meaningless phrase in many churches. Expectations for members, even when clearly identified and publicized, are rarely monitored. The result can be an assumption that membership is a lifelong privilege even for those who are nonsupportive of the church by prayer or financial commitment or that the most inactive member can occasionally exercise destructive influence in church affairs as a matter of "right." Left undisciplined, these matters will ruin the witness and purpose of a church.

In approaching this subject, Hiscox concluded that there was scriptural authority for discipline and defined it by what he called the "Three Laws of Christ's House." They are, he proposed, royal decrees given by Christ who is head of the church (p. 133). We might agree that they are timeless rules of discipline that are invested with divine sanction and worthy of reinstitution by a good many Baptist churches today:

First, for every disciple, the law of love. "A new commandment I give to you, that you love one another; even as I have loved you, that you also love one another. By this all men will know that you are my disciples" (John 13:34-35). Is there any doubt that consistently applied, this law would prevent much acrimony, grief, and destruction in church life? On the one hand, it would prevent cold, uncaring indifference between church members, and on the other, it would discourage unfounded suspicion, accusations without cause, jealousies, animosities, bitterness, hatred, and strife. Those who love rarely need discipline.

Second, for the offender, the law of confession. "So if you are offering your gift at the altar, and there remember that your brother has something against you, leave your gift there before the altar and go; first be reconciled to your brother, and then come and offer your gift" (Matthew 5:23-24). This law places the obligation of reconciliation on everyone. It urges the guilty to first go and confess a transgression against another. It compels the innocent to go and discover what misperception has led to a bad feeling, granting him or her an opportunity to try to correct it. It leads to justice, and it opens the door for mercy.

Third, for the offended, the law of forgiveness. "If your brother sins, rebuke him, and if he repents, forgive him, and if he sins against you seven times in the day, and turns to you seven times, and says, 'I repent,' you must forgive him" (Luke 17:3-4). Like the second law, which places the obligation of confession on everyone, this law places the responsibility of forgiveness on all. It does not require that friendship continue as it was before, or even that the same cordiality, affection, and esteem exist as before; such feelings are impossible when hurts are deep. But it does require that things be set aside and put behind when they have been recognized. And it requires that there be no end to new opportunities for reconciliation. When Peter asked Jesus, for example, how often he must forgive his brother, he said, "I do not say to you seven times, but seventy times seven" (Matthew 18:22). That is, there is no end to the cycle of repentance and forgiveness.

Regrettably, not all church members observe these laws. Sometimes they observe them inconsistently or with conditions, or they excuse themselves from their domain while requiring them of others. In some circumstances the church must be prepared to exercise discipline among those who have ignored the "Laws of Christ's House" to the detriment of its harmony and order.

The Scope of Discipline

As Hiscox put it, "the object and purpose of discipline is to prevent, restrain, or remove the evil that may exist, to encourage and protect the right, and cherish the good, 'for the edifying of the body of Christ,' that it may be 'perfect in love,' and without reproach" (p. 134). The church that expects great things of its members; that holds a high standard not only of Christian morals but of Christian compassion, justice, and love; and that is willing to exercise a watchcare over one another, is bound to be held in high esteem by its own members. More, it is bound to have a positive influence on the world.

Discipline has not been a popular concept in church life of recent years because it is thought to be an invasion of privacy or confused with "judgmentalism." Of course, a church has the obligation to respect privacy and a Baptist church, above all others, has the obligation to cherish differences in spiritual perspective. Nevertheless, discipline has a positive and definite purpose in trying to heal offenses and encourage reconciliation between members or between an offending member and the church. "If he repents, forgive him" (Luke 17:3). In this way the church is preserved in form and spirit.

If such efforts are ultimately unsuccessful, then the church may have further obligation to remove the member from the church. Painful as this action always is for a church, it is the action of preservation of the church—not the church as a corporation or the church as a building but the church as the living Spirit and embodiment of Christ. The early church jealously guarded this principle. In 2 Thessalonians 3:6 Paul instructed: "Now we command you, brethren, in the name of our Lord Jesus Christ, that you keep away from any brother who is living in idleness and not in accord with the tradition that you received from us." And even more strongly, in Titus 3:10 we hear this specific instruction: "As for a man who is factious, after admonishing him once or twice, have nothing more to do with him, knowing that such a person is perverted and sinful; he is self-condemned."

The church has a strong tradition of showing great compassion for personal indiscretions and sin and has reserved its most vigorous discipline for those whose behavior has hurt others and, most severe of all, for those whose continued behavior has damaged the church in its relationships, purpose, and witness. Nevertheless, the manner in which discipline is effected must always be governed by gentleness, compassion, and love and never exercised in a spirit of arrogance, dictatorial power, vindictiveness, or moral superiority. Indeed, to the Galatians Paul said, "Brethren, if a man is overtaken in any trespass, you who are spiritual should restore him in a spirit of gentleness. Look to yourself, lest you too be tempted" (Galatians 6:1).

So the work of discipline is done first in love, and always with the priority of the health of the body of Christ. Its first purpose is reconciliation and restoration. Only in its most extreme moment should separation and abandonment be considered. If the latter is the only course, it should be approached with great sadness, as well as gentleness, for it represents a great loss in the community of Christ.

Dealing with Offenses

"I commend you because you remember me in everything and maintain the traditions even as I have delivered them to you," said Paul (1 Corinthians 11:2). In approaching the question of discipline, the nature of the offense must be considered. Matters that might require discipline in the church may most conveniently be considered in two categories: private and public, that is, personal and general.

Private Offenses: Baptists, above all others, have a profound respect for personal differences and perspectives. Many have, in fact, died for the privilege of personal conscience and private belief—for themselves as well as others. Church discipline should not be directed at honest differences of faith, piety, or practice. It is a proper response, however, when there is reference to an injury done—or claimed to have been done—by one member to another, intentionally or unintentionally. Because of its personal nature, it might be questioned why a church should get involved, why it is not a matter best left to the civil courts. The answer is first that church members have a greater commitment to one another in Christ than can be evaluated in a civil court, and second, injuries between members are bound, inevitably, to affect the health of the whole congregation.

Fortunately, a pattern of approach was prescribed by Christ in Matthew 18:15-17.

First, the one who considers himself or herself injured should go to the offender, convey the cause or concern and, if possible, settle the difficulty. "If your brother sins against you, go and tell him his fault, between you and him alone. If he listens to you, you have gained a brother" (v. 15). This step might be recommended by the leaders of the church on an informal basis. It preserves the privacy of both parties and allows them first to approach a manner by which the difficulty can be resolved. The purpose is to gain a brother or sister and not to pursue a cause.

Second, if the first step fails, then the injured one must seek another interview with the one believed to have offended him or her, and this time be accompanied by one or two other members of the church, preferably members esteemed and trusted by both parties. "But if he does not listen, take one or two others along with you, that every word may be confirmed by the evidence of two or three witnesses" (v. 16). The purpose of two or three witnesses is twofold: First, those accompanying a presumed injured person may have a greater ability to focus the issue so that both the injured and the accused can perceive the difficulty and the possible solution. They are to be reconcilers and mediators when possible. Second, if this step fails, they are presumably to be witnesses to both the attempt and to the nature of the trouble, if further action must be taken. They can witness to truth when that is possible and also to demeanor, temper, spirit, and attitude. Great care should be exercised, therefore, in selecting those who might accompany an injured party.

Third, should the second attempt also be unsuccessful, the offended or injured one has the opportunity, and most often the obligation, to tell it to the church (or, more appropriately, a responsible church council). "If he refuses to listen to them, tell it to the church" (Matthew 18:17). The reason for this is not only that he or she might gain "justice" but that the matter not fester between them and that the church have a chance to exercise mediation and judgment in attempting to reconcile them. Here the injured party must be reminded that he or she is still attempting to "gain a brother" (or sister), and the church must remember it is trying to mend a tear in the fabric of fellowship. In many churches, a council of mediators able to deal with such difficulty might be a great contribution to the life of the church.

Fourth, if the matter is determined to be a clear case of infraction of one against another, then the council has an obligation to make that judgment and to let it be known within the church. If the infraction is judged serious and likely to be of continuing damage to the life of the church, then it must recommend that the offending member be separated from activity in the church. "If he refuses to listen even to the church, let him be to you as a Gentile and a tax collector" (Matthew 18:17). This seems a harsh judgment, yet by refusing to consider the church's counsel, the unrepentant member has, in effect, already separated himself or herself from the church in principle. It is sometimes the case that both members may be considered unrepentant and, therefore, subject to dismissal from the fellowship. This is the case when fault is difficult to assign to either party and when both parties seem more inclined to pursue animosity than to seek reconciliation. In such a case, left undisciplined, either or both members are certain to attempt to advance their personal causes among other members, cause a division, and seriously damage the ability of the church to fulfill its calling and to perform its witness.

Public Offenses: In an earlier day, church courts tried members for violations of religious or civil laws. In part this was because the distinction between church and civil courts was unclear and in part because a more close-knit culture expected it of them. Churches today are much less frequently advised to respond to the public offenses of their members, whether they be legal, moral, or civil in nature. Indeed, the appropriate response is more often to invite members who have committed public offense to be restored and healed by the compassion and love of the fellowship of the church.

There are, however, some circumstances when a church believes the public activity of a member has not only damaged a social law, a community principle, or a moral position, but, by his or her action, has brought into serious question the nature and purpose of the church. Such an infraction might include corruption or immorality in business dealings or in political leadership or in an activity counter to Christian principles of justice or mercy or others.[4] In such a circumstance, a church "trial" may need to be considered. Its purpose is, again, to investigate the means of restoration as its first cause. But, if restoration is not possible, its second purpose may be to indicate to the community at large, and to the church members in particular, that there are some matters that destroy the very meaning of church witness and must therefore be repudiated.

In such circumstances a church is wise to follow a procedure similar to that outlined in Matthew 18:15-17.

First, those who have knowledge of the offense should seek the offender, advise him or her of their knowledge or concern, and give the person the opportunity to remove the difficulty. This is, of course, a difficult thing for a member to do. And if more than one member is aware of the situation, several might ask for a meeting with the offender for reasons of mutual support.

Second, if the offender is unwilling or unable to end the behavior, or if no one is willing to bring it to his or her attention, then those having knowledge of the circumstance should report it to the pastor or, perhaps, a few of the most responsible church leaders.[5] In all likelihood, having been informed, the pastor and or deacons might themselves try the first step in private.[6] All such cases should be kept private for the sake of both the member and the church if there is an opportunity for the offender to rectify the actions or to make proper amends.

Third, if the matter cannot be dealt with privately, then the case must come before the church, or possibly first before a responsible church council. Here the charges should be specific, avoiding at all counts vague references to undefined and therefore unable-to-be-defended concerns. Only in this way might an offending member attempt to clarify the actions and defend himself or herself. As much time as is deemed appropriate both to hear the concerns and to consider the response should be allowed, and strongly defined rules of proceedings should be established. Following the review of the case, proposals should be recommended by a church council, or by a church member, regarding the proper action. Such actions might include reprimand, censure, a course of remedy, or, in extreme cases, removal from the church.

Fourth, if the offending member (or accused) will not appear before the church or church council or denies their authority to request his or her appearance, by that refusal he or she defies his or her relationship to the congregation in an important way.[7] The council or church is then required to act according to its best knowledge and judgment. If the person is prevented from appearing before it by reason of illness, distance, or imprisonment, then the church must diligently seek whatever information might be available and act according to its best judgment.

Fifth, if at any stage of such a review the accused brother or sister disproves the charges or establishes sufficient doubt regarding their truth, then this should be deemed sufficient and the proceedings abandoned. Alternatively, if at any stage the person admits the charges, confesses wrong, and makes suitable acknowledgment and reparation, the church should affirm the conditions of restitution and restore the individual to full fellowship.

Finally, if any person is removed from the fellowship of a church, let it be stated that the church remains open to restore fellowship if repentance, restitution, and redirection of life are offered. The church should restore to its fellowship at any time, at the appropriate request, any excluded member, if the church is satisfied that the repentance is sincere, the way of life restored, and the desire to return to membership is for the purpose of advancing the church's purpose and witness. Meanwhile, let church members be reminded that even as the person is separated from them, they are to treat him or her with compassion and love in departing, and in greeting him or her in the community.

In all that a church does with regard to discipline, it must be reminded constantly that its purpose is not to sit in judgment against one another but to encourage one another that the way of Christ might be strengthened and followed. Membership in a church makes no sense if it is merely membership in an organization that has no principles. Discipline, therefore, is required to maintain the health of those principles and their clarity before others. But discipline for discipline's sake serves no useful purpose and can, in contrast, do great harm both to individuals and to the church.

In the great majority of cases, before a church chooses any path of discipline, it should encourage its members first to review their own lives, as Jesus encouraged the tribunal that was about to condemn the adulterous woman (John 8:7). Let them see first the great stain in their own eye before they rush to judgment about the small blemish in the eye of another.

Positive Church Disciplines

Church discipline must also include the positive disciplines that, under most circumstances, will keep negative judgments from being necessary. The disciplines of prayer, worship, personal devotions, spiritual growth, and discipleship, for example, should be encouraged. The church that keeps in focus a clear vision of the call to the service of Christ and the discipline of discipleship that such service requires will not fail to develop the practices that make possible service to its Lord. A church dedicated to the service of the Lord Jesus Christ and to leading others into the presence of Christ will rarely, if ever, need to seek harsh judgments upon one another. For in Christ all who have sinned have been forgiven, all who are dead in sin have been brought to life, and all who were without hope now live in hope. Any discipline that the church can affirm and recommend that keeps these gospel truths clear and present will strengthen both the individual who hears them and the church whose people live by them.

NOTES

1. *Robert's Rules of Order* is the established guide to meetings in North American culture. However, this is an often complex procedure that favors those who have mastered its finer points and that, conversely, frustrates those

who are not confident in their use of them. Understanding a simplified or summarized version is often worth the time a church might devote to developing them for their own purpose. A brief "Rules of Order" is therefore included in this book as appendix D. Its abbreviated form is adequate for most churches under all but the most extreme circumstances.

2. In guiding church life, leaders must be aware of generational characteristics among previous, emerging, and dominant generations included in the congregation. At present, for example, much analysis and comment has been published regarding the "baby boomer" (born between 1945 and 1960) generation's attitude toward institutions, including churches. Whereas the previous generation valued concepts of strong leadership, hierarchy, commitment, and sacrifice in church life, "baby boomers" are observed to prefer collegial relationships and participation in decision making, are consumerist in their relationships to churches and other institutions, and often fail to develop a lasting commitment to church life. Those following the baby-boomer generation have still different characteristics. To remain healthy, churches must seek to understand such differences and account for them in establishing process. Much present church conflict seems rooted, in part, in the presence of such differences of expectation in church life.

3. A great deal of literature has been published to help develop church organizational life. Most denominations have published good examples of them. The Alban Institute, located in Washington, D.C., is also a good source, as are the writings of Lyle Schaller, a noted consultant and writer on church processes and programs.

4. The church should not commence disciplinary proceedings of any sort, or even entertain a charge against a member, unless the evidence be such as to make the truth of the charge probable, if not certain. Conversely, it should sternly rebuke any members who lightly bring charges against another member as a matter of personal vindictiveness or gain.

5. The relationship of the pastor to persons accused should be carefully considered. In many circumstances a pastor should remove himself or herself from official leadership of meetings and keep conversations between himself or herself and the accused focused in the spirit of pastoral care.

6. In contrast, Jewish rabbinical tradition includes a strong role for a rabbi to function as a judge or arbiter in disputes or grievances between members of the synagogue or community. This, however, reflects the strong basis of law upon which much of Jewish community life is founded. Ministers do not have such a tradition on which to ground a judicial function. Likewise, when churches have established ordained ministers in prosecutorial or judicial functions, it has often led to division or polarization within the community. The Christian church is founded more on grace than on law. Therefore, the role of the pastor is to provide pastoral care in the form of guidance to the church and care and counsel to the accused offender.

7. For Baptists, particularly, this raises a significant question of authority in light of the principle of the "priesthood of the believer," which many

Baptists interpret and cherish as a tradition of spiritual individualism. In matters of church authority, no one can force another to submit to a church decision or even a review. But what is at stake here is not an ultimate question of justice, right, or wrong, but of mutual expectations in Christian relationship. A church does not have a prerogative to determine authoritatively anything pertaining to a member's likely salvation. But it does have a right to determine with whom it shall be in spiritual relationship. Therefore, in all things not contrary to his or her conscience, the member should be willing to come before the church. But in matters of faith and conscience, he or she should do what he or she honestly believes is right, whether the church in the administration of its function chooses to condemn or to commend him or her. And, both churches and individuals must ultimately recognize, especially when matters are not strictly defined with regard to moral or legal principle, that there are times when a minority of one must, with Martin Luther, simply confess: "Here I stand; I cannot do otherwise."

Conclusion

Edward T. Hiscox first wrote during a cycle of vigorous and at times chaotic formation among Baptists and Baptist churches. Hiscox's purpose was to provide guidance and direction for the effective biblical and practical ordering of church life among Baptists. Guidance and direction is still much in need among Baptists because life is even more complex and the leadership of Baptist churches more challenging than ever.

One hundred forty years after the first publication of some of these materials in their original form, Baptist churches are much more developed institutionally, often possess more significant financial resources, and have developed more complex styles of management and program. Such achievement would suggest stability and good order in Baptist church life. Yet there are disturbing changes and trends that seem to be challenging to Baptist churches especially.

For one thing, diversity of opinion and, indeed, diversity of life experience are much greater now than in the 1890s. This makes the establishment of internal harmony in church life more difficult. Human affairs in the social context in which the church lives are arranged in endless variation and complexity. Consensus regarding fundamental values, community goals, and authority for leadership is often weak or lacking. In many churches, nearly half of the congregation began their spiritual lives in some other denomination and bring with them habits of thought, experiences, and perspectives formed in that time and experience. Also, despite continuing research results that indicate the great majority of Americans think of themselves as religious or have a belief in God and some kind of identification with a church, a growing number of church participants have previously had only a marginal connection or contact with a church. And familiarity with the material and teachings of the Bible, a basic assumption for many people a century ago, is lacking even among those who frequently attend churches.

Related to this, the issues of race and class have proved to be more difficult to bridge in churches than almost any other institution. Likewise, the issue of sexual identity and expression has become confusing and threatening for the church. Churches, along with much of the culture beyond them, are wrestling with the issues of homosexuality, the role of women in the church, the family, and the nature of economic order, as well as with such issues of personal sexual behavior as abortion or sexual relationships outside of marriage. These are divisive in the community at large, and congregations also divide in opinion on these issues more quickly than any others. And because debate on these issues permeates the culture, they seem unable to be avoided in the church.

In addition, spiritual identity and commitment among Christians in general and Baptists in particular seem often to be secondary to other points of reference. Political loyalties, peer-group conformity, class consciousness, educational backgrounds and perspectives, and many other points of reference are often more personally definitive for church participants than their religious belief or church commitment. The result is that churches have great difficulty in agreeing upon a common course and developing a unity of spirit.

This general condition has led to a second concern, for among Baptists, diversity has worked specific evils. For example, in recent years denominational strife, church division, pastoral terminations, and chronic congregational discord have risen in frequency and intensity. Internal strife within the Southern Baptist Convention has been the most newsworthy, but it is by no means exclusive. Profound disagreement regarding the role and authority of the Scriptures, issues of style and authority for leaders, goals and strategies for church development and success—these are but a few of a long list of issues that regularly divide Baptists.

These points of division are aggravated by some commonly

defined demographic and cultural changes. For example, those who were born before World War II more often believe obedience to authority enhances the common good. Thus they have tended to accept authority readily, have aspired to have authority more enthusiastically, and have been impatient with pastors and other leaders who do not exercise authority in the manner they are accustomed to. Those born since World War II, particularly those who came of age during the Vietnam War era, learned to question authority and often look askance at those who readily obey it. The former generation has provided church leadership until now and is usually not comfortable with the style of leadership the younger generation seems to offer. This fosters frequent intergenerational conflict in churches.

In addition young adults are more ambiguous about church life in general. On the one hand, young persons are often quite conservative—often more conservative than their parents in theology. And, if they embrace church life, this theological preference often adds to generational differences. But many young persons are not church-oriented at all. Either they have little theological and faith interest or they express it in one of the variety of noninstitutional church ways that have developed in the later decades of the twentieth century. This leads to anxiety and confusion among older generations and puts the future of many churches in doubt. And when young persons investigate church life, their relative lack of knowledge of Scripture, traditions, and practices and their desire to investigate varieties of spiritual disciplines, traditions, and practices can be destabilizing.

Some new churches have grown and developed rapidly—and have often done so without much understanding of Baptist history and principles. In such churches, creating appropriate order out of the chaos of growth is a continuing challenge for pastors and leaders. Amidst the excitement of such growth it is important for Baptist principles and traditions to be understood and reinterpreted.

On the other hand, many long-established churches have declined in membership and in program capacity, in the last twenty-five years especially. This is particularly true of central urban churches and churches in older suburbs where marked changes in population have profoundly affected neighborhoods and church traditions. Long-term, older members of such churches often have experienced a profound sense of loss and failure. In contrast to earlier times when churches were full and programs were active and successful, empty sanctuaries, depleted Sunday schools, and changing styles of worship encourage a sense of impending collapse for their most cherished memories and points of spiritual reference. One result is often to blame the pastor and ministerial leaders or the "younger generation." This is particularly acute where longtime members in retirement desire to focus their time in church leadership or service and find such experience disheartening. This leads to conflict between ministers and significant leaders of their congregations and often results in short pastoral terms.

In addition, rising costs of operating churches have resulted from inflation, particularly in maintenance, fuel, and electricity costs and salaries. Compensation of staff is often therefore a major point of difficulty for churches. Professional church leaders expect and deserve adequate compensation. And more than in previous eras, such compensation is expected in monetary form rather than through provided housing and in-kind gifts from members of the congregation or community. Also, the decreasing availability of volunteer labor and assistance due to changes in church members' work; the entry of women into the marketplace; and the tendency for retired persons to be more active in recreation, travel, and community involvement have caused churches to retain or build larger paid staffs even when programming or membership has declined. The resulting financial pressure has caused friction between church leaders in establishing congregational priorities, between churches and the denominations that need their support, and between the congregations and their staff members. In such churches great effort should be expended to celebrate the Baptist past and to form a new vision, consistent with Baptist spirit and vitality. Instead, old institutional forms are often idealized, and much energy is focused on unsuccessful attempts to revive them.

This is a challenge particularly in old, well-established congregations. Intergenerational conflict and the confrontations of opinion, life experience, and perspective are frequently aggravated by the rapidity of change in the last generation in particular. In times of change, many persons turn to the church for security and stability.

Tragically, this search for spiritual security often comes to focus on the institutional forms and styles of churches rather than on the eternal Word that gives them life. All too often churches are driven by anger, jealousy, and strife. It is, in fact, one of the great ironies of our age that in a time of spiritual uncertainty and chaos, churches have sought stability by building ever more complex and impressive institutional structures.

In many places, therefore, Baptist churches are suffering great stress and attempting to define their mission and ministry in the midst of countervailing forces and even chaos. The spiritual health of many churches is thus at stake. In writing to an international constituency, one Baptist leader noted that when such dynamics are let loose, "proselytism replaces evangelism. Propaganda replaces education. Materialism replaces the Spirit. Suspicion replaces trust. Power replaces the cross. And sadly, the world replaces the church, and Christ is crucified again by his own people!"[1] "For where jealousy and selfish ambition exist, there will be disorder and every vile practice" (James 3:16).

Third, since Hiscox's time denominations have been created, have risen to a high level of corporate development and complexity, and are now declining again in size and importance. This places new pressure on the local congregations to be focused and specific in defining their mission and in valuing their ministry. It also heightens the temptation to overinstitutionalize and denies churches the support and interrelationship with the denominational programs and structure they had become used to. Thus, churches and their leaders often feel isolated.

Amidst all of this is a commonly perceived change taking place regarding leadership style and expectations. In business, in political organizations, in government, in education—everywhere there is evidence that leadership is a far more challenging profession than ever before. That is certainly true of churches. What once worked works no longer. And where churches could once rely on repeating time-honored, traditional programs, they must now explore new methods, programs, and opportunities to minister effectively both to their current congregations and to those beyond the church whom they desire to evangelize.

In addition to the resources of previous chapters, therefore, the following principles may be of value:

• Baptist churches and their leaders must become reconciled to the evident diversity of our present age and therefore to reject no one because of differences, but instead to accept Christ's call in the midst of diversity to minister to everyone.

• Baptist churches must be led to establish as a high priority the development of spiritual unity that may be found in Christian discipleship, despite the difference and diversity of human experience.

• Baptist churches must avoid overreliance on structures, programs, and institutional formations of human creation, and instead witness to the principle that Christ alone is the sure foundation.

•Baptist churches and their leaders must renew their response to the Great Commission to make disciples rather than to build empires or amass power.

• Baptist churches and their leaders must renew their historic commitment to saving souls and transforming persons and not be diverted by lesser, even though more measurable, tasks.

This review of some of the challenges facing Baptist churches is not to suggest this volume restating Hiscox's prescription for effective order and vitality for Baptist church life has an answer for every problem. Nevertheless, as Hiscox tirelessly reminded an earlier generation, leaders of churches do have the great resource of the example of Christ, the enduring witness of the church, and the renewing power of the Holy Spirit to guide their labors. Thus while it is a time to express sympathy for pastors, ministers, and church leaders in general—and certainly it is a time to support them—it is also a time to call them and Baptist congregations to renewed commitment. Leaders of churches need to keep Christ before them and to discourage congregations from becoming diverted by lesser images and more mundane goals. Leaders of churches are called to make life in spiritual community a transforming experience for all—and not just arenas for political, social, or personal contest. That is a high challenge. But life in Christ is also a high privilege.

Those who analyze churches today note the remarkable diversity of church sizes, styles, and organizations: from house churches to megachurches, from traditional styles to contemporary expressions that change from day to day, and from churches focused on worship and correct doctrine to churches that prioritize missions, outreach, and community transformation. We have avoided specific mention of these categories and examples in this volume and have no special word to offer regarding a particular church model or style. The resources outlined in Appendix G may direct the reader to many traditional Baptist sources for leadership in churches and also to some of the contemporary writings and resources dealing with specific church needs.

Whatever its specific expression, "a church is a church is a church." And if it is a church, it has one Lord; one faith; and, despite the differences of interpretation, one authority in Scripture, one expression in baptism, and one fellowship in unity. It is hoped that the reader of these pages will rediscover timeless approaches to Baptist leadership, organization, and procedure in developing healthy churches for the work of Christ. It is also especially hoped that Baptists in particular will be reminded, again, that it is not fundamentally to the will and work of a human majority that they are called, nor even to the development of great institutions, no matter how powerful and effective they might be, but to the building up of the body of Christ, who is its Lord. Baptist churches have developed and endured as a result of the spirit and labors of those such as Edward T. Hiscox and many others who have seen that vision and have been obedient in working for its accomplishment. Their practices and principles have nurtured Baptists for generations—and are able to be adapted and reinterpreted even now. We invite the reader's response to that goal.

NOTES

1. Denton Lotz, general secretary of the Baptist World Alliance, in *BWA News*, February 1993.

A Baptist Chronology

The following events are recorded as some significant milestones in the development of Baptist doctrine, organization, practices, and institutional development. It is in no regard an exhaustive list and does not attempt to record the foundation of the many Baptist colleges, hospitals, centers, and other institutions of mission outreach, education, assistance, and evangelism. It does, however, outline many of the events that have defined the Baptist experience. In that respect it is intended to outline some of the scope, as well as divergent issues, of Baptist church development.

Many scholars agree that the Baptist movement in North America has roots in the English Baptist movements of the seventeenth century but is, essentially, a New World movement. Nevertheless, a few dates suggesting the early development of Baptists in England are included, as are a few from the Anabaptist movements in Europe during the Reformation. Baptists as we know them do not have a direct connection to the Anabaptist communities and movements. Nevertheless, it is known that English Baptists did have contact with Anabaptist leaders and members, especially in Holland, and present-day Baptists often perceive similarities in church organization, doctrine, and perspective with descendants of the Anabaptists, especially the Mennonites, Brethren, and a few others. It was not until much later—in the nineteenth century—that Baptists in America largely helped to support the development of Baptist churches in Europe, and, indeed, around the world.

For a more detailed annotation of dates, the reader is urged to consult a standard Baptist text. Robert G. Torbet's *A History of the*

Baptists, Revised Edition remains the most thorough treatment of
Baptist life both in historical development and in the context of
North America. The reader is also directed to bibliographies and
lists of Baptist achievements developed by the several Baptist
historical societies, such as the American Baptist Historical Society
and the Southern Baptist Historical Commission. Other historical
works are noted in Appendix G.

Some Significant Baptist Events and Dates

1525 Swiss Anabaptists break with Zwingli to establish an independent
worship and begin practice of adult baptism by immersion in
Zurich.
Balthasar Hubmaier is baptized.
A Peasants' Revolt, led by Thomas Munzer, gives rebellious,
anti-authoritarian character to Anabaptists.

1535 Anabaptists in Zurich are suppressed.
The populist rebellion in Munster establishes a reign claimed to
be millennial; violent behavior discredits Anabaptists in public
opinion. Revolution is suppressed and leaders executed.

1537 Menno Simons becomes leader of Dutch Anabaptists.

1538 English Anabaptists are persecuted. Many leave England.

1609 First English General Baptist Church is formed in Holland under
John Smyth.

1611 First General Baptist Church in England is organized by Thomas
Helwys and John Murton.

1638 First Particular Baptist Church in England is organized by John
Spilsbury.

1638–1639 Organization of the First Baptist Church in America at
Providence, Rhode Island, in association with Roger Williams,
and in Newport under the leadership of John Clarke. (Dates are
somewhat uncertain, and both congregations make historical
claim to being the actual first organized, continuing church.)

1641 John Spilsbury emphasizes baptism by immersion.

1644 London Confession of 1644. This was a confession influenced
by Calvinism and especially emphasized religious liberty and
baptism by immersion, which became Baptist points of identity.
Organization of the Association of London Particular Baptists.

1650 Welsh Association is formed, beginning with three churches.

1651 Midland Association of General Baptists is formed with thirty churches.

1660 Organization of General Assembly of all Associations of General Baptists in London.

1670 General Six-Principle Baptist Church is organized in Rhode Island.

1689 General Assembly of Particular Baptists is organized in London. London Confession of Particular Baptists is formulated.

1707 The Philadelphia Association is formed, the first Baptist association in the North American colonies.

1727 The Original Freewill Baptists are organized in Virginia and North Carolina.

1728 First Seventh-Day Baptist Church in America is organized in Germantown, Pennsylvania.

1739 Baptists in American colonies divide into Regular and Separate Baptists as a result of differences resulting from evangelical movement known as the Great Awakening. (The date is for reference and does not reflect one specific event.)

1742 The Philadelphia Association adopts the London Confession of Particular Baptists (1689).

1764 College of Rhode Island, later known as Brown University, is founded.

1787 General Baptists in England send petition to Parliament urging the abolition of slavery.

1792 William Carey urges the organization of the English Baptist Missionary Society at Kettering, England.

1793 William Carey arrives in Calcutta, India, as an appointee of the English Baptist Missionary Society.

1797 Formation of the English Baptist Home Mission Society.

1799 Formation of the Baptist Union of Wales.

1802 The Massachusetts Baptist Missionary Society is organized to raise support for Carey in India. It is the first statewide Baptist association structure in America.
The First Baptist Church is founded in Washington, D.C., the new national capital.

1811 Baptists contribute three thousand dollars to the American Board of Commissioners for Foreign Missions to support Adoniram and Ann Judson and Luther Rice in a mission to India.

1813 The General Union of Baptist Ministers and Churches in England is organized—the forerunner of the Baptist Union of Great Britain and Ireland.
Adoniram Judson is persuaded by Baptist principles en route to India. He goes on to Burma as a Baptist and gains further Baptist support. Luther Rice returns to the United States to develop mission support among Baptists.

1814 Formation of the Triennial Meeting of the General Missionary Convention in Philadelphia.

1817 John Mason Peck and James Welch are sent out as home missionaries to the Midwest by the Triennial Convention.

1818 Hamilton Literary and Theological Institution is founded in New York.

1824 The Baptist General Tract Society is founded in Washington, D.C. It is later known as the American Baptist Publication Society.

1825 The Newton Theological Institution is founded in Newton, Massachusetts (near Boston) and is the first graduate theological institution in America.

1832 American Baptist Home Mission Society is organized in New York City.

1832 Beginning of William Knibb's agitation against slave traffic in the British Colonial Empire.

1833 New Hampshire Confession is developed as a defense against Freewill Baptist Arminianism.

1834 First Australian Baptist Church is organized in Sydney, Australia. Johann Oncken is sent by the Triennial Convention to Germany and there establishes the first Baptist church in Hamburg.

1835 Primitive Baptists are organized in New York and Pennsylvania. William Dean baptizes three Chinese converts in Bangkok and thereby organizes the first church among the Chinese in Asia.

1837 The American and Foreign Bible Society is organized in Philadelphia by Baptists.

1839 First Danish Baptist Church is organized by Johann Oncken and Julius Kobner.

1841 Organization of the First Lithuanian Baptist Church under Oncken's guidance.

1843 American and Foreign Free Baptist Missionary Society is organized in Boston by abolitionists.

1845 Controversy over slavery divides Baptists. As a consequence, the Southern Baptist Convention (SBC) is organized at Augusta, Georgia, and (in 1846) the Triennial Convention is renamed the American Baptist Missionary Union.
Baptist work begins in the Netherlands, Hungary, and Romania.

1848 First Baptist Church is organized in Sweden (near Gothenburg) by F. O. Nilson.

1849 Baptist work begins in Switzerland.

1851 First Baptist Church is organized in New Zealand.

1853 Jonathan Goble visits Tokyo as part of Commodore Perry Expedition and develops a plan for Baptist mission. First appointed by the Freewill Baptists.

1860 First Baptist Church is organized in Norway.

1861 First baptism occurs in Latvia.

1865 Bible Translation Society and the Irish Missionary Society merge to become the British and Irish Baptist Home Mission Society.

1868 Native American work is transferred from the American Baptist Union to the American Baptist Home Mission Society.

1869 Baptist Union of Scotland is formed.
Organization of first Baptist church in Finland.

1870 Southern Baptists begin work in Italy.

1877 Women's Baptist Home Mission Society of the East and Women's Baptist Home Mission Society of the West are organized.

1878 Baptist work begins in the Belgian Congo (later Zaire) as part of the Livingstone Mission.

1879 Southern Baptist Convention decides to maintain its organization apart from the American Baptist Missionary Union.

1883 German American Baptists establish an independent mission.

1884 First baptism occurs in Estonia.

1885 Baptist work begins in Czechoslovakia.

1888 Organization of the American Baptist Education Society in Washington, D.C.

1889 Southern Baptist work begins in Japan.

1891 Formation of the Baptist Union for Great Britain and Ireland. Merger of the Particular Baptists and the New Connexion General Baptists.

1891 Baptist Young People's Union is organized in North America. First "chapel car"—a railroad car equipped as a worship, education, and mission administration center—is dedicated as an evangelism tool in establishing churches and Sunday schools in the Midwest and West.

1893 First Baptist participation in the National Free Church Council in England.

1895 The National Baptist Convention of America is organized.

1901 Baptist work begins in the Philippines.

1905 Baptist World Alliance is organized in London.

1906 Freewill and Particular Baptists in Canada merge to become the United Baptist Convention of Canada.

1907 Northern Baptist Convention is organized at Calvary Baptist Church in Washington, D.C.

1908 The first Congress of European Baptists meets in Berlin.

1909 The separate East and West Women's Baptist Home Missions Societies merge to become the Woman's American Baptist Home Mission Society.

1911 Free Baptists merge with Northern Baptist Convention.

1913 Department of Evangelism is created by the Southern Baptist Convention.

1915 Division within the National Baptist Convention leads to incorporation of the National Baptist Convention, U.S.A., Inc. as separate body.

1919 Five-Year New World movement is undertaken by Northern Baptist Convention to raise $100 million for worldwide missions. White Cross Service is developed to channel materials to mission hospitals and schools. It is modeled after the Red Cross work in World War I.

1921 Helen Barrett Montgomery is elected president of Northern Baptist Convention—the first woman presiding officer of a Baptist denominational body.

1936 Action by Northern Baptist Convention and Southern Baptist Convention creates the first meetings of the organization that becomes the Baptist Joint Committee on Public Affairs.

1939 American Baptist Bill of Rights is promulgated by Northern Baptist Convention, the Southern Baptist Convention, and the National Baptist Convention, U.S.A., Inc. in separate actions at annual meetings.

1941 Baptist Youth Fellowship of the Northern Baptist Convention is developed.

1943 Conservative Baptist Foreign Mission Society is formed.

1944 Northern Baptist Assembly is established in Green Lake, Wisconsin.

1945 Northern Baptists and Southern Baptists undertake parallel World Mission Crusade movements.

1947 Formation of the Conservative Baptist Association of America. Northern Baptist Convention sends representatives to the organizational meeting of the World Council of Churches in Amsterdam, Holland.

1948 Formation of the European Baptist Union.
Proposals are made for the formation of a Baptist Union of North America.

1949 European Baptist Federation is organized in Zurich, Switzerland. International Baptist Seminary opens at Rüschlikon, Switzerland.

1950 The Northern Baptist Convention undertakes structural changes and changes its name to the American Baptist Convention. Conservative Baptist Theological Seminary is founded in Denver, Colorado, by the Conservative Baptist Association.

1954 Baptist delegates participate in the Second Assembly of the World Council of Churches at Evanston, Illinois.

1955 American Baptists integrate Woman's American Baptist Foreign Mission Society and American Baptist Foreign Mission Society, and also the Woman's American Baptist Home Mission Society with the American Baptist Home Mission Society.

1955 American Baptists reorganize their administrative structure and coordinate their work in one building.

1957 American Baptist Convention votes to oppose segregation.

1958 American Baptist Convention selects Valley Forge, Pennsylvania, as the new site for its national headquarters.

1959 Baptists in North America adopt Baptist Jubilee Advance evangelism program.
Foreign Mission Board of the Southern Baptist Convention expands missions to six new countries, now totals forty-four.

1960 American Baptist Convention reaffirms its commitment to the ecumenical movement and also authorizes the financing of a new building at the Valley Forge headquarters site.

1961 Progressive Baptist Convention of America is organized in Cincinnati, Ohio, by churches formerly in the National Baptist Convention, U.S.A.
Baptist delegates from many world regions participate in the Third Assembly of the World Council of Churches in New Delhi, India.

1962 Puerto Rico Baptist Convention is received as an affiliated convention of the American Baptist Convention—the first instance of a former mission-receiving region being welcomed as an equal partner by a former mission-sending convention.
Headquarters of the American Baptist Convention in Valley Forge is occupied and dedicated.

1963 Ralph Elliott is dismissed from the faculty of Midwestern Baptist Theological Seminary following intense criticism of his biblical commentary *The Message of Genesis.*
In the annual session in Kansas City, Missouri, the Southern Baptist Convention approves a revised version of the 1925 doctrinal statement "The Baptist Faith and Message."

1964 American Baptist Convention and Southern Baptist Convention hold parallel meetings in Atlantic City, New Jersey, as part of the Baptist Jubilee celebration.

1968 Baptist pastor and civil rights leader, Martin Luther King Jr. is slain in Memphis, Tennessee.

1972 American Baptist Convention changes its name to American Baptist Churches in the U.S.A.

1976 A Baptist, Jimmy Carter, is elected president of the United States. He speaks openly of his faith, regularly attends Washington's First Baptist Church, and teaches Sunday school.

1979 Memphis pastor Adrian Rogers is elected as president of the Southern Baptist Convention, marking the renewal of theological debate, especially regarding biblical inerrancy, authority, social values, and the identity of Southern Baptist Churches. The convention begins to polarize into conservative (fundamentalist) and moderate factions.

1984 Equal Access Act is passed with Baptist Joint Committee on Public Affairs leadership of Baptist involvement. The Act establishes equal access of religious groups for use of public buildings, especially educational facilities.

1987 Formation of the Southern Baptist Alliance (later Alliance of Baptists) is announced by the progressive wing of the "moderates" within the SBC. Its stated intention is to preserve historic Baptist principles and to address their perceived abandonment by SBC leadership.

1990 Moderate wing of the Southern Baptist Convention announces it will no longer contest the office of president. This follows ten years of unsuccessful attempts to regain leadership.
Dismissal of two chief editors of the Baptist Press (SBC) further escalates factional strife in SBC constituencies. A new "fellowship" style of organization is developed among moderates and an interim steering committee is elected.

1991 Cooperative Baptist Fellowship (SBC moderates) is formally constituted in Atlanta at a meeting attended by more than six thousand individuals and congregational representatives; an administrative office is opened in Atlanta.

1993 Religious Freedom Restoration Act is passed by Congress and signed by Baptist President Bill Clinton. The Act clarified access to public buildings, schools, and properties by religious groups, but was declared unconstitutional by the U.S. Supreme Court in 1997. The Baptist Joint Committee on Public Affairs was a catalyst in shaping the original bill and continued in efforts to shape a constitutionally acceptable version.

1998 Baptist former President Jimmy Carter invites Baptist leaders
     to sign "A Declaration of Cooperation" affirming joint Baptist
     advocacy of racial reconciliation and opposition to religious
     persecution as areas of Baptist unity.

Creeds and Confessions

While all evangelical Christians hold that the Bible alone is the complete and sufficient guide in matters of religious faith and practice, most denominations have certain doctrinal statements setting forth, more or less fully, the fundamental truths they understand the Scriptures to teach. These usually serve for the instruction and unity of the people and, in some circumstances, for appeal in controversy. However, creeds and confessions are not held as binding the conscience, or limiting the faith of believers, save in a few cases. These documents are very numerous, and some of them very widely accepted.

Many of these confessions have become historic. Those of Augsburg, Basle, Heidelberg, the Helvetic, Belgic, Saxony, the Synod of Dort, the Thirty-nine Articles of the Anglican Church, the Westminster Assembly Confession (based on, and similar to, the Thirty-nine Articles), and the Savoy (a modification of the Westminster's) served to establish reference points for churches or denominations. Each denomination of Christians has its own; and, save the Apostles' Creed, the oldest and briefest of them all, there is no one in which all professed Christians can agree as to its entire statements.

The Apostles' Creed

The Apostles' Creed, so-called, originated first in Greek and then in Roman from as early as the fourth century. It is not known by whom it was prepared—certainly not by the apostles, whose name it bears and to whom tradition long ascribed it. Truly, in fact, it teaches apostolic truth. Its earliest origins may have been as a catechism for baptismal candidates and developed over time as most enduring things have done. Possibly, also, the brevity of its form, as well as the substance of its truth, has helped to preserve it from oblivion. Augustine pronounced it *brevis et grandis*—brief as to the number of its words, grand as to the weight of its teaching.

It is as follows:

"I believe in God the Father Almighty, maker of heaven and earth: And in Jesus Christ, His only Son, our Lord, Who was conceived by the Holy Ghost, Born of the Virgin Mary, Suffered under Pontius Pilate, Was crucified, dead and buried. He descended into hades: The third day He rose again from the dead. He ascended into heaven, and sitteth on the right hand of God the Father Almighty; From thence He shall come to judge the quick and the dead. I believe in the Holy Ghost; the holy catholic church; the communion of saints; the forgiveness of sins; the resurrection of the body; and the life everlasting. Amen."

The Nicene Creed

The Nicene Creed also belongs to the fourth century—which was a creed-making era—having been adopted by the Council of Nicea in A.D. 325 and enlarged and approved by the second Council of Constantinople A.D. 381, in which form it is commonly used, and is given below. It is somewhat longer than the Apostles' but shorter and more satisfactory than the Athanasian. It made emphatic the divinity of Christ, and was designed as a breakwater against the incoming heresy of the Arians.

It is as follows:

"We believe in one God, the Father Almighty, Maker of heaven and earth, and of all things visible and invisible: And in one Lord Jesus Christ, the only begotten Son of God, begotten of His Father before all worlds; God of God, Light of Light, very God of very God, begotten, not made, being of one substance with the Father, by whom all things were made: who for us men, and for our salvation, came down from heaven, and was incarnate by the Holy Ghost and the Virgin Mary, and was made man, and was crucified also for us under Pontius Pilate. He suffered and was buried, and the third day he rose again according to the Scriptures, and ascended into heaven, and sitteth on the right hand of the Father. And he shall come again with glory to judge the quick and the dead: whose kingdom shall have no end. And we believe in the Holy Ghost, the Lord and Giver of Life, who proceedeth from the Father, and with the Father and the Son together is worshiped and glorified, who spake by the prophets. And we believe in one catholic and apostolic Church, we acknowledge one baptism for the remission of sins; and we look for the resurrection of the dead; and the life of the world to come. Amen."

The Athanasian Creed

This also was the product of the fourth century but is not thought to have been prepared by Athanasius himself, though he may have produced the original basis on which it was built. The superstructure underwent various modifications by other hands before it crystallized into its final form after several centuries of use and change. It is longer than the other ancient symbols and less satisfactory to the faith of the present age. In its final shape it was designed to stem the current of Arian heresy by strongly teaching the absolute divinity of Christ and his coequality with the Father. A large part of the text is devoted to this doctrine, the phraseology of which is as perplexing to modern syntax as the doctrinal teaching is confounding to a simple Christian faith. Nevertheless, it demonstrates the intensity and seriousness with which early theologians considered theological definition and metaphysical subtlety. Despite the challenge it presents to modern thought and expression, it conveys the mind of the early church and its understanding of truth. It reads as follows:

"Whosoever will be saved, before all things it is necessary that he hold the catholic faith. Which faith, except every one do keep whole and undefiled, without doubt he shall perish everlastingly. And the catholic faith is this: That we worship one God in Trinity, and Trinity in Unity; neither confounding the persons nor dividing the substance. For there is one person of the Father, another of the Son, and another of the Holy Ghost. But the Godhead of the Father and of the Son, and of the Holy Ghost is all one; the glory equal, the majesty coeternal. Such as the Father is, such is the Son, and such is the Holy Ghost. The Father uncreated, the Son uncreated, and the Holy Ghost uncreated. The Father immeasurable, the Son immeasurable, and the Holy Ghost immeasurable. The Father eternal, the Son eternal, and the Holy Ghost eternal. And yet they are not three eternals, but one eternal. As also there are not three immeasurables, nor three uncreated, but one uncreated and one immeasurable, so likewise is the Father almighty, the Son almighty, and the Holy Ghost almighty. And yet there are not three almighties, but one almighty. So the Father is God, the Son is God, and the Holy Ghost is God. And yet there are not three Gods, but one God. So also the Father is Lord, the Son is Lord, and the Holy Ghost is Lord. And yet there are not three Lords, but one Lord. For like as we are compelled by the Christian verity to acknowledge every person by himself to be God and Lord, so are we forbidden by the catholic religion to say there be three Gods and three Lords.

"The Father is made of none, neither created nor begotten. The Son is of the Father alone: not made, nor created; but begotten. The Holy Ghost is of the Father and the Son: not made; neither created; nor begotten; but proceeding. Thus there is one Father, not three Fathers; one Son, not three Sons; one Holy Ghost, not three Holy Ghosts. And in this Trinity none is before or after the other; none is greater or less than another. But the whole three persons are co-eternal together, and co-equal. So that in all things, as aforesaid, the Unity in Trinity and the Trinity in Unity is to be worshiped. He, therefore, that will be saved, must thus think of the Trinity.

"Furthermore, it is necessary to everlasting salvation that we believe also rightly in the incarnation of our Lord Jesus Christ. Now the right faith is that we believe and confess that our Lord Jesus Christ, the Son of God, is God and man. God, of the substance of the Father, begotten before the worlds: and man, of the substance of his mother, born in the world. Perfect God perfect man, of a reasonable soul and human flesh subsisting. Equal to the Father as touching His Godhead: inferior to the Father as touching His manhood. And although He be God and man; yet He is not two, but one Christ. One, not by conversion of the Godhead into flesh: but assumption of the manhood into God. One altogether not by confusion of substance, but by unity of person. For, as the reasonable soul and flesh is one man, so God and man is one Christ.

"Who suffered for our salvation, descended into hades: rose again the third day from the dead. He ascended into heaven, He sitteth on the right hand of God, the Father Almighty. From whence He shall come to judge the quick and the dead. At whose coming all men shall rise again with their bodies; and shall give account of their own works. And they that have done good shall go into life everlasting; and they that have done evil, into everlasting fire.

"This is the catholic faith; which except a man believe faithfully, he cannot be saved."

Later Confessions

The Augsburg Confession is the principal standard of doctrine for the Lutheran churches and constitutes what is considered "the first Protestant Confession." However, Luther had previously prepared articles for the Convention of Schwabach, which had not yet been published but which were the basis of Lutheran doctrine. The Emperor Charles V called a German Diet to meet at Augsburg, 1530, and directed the Protestants to present a statement of their faith. The assignment was given to Melanchthon and he carried it through, after consultation with Luther.

The Schmalkald Confession, drawn chiefly by Luther as a protest against the traditions and false teachings of the papacy, was presented to the Protestant league of princes, electors, and nobles, at Schmalkald, and by them approved in 1537, and published in German and Latin at Wittenberg the next year. These articles are regarded as authoritative by the Lutheran churches throughout the world.

The Thirty-nine Articles, so-called, constitute the *Confession of the Church of England.* Originally these were forty-two. They were prepared by royal commission, appointed in 1551, under Edward VII, for this purpose. At the head of it was Archbishop Cranmer, who had previously prepared some articles, drawn largely from the Augsburg Confession. These became the basis of the thirty-nine. Calvin, Melanchthon, Bullinger, Peter Martyr, and others conferred as to their preparation. In 1553 they were presented to the convocation. Various changes were made in them before they were confirmed by Parliament. Various further changes were made by the convocation in 1562, 1566, and 1571, but it was not until 1628 that they were issued by royal authority under Charles I.

The Heidelberg Confession, called also the Heidelberg Catechism, was prepared under the direction of Frederick III, prince of the Palatinate, who had espoused the cause of the Reformation. Its preparation was committed to Ursinus, a pupil of Melanchthon (who is regarded as its principal author), aided by Olevianus, court preacher and professor at Heidelberg. Catechisms of Luther, Calvin, Melanchthon, and Lasco furnished materials, and the work was completed, presented to, and accepted by a synod of the Palatinate in December 1562 and published in 1563. It has been published by millions and translated into nearly every known language. It has become the venerated symbol and the accepted doctrinal standard of the German and Dutch Reformed Churches everywhere. It is strongly Calvinistic in tone and is beyond question one of the most admirable compendiums of the Christian doctrine extant.

The Canons of Dort were prepared by a national synod called to settle the disputes that had arisen between the Calvinists and the Arminians. In this bitter controversy the great Grotius and the equally noble Barneveldt were engaged; the latter of whom lost his life through the hostile and heartless jealousy of Maurice, stadtholder of Nassau. The synod opened its sessions in November 1618 in the great church of Dort, Holland, and closed them in May 1619. They approved as orthodox both the Heidelberg and Belgic Confessions and issued their own Canons of Doctrine, which are accepted as authoritative by the Reformed Dutch Church and some other communions.

The Westminster Confession is the leading doctrinal standard of the Presbyterian churches throughout the world, and, with some exceptions, is one of the best compends of Christian faith of modern history. It was prepared by the Westminster synod, known as the "Assembly of Divines," appointed by Parliament, and composed of Presbyterians, Episcopalians, Independents, and Erastians:[1] 121 divines and 30 laymen from England, and 5 from Scotland. The meetings were held in Westminster Abbey, London, having been convened in the presence of both houses of Parliament on July 1, 1643.

The assembly continued its sessions until the dissolution of the Long Parliament by Cromwell in 1653. Their labors included the larger and smaller catechism and a directory for public worship, in addition to the confession. This was based on, and largely conformed to, the Thirty-nine Articles of the English Church; indeed, it was little more than a revision of that document, prepared 100 years before, adopting it, article by article, with few changes, to the close of the fifteenth article, where their revision terminated. The work was approved by the House of Commons in 1647 and adopted by the Presbyterian General Assembly of Scotland in 1648.

The Savoy Confession was so-called from the Savoy Palace, the residence of the bishop of London, in which was held the conference in 1658, appointed by royal commission to formulate a declaration of faith, which should, if possible, harmonize the Nonconformists with the Anglican Church. Both the Anglican and the dissenting clergy were engaged in the conference, but the effort proved unavailing. The confession prepared is largely a reproduction of the Westminster Assembly's and to a considerable extent verbally identical with it, containing thirty-two articles, one less than the assembly's.

Baptist Confessions

The Protestant doctrine that the Bible alone is an authoritative standard of religious truth, and the only sufficient guide in faith and doctrine, is emphasized by Baptists. Baptists have their confessions, or, as they are more commonly called, "Articles of Faith." Most churches have these summaries, and each church uses such form as it may prefer—or no form at all. Some Baptist churches restrict common expressions of faith and doctrine to a simple church covenant (addressed in Appendix F). None is binding on the conscience of any, and members are not required to subscribe to any.

A complete survey of Baptist confessions of faith would be too lengthy to include in this volume. Instead, the reader is referred to the book *Baptist Confessions of Faith*, edited by William L. Lumpkin (Valley Forge, Pa.: Judson Press, 1959). Here it will suffice to mention three. One is the Second London Confession, which was the climactic work in this field by the English Baptists, and was published first in 1677, then in several other editions through the years. The Second London Confession is actually a revision of the Westminster Confession to meet Baptist needs. The two American Baptist confessions that have been of particular interest through the years are the Philadelphia Confession and the New Hampshire Confession. They are discussed and reprinted here for their historical interest.

The Philadelphia Confession

It was in 1724, so far as available records indicate, that the Philadelphia Baptist Association first acknowledged the use of the Second London Confession (1689 edition), but not until 1742 do we find a record of any official action to indicate its official status. At that time the association ordered the Second London Confession printed, with two additional articles (numbers XXIII and XXXI). Thus, the Philadelphia Confession differs only in these two articles from that used by the English Baptists. It is noteworthy for its strong Calvinistic flavor, which later became less prevalent among Baptists.

Text of the Philadelphia Confession

I. Of the Holy Scriptures

1. The Holy Scripture is the only sufficient, certain, and infallible rule of all saving knowledge, faith, and obedience; Although the light of nature and the works of creation and providence do so far manifest the goodness, wisdom, and power of God, as to leave men unexcusable; yet they are not sufficient to give that knowledge of God and his will, which is necessary unto salvation. Therefore it pleased the Lord at sundry times, and in divers manners, to reveal himself and to declare his will unto his church; and afterward for the better preserving and propagating of the truth, and for the more sure establishment and comfort of the church against the corruption of the flesh and the malice of Satan and of the world, to commit the same wholly unto writing; which maketh the Holy Scriptures to be most necessary, those former ways of God's revealing his will unto his people being now ceased.

2. Under the name of Holy Scripture, or the Word of God written, are now contained all the books of the Old and New Testament, which are these:

Of the Old Testament: Genesis, Exodus, Leviticus, Numbers, Deuteronomy, Joshua, Judges, Ruth, I Samuel, II Samuel, I Kings, II Kings, I Chronicles, II Chronicles, Ezra, Nehemiah, Esther, Job, Psalms, Proverbs, Ecclesiastes, The Song of Songs, Isaiah, Jeremiah, Lamentations, Ezekiel, Daniel, Hosea, Joel, Amos, Obadiah, Jonah, Micah, Nahum, Habakkuk, Zephaniah, Haggai, Zechariah, Malachi.

Of the New Testament: Matthew, Mark, Luke, John, The Acts of the Apostles, Paul's Epistle to the Romans, I Corinthians, II Corinthians, Galatians, Ephesians, Philippians, Colossians, I Thessalonians, II Thessalonians, I Timothy, II Timothy, to Titus, to Philemon, the Epistle to the Hebrews, the Epistle of James, the first and second Epistles of Peter, the first, second, and third Epistles of John, the Epistle of Jude, the Revelation; all which are given by the inspiration of God to be the rule of faith and life.

3. The books commonly called Apocrypha, not being of divine inspiration, are no part of the Canon (or rule) of the Scripture, and therefore of no authority to the church of God, nor to be any otherwise approved or made use of than other human writings.

4. The authority of the Holy Scripture for which it ought to be believed dependeth not upon the testimony of any man or church; but wholly upon God (who is truth itself) the author thereof; therefore it is to be received, because it is the Word of God.

5. We may be moved and induced by the testimony of the church of God, to a high and reverent esteem of the Holy Scriptures; and the heavenliness of the matter, the efficacy of the Doctrine, and the majesty of the style, the consent of all the parts, the scope of the whole (which is to give all glory to God), the full discovery it makes of the only way of man's salvation, and many other incomparable excellencies and entire perfections thereof, are arguments whereby it doth abundantly evidence itself to be the Word of God; yet, notwithstanding, our full persuasion and assurance of the infallible truth and divine authority thereof is from the inward work of the Holy Spirit, bearing witness by and with the Word in our hearts.

6. The whole counsel of God concerning all things necessary for

his own glory, man's salvation, faith, and life, is either expressly set down or necessarily contained in the Holy Scripture; unto which nothing at any time is to be added, whether by new revelation of the Spirit or traditions of men.

Nevertheless we acknowledge the inward illumination of the Spirit of God to be necessary for the saving understanding of such things as are revealed in the Word, and that there are some circumstances concerning the worship of God and government of the church common to human actions and societies which are to be ordered by the light of nature and Christian prudence according to the general rules of the Word, which are always to be observed.

7. All things in Scripture are not alike plain in themselves nor alike clear unto all; yet those things which are necessary to be known, believed, and observed for salvation, are so clearly propounded, and opened in some place of Scripture or other, that not only the learned, but the unlearned, in a due use of ordinary means, may attain to a sufficient understanding of them.

8. The Old Testament in *Hebrew* (which was the native language of the people of God of old) and the New Testament in *Greek* (which at the time of the writing of it was most generally known to the nations being immediately inspired by God, and by his singular care and providence kept pure in all ages) are therefore authentic; so, as in all controversies of religion, the church is finally to appeal unto them. But because these original tongues are not known to all the people of God, who have a right unto and interest in the Scriptures and are commanded in the fear of God to read and search them, therefore they are to be translated into the vulgar language of every nation unto which they come, that the Word of God dwelling plentifully in all, they may worship him in an acceptable manner and through patience and comfort of the Scriptures may have hope.

9. The infallible rule of interpretation of Scripture is the Scripture itself: And therefore, when there is a question about the true and full sense of any Scripture (which is not manifold but one) it must be searched by other places that speak more clearly.

10. The supreme judge by which all controversies of religion are to be determined, and all decrees of councils, opinions of ancient writers, doctrines of men, and private spirits are to be examined, and in whose sentence we are to rest, can be no other but the Holy

Scripture delivered by the Spirit; into which Scripture, so delivered, our faith is finally resolved.

II. Of God and of the Holy Trinity

1. The Lord our God is but one only living and true God; whose subsistence is in and of himself, infinite in being and perfection, whose essence cannot be comprehended by any but himself; a most pure spirit, invisible, without body, parts, or passions, who only hath immortality, dwelling in the light, which no man can approach unto, who is immutable, immense, eternal, incomprehensible, almighty, every way infinite, most holy, most wise, most free, most absolute (working all things according to the counsel of his own immutable and most righteous will for his own glory), most loving, gracious, merciful, long-suffering, abundant in goodness and truth, forgiving iniquity, transgression and sin, the rewarder of them that diligently seek him, and withal most just and terrible in his judgments, hating all sin, and who by no means clear the guilty.

2. God, having all life, glory, goodness, blessedness, in and of himself, is alone in and unto himself all-sufficient, not standing in need of any creature which he hath made, nor deriving any glory from them, but only manifesting his own glory in, by, unto, and upon them. He is alone the fountain of all being, of whom, through whom, and to whom are all things, and he hath most sovereign dominion over all creatures, to do by them, for them, and upon them, whatsoever himself pleaseth. In his sight all things are open and manifest, his knowledge is infinite, infallible, and independent upon the creature, so as nothing is to him contingent or uncertain. He is most holy in all his counsels, in all his works, and in all his commands; to him is due from angels and men, whatsoever worship, service, or obedience as creatures they owe unto the Creator, and whatever he is further pleased to require of them.

3. In this divine and infinite being there are three subsistences, the Father, the Word (or Son), and the Holy Spirit, of one substance, power, and eternity, each having the whole divine essence, yet the essence undivided. The Father is of none neither begotten nor proceeding, the Son is eternally begotten of the Father, the Holy Spirit proceeding from the Father and the Son, all infinite, without beginning; therefore but one God, who is not to be divided in nature

and being, but distinguished by several peculiar, relative properties and personal relations; which doctrine of the Trinity is the foundation of all our communion with God, and comfortable dependence on him.

III. Of God's Decree

1. God hath decreed in himself from all eternity, by the most wise and holy counsel of his own will, freely and unchangeably, all things whatsoever come to pass; yet so as thereby is God neither the author of sin nor hath fellowship with any therein, nor is violence offered to the will of the creature, nor yet is the liberty or contingency of second causes taken away, but rather established; in which appears his wisdom in disposing all things, and power and faithfulness in accomplishing his decree.

2. Although God knoweth whatsoever may or can come to pass upon all supposed conditions, yet hath he not decreed anything because he foresaw it as future or as that which would come to pass upon such conditions.

3. By the decree of God, for the manifestation of his glory some men and angels are predestined or foreordained to eternal life, through Jesus Christ, to the praise of his glorious grace; others being left to act in their sin to their just condemnation, to the praise of his glorious justice.

4. These angels and men, thus predestined and foreordained, are particularly and unchangeably designed, and their number so certain and definite that it cannot be either increased or diminished.

5. Those of mankind that are predestined to life, God (before the foundation of the world was laid, according to his eternal and immutable purpose and the secret counsel and good pleasure of his will) hath chosen in Christ unto everlasting glory out of his mere free grace and love, without any other thing in the creature as a condition or cause moving him thereunto.

6. As God hath appointed the elect unto glory, so he hath, by the eternal and most free purpose of his will, foreordained all the means thereunto wherefore they who are elected, being fallen in Adam, are redeemed by Christ, are effectually called unto faith in Christ (by his Spirit working in due season), are justified, adopted, sanctified, and kept by his power through faith unto salvation, neither

are any other redeemed by Christ, or effectually called, justified, adopted, sanctified, and saved, but the elect only.

7. The doctrine of this high mystery of predestination is to be handled with special prudence and care; that men attending the will of God revealed in his Word, and yielding obedience thereunto, may from the certainty of their effectual vocation be assured of their eternal election; so shall this doctrine afford matter of praise, reverence, and admiration of God, and of humility, diligence, and abundant consolation, to all that sincerely obey the gospel.

IV. Of Creation

1. In the beginning it pleased God the Father, Son, and Holy Spirit, for the manifestation of the glory of his eternal power, wisdom, and goodness, to create or make the world, and all things therein, whether visible or invisible, in the space of six days, and all very good.

2. After God had made all other creatures, he created man, male and female, with reasonable and immortal souls, rendering them fit unto that life to God for which they were created; being made after the image of God in knowledge, righteousness, and true holiness; having the Law of God written in their hearts, and power to fulfill it; and yet under a possibility of transgressing, being left to the liberty of their own will, which was subject to change.

3. Besides the law written in their hearts, they received a command not to eat of the tree of knowledge of good and evil; which, whilst they kept, they were happy in their communion with God and had dominion over the creatures.

V. Of Divine Providence

1. God, the good creator of all things, in his infinite power and wisdom doth uphold, direct, dispose, and govern all creatures and things, from the greatest even to the least, by his most wise and holy providence, to the end for which they were created, according unto his infallible foreknowledge and the free and immutable counsel of his own will, to the praise and glory of his wisdom, power, justice, infinite goodness, and mercy.

2. Although in relation to the foreknowledge and decree of God, the first cause, all things come to pass immutably and infallibly (so

that there is not any thing befalls any by chance or without his providence), yet by the same providence he ordereth them to fall out according to the nature of second causes, either necessarily, freely, or contingently.

3. God in his ordinary providence maketh use of means; yet is free to work without, above, and against them at his pleasure.

4. The almighty power, unsearchable wisdom, and infinite goodness of God so far manifest themselves in his providence that his determinate counsel extendeth itself even to the first fall and all other sinful actions both of angels and men (and that not by a bare permission); which also he most wisely and powerfully boundeth and otherwise ordereth and governeth in a manifold dispensation to his most holy ends: yet so, as the sinfulness of their acts proceedeth only from the creatures and not from God, who being most holy and righteous, neither is nor can be the author or approver of sin.

5. The most wise, righteous, and gracious God doth oftentimes leave for a season his own children to manifold temptations and the corruptions of their own heart, to chastise them for their former sins or to discover unto them the hidden strength of corruption and deceitfulness of their hearts that they may be humbled; and to raise them to a more close and constant dependence for their support upon himself; and to make them more watchful against all future occasions of sin, and for other just and holy ends.

So that whatsoever befalls any of his elect is by his appointment, for his glory and their good.

6. As for those wicked and ungodly men whom God as a righteous judge for former sin doth blind and harden; from them he not only withholdeth his grace, whereby they might have been enlightened in their understanding and wrought upon in their hearts: but sometimes also withdraweth the gifts which they had, and exposeth them to such objects as their corruptions make occasion of sin; and withal gives them over to their own lusts, the temptations of the world, and the power of Satan, whereby it comes to pass that they harden themselves, even under those means which God useth for the softening of others.

7. As the providence of God doth in general reach to all creatures, so after a most special manner it taketh care of his church, and disposeth of all things to the good thereof.

VI. Of the Fall of Man, of Sin, and of the Punishment Thereof

1. Although God created man upright and perfect, and gave him a righteous law which had been unto life had he kept it, and threatened death upon the breach thereof, yet he did not long abide in this honor; Satan using the subtlety of the serpent to seduce Eve, then by her seducing Adam, who without any compulsion did wilfully transgress the law of their creation, and the command given unto them in eating the forbidden fruit; which God was pleased according to his wise and holy counsel to permit, having purposed to order it to his own glory.

2. Our first parents by this sin fell from their original righteousness and communion with God, and we in them, whereby death came upon all, all becoming dead in sin, and wholly defiled in all the faculties and parts of soul and body.

3. They being the root, and by God's appointment, standing in the room and stead of all mankind, the guilt of the sin was imputed (and corrupted nature conveyed) to all their posterity descending from them by ordinary generation, being now conceived in sin, and by nature children of wrath, the servants of sin, the subjects of death and all other miseries spiritual, temporal, and eternal, unless the Lord Jesus set them free.

4. From this original corruption—whereby we are utterly indisposed, disabled, and made opposite to all good and wholly inclined to all evil—do proceed all actual transgressions.

5. This corruption of nature during this life doth remain in those that are regenerated; and, although it be through Christ pardoned and mortified, yet both itself and the first motions thereof are truly and properly sin.

VII. Of God's Covenant

1. The distance between God and the creature is so great that, although reasonable creatures do owe obedience unto him as their creator, yet they could never have attained the reward of life but by some voluntary condescension on God's part, which he hath been pleased to express by way of covenant.

2. Moreover, man having been brought himself under the curse of the law by his fall, it pleased the Lord to make a covenant of grace wherein he freely offereth unto sinners life and salvation by

Jesus Christ, requiring of them faith in him that they may be saved; and promising to give unto all those that are ordained unto eternal life his Holy Spirit to make them willing and able to believe.

3. This covenant is revealed in the gospel; first of all to Adam in the promise of salvation by the seed of the woman and afterwards by farther steps until the full discovery thereof was completed in the New Testament; and it is founded in that eternal covenant transaction that was between the Father and the Son, about the redemption of the elect; and it is alone by the grace of this covenant, that all of the posterity of fallen Adam that ever were saved did obtain life and a blessed immortality; man being now utterly incapable of acceptance with God upon those terms on which Adam stood in his state of innocency.

VIII. Of Christ the Mediator

1. It pleased God in his eternal purpose to choose and ordain the Lord Jesus his only begotten Son according to the covenant made between them both, to be the mediator between God and man; the Prophet, Priest, and King; Head and Savior of his church, the heir of all things, and judge of the world: Unto whom he did from all eternity give a people to be his seed and to be by him in time redeemed, called, justified, sanctified, and glorified.

2. The Son of God, the second person in the Holy Trinity, being very and eternal God, the brightness of the Father's glory, of one substance and equal with him—who made the world, who upholdeth and governeth all things he hath made—did when the fullness of time was come take upon him man's nature, with all the essential properties, and common infirmities thereof, yet without sin: Being conceived by the Holy Spirit in the womb of the Virgin Mary, the Holy Spirit coming down upon her, and the power of the most high overshadowing her, and so was made of a woman, of the tribe of Judah, of the seed of Abraham and David according to the Scriptures: So that two whole, perfect, and distinct natures were inseparably joined together in one person, without conversion, composition, or confusion, which person is very God and very man, yet one Christ, the only mediator between God and man.

3. The Lord Jesus in his human nature thus united to the divine in the person of the Son, was sanctified, anointed with the Holy

Spirit above measure, having in him all the treasures of wisdom and knowledge; in whom it pleased the Father that all fullness should dwell: To the end that being holy, harmless, undefiled, and full of grace and truth, he might be thoroughly furnished to execute the office of a mediator and surety; which office he took not upon himself, but was thereunto called by his Father, who also put all power and judgment in his hand, and gave him commandment to execute the same.

4. This office the Lord Jesus did most willingly undertake, which that he might discharge he was made under the law and did perfectly fulfill it and underwent the punishment due to us, which we should have borne and suffered, being made sin and a curse for us, enduring most grievous sorrows in his soul and most painful sufferings in his body; was crucified and died, and remained in the state of the dead, yet saw no corruption. On the third day he arose from the dead with the same body in which he suffered, with which he also ascended into heaven and there sitteth at the right hand of his Father making intercession, and shall return to judge men and angels at the end of the world.

5. The Lord Jesus by his perfect obedience and sacrifice of himself, which he through the Eternal Spirit once offered up unto God, hath fully satisfied the justice of God, procured reconciliation, and purchased an everlasting inheritance in the kingdom of heaven for all those whom the Father hath given unto him.

6. Although the price of redemption was not actually paid by Christ till after his incarnation, yet the virtue, efficacy, and benefit thereof were communicated to the elect in all ages successively from the beginning of the world, in and by those promises, types, and sacrifices wherein he was revealed and signified to be the seed of the woman which should bruise the serpent's head, and the lamb slain from the foundation of the world: Being the same yesterday and today and forever.

7. Christ in the work of mediation acteth according to both natures, by each nature doing that which is proper to itself; yet, by reason of the unity of the person, that which is proper to one nature is sometimes in Scripture attributed to the person denominated by the other nature.

8. To all those for whom Christ hath obtained eternal redemption,

he doth certainly and effectually apply and communicate the same; making intercession for them, uniting them to himself by his Spirit, revealing unto them, in and by the Word, the mystery of salvation; persuading them to believe and obey, governing their hearts by his Word and Spirit, and overcoming all their enemies by his almighty power and wisdom, in such manner and ways as are most consonant to his wonderful and unsearchable dispensation; and all of free and absolute grace, without any condition foreseen in them, to procure it.

9. This office of mediator between God and man is proper only to Christ, who is the prophet, priest, and king of the church of God, and may not be either in whole or any part thereof transferred from him to any other.

10. This number and order of offices is necessary, for in respect of our ignorance we stand in need of his prophetical office; and in respect of our alienation from God and imperfection of the best of our services, we need his priestly office to reconcile us and present us acceptable unto God; and in respect of our averseness and utter inability to return to God, and for our spiritual adversaries, we need his kingly office to convince, subdue, draw, uphold, deliver, and preserve us to his heavenly kingdom.

IX. Of Free Will

1. God hath endued the will of man with that natural liberty and power of acting upon choice, that it is neither forced nor by any necessity of nature determined to do good or evil.

2. Man in his state of innocency had freedom and power to will and to do that which was good and well-pleasing to God; but yet was mutable, so that he might fall from it.

3. Man, by his fall into a state of sin, hath wholly lost all ability of will to any spiritual good accompanying salvation; so, as a natural man, being altogether averse from that good and dead in sin, is not able by his own strength to convert himself, or to prepare himself thereunto.

4. When God converts a sinner and translates him into the state of grace, he freeth him from his natural bondage under sin and, by his grace alone, enables him freely to will and to do that which is spiritually good; yet so as that by reason of his remaining corruptions he doth not perfectly nor only will that which is good,

but doth also will that which is evil.

5. The will of man is made perfectly and immutably free to good alone, in the state of glory only.

X. Of Effectual Calling

1. Those whom God hath predestined unto life, he is pleased, in his appointed and accepted time, effectually to call by his Word and Spirit, out of that state of sin and death in which they are by nature, to grace and salvation by Jesus Christ; enlightening their minds, spiritually and savingly, to understand the things of God; taking away their heart of stone and giving unto them a heart of flesh; renewing their wills, and by his almighty power determining them to that which is good, and effectually drawing them to Jesus Christ; yet so as they come most freely, being made willing by his grace.

2. This effectual call is of God's free and special grace alone, not from anything at all foreseen in man, nor from any power or agency in the creature co-working with his special grace, the creature being wholly passive therein, being dead in sins and trespasses; until, being quickened and renewed by the Holy Spirit, he is thereby enabled to answer this call and to embrace the grace offered and conveyed in it; and that by no less power than that which raised up Christ from the dead.

3. Elect infants dying in infancy are regenerated and saved by Christ through the Spirit; who worketh when and where and how he pleaseth: so also are all other elect persons who are incapable of being outwardly called by the ministry of the Word.

4. Others not elected (although they may be called by the ministry of the Word and may have some common operations of the Spirit, yet not being effectually drawn by the Father), they neither will nor can truly come to Christ, and therefore cannot be saved. Much less can men that receive not the Christian religion be saved, be they never so diligent to frame their lives according to the light of nature and the law of that religion they do profess.

XI. Of Justification

1. Those whom God effectually calleth, he also freely justifieth, not by infusing righteousness into them, but by pardoning their sins and by accounting and accepting their persons as righteous; not for anything wrought in them, but for Christ's sake alone; not by

imputing faith itself, the act of believing, nor any other evangelical obedience to them as their righteousness, but by imputing Christ's active obedience unto the whole law and passive obedience in his death for their whole and sole righteousness, they receiving and resting on him and his righteousness by faith, which faith they have not of themselves; it is the gift of God.

2. Faith, thus receiving and resting on Christ and his righteousness, is the lone instrument of justification; yet it is not alone in the person justified, but is ever accompanied with all other saving graces and is no dead faith, but worketh by love.

3. Christ by his obedience and death did fully discharge the debt of all those that are justified; and did by the sacrifice of himself, in the blood of his cross, undergoing in their stead the penalty due unto them, make a proper, real, and full satisfaction to God's justice in their behalf. Yet, inasmuch as he was given by the Father for them and his obedience and satisfaction accepted in their stead, and both freely, not for anything in them, their justification is only of free grace, that both the exact justice and rich grace of God might be glorified in the justification of sinners.

4. God did from all eternity decree to justify all the elect, and Christ did in the fullness of time die for their sins and rise again for their justification; nevertheless they are not justified personally until the Holy Spirit doth in due time actually apply Christ unto them.

5. God doth continue to forgive the sins of those that are justified; and, although they can never fall from the state of justification, yet they may by their sins fall under God's fatherly displeasure, and in that condition they have not usually the light of his countenance restored unto them until they humble themselves, confess their sins, beg pardon, and renew their faith and repentance.

6. The justification of believers under the Old Testament was in all these respects one and the same with the justification of believers under the New Testament.

XII. Of Adoption

All those that are justified, God vouchsafed in and for the sake of his only son Jesus Christ, to make partakers of the grace of adoption, by which they are taken into the number, and enjoy the liberties and privileges of children of God; have his name put upon them, receive the spirit of adoption, have access to the throne of grace with boldness, are enabled to cry Abba Father, are pitied, protected, provided for, and chastened by him as by a Father; yet never cast off, but sealed to the day of redemption, and inherit the promises, as heirs, of everlasting salvation.

XIII. Of Sanctification

1. They who are united to Christ, effectually called and regenerated, having a new heart and a new spirit created in them through the virtue of Christ's death and resurrection, are also further sanctified, really and personally, through the same virtue, by his Word and Spirit dwelling in them; the dominion of the whole body of sin is destroyed, and the several lusts thereof are more and more weakened and mortified; and they more and more quickened and strengthened in all saving graces, to the practice of all true holiness, without which no man shall see the Lord.

2. This sanctification is throughout, in the whole man, yet imperfect in this life; there abideth still some remnants of corruption in every part, whence ariseth a continual and irreconcilable war, the flesh lusting against the spirit, and the spirit against the flesh.

3. In which war, although the remaining corruption for a time may yet prevail, yet through the continual supply of strength from the sanctifying spirit of Christ the regenerate part doth overcome; and so the saints grow in grace, perfecting holiness in the fear of God, pressing after a heavenly life in evangelical obedience to all the commands which Christ as head and king, in his word, hath prescribed to them.

XIV. Of Saving Faith

1. The grace of faith, whereby the elect are enabled to believe to the saving of their souls, is the work of the Spirit of Christ in their hearts; and is ordinarily wrought by the ministry of the Word, by which also (and by the administration of baptism and the Lord's Supper, prayer, and other means appointed of God) it is increased and strengthened.

2. By this faith a Christian believeth to be true whatsoever is revealed in the Word, for the authority of God himself; and also apprehendeth an excellency therein above all other writings and all

things in the world, as it bears forth the glory of God in his attributes, the excellency of Christ in his nature and offices, and the power and fullness of the Holy Spirit in his working and operations, and so is enabled to cast his soul upon the truth thus believed; and also acteth differently upon that which each particular passage thereof containeth, yielding obedience to the commands, trembling at the threatenings, and embracing the promises of God for this life and that which is to come. But the principal acts of saving faith have immediate relation to Christ, accepting, receiving, and resting upon him alone for justification, sanctification, and eternal life by virtue of the covenant of grace.

3. This faith, although it be different in degrees and may be weak or strong, yet it is in the least degree of it different in the kind or nature of it (as is all other saving grace) from the faith and common grace of temporary believers; and therefore, though it may be many times assailed and weakened, yet it gets the victory, growing up in many, to the attainment of a full assurance through Christ, who is both the author and finisher of our faith.

XV. Of Repentance unto Life and Salvation

1. Such of the elect as are converted at riper years, having sometimes lived in the state of nature and therein served divers lusts and pleasures, God in their effectual calling giveth them repentance unto life.

2. Whereas there is none that doth good and sinneth not, and the best of men may (through the power and deceitfulness of their corruption dwelling in them, with the prevalency of temptation) fall into great sins and provocations, God hath in the covenant of grace mercifully provided that believers so sinning and falling be renewed through repentance unto salvation.

3. This saving repentance is an evangelical grace whereby a person, being by the Holy Spirit made sensible of the manifold evils of his sin, doth, by faith in Christ, humble himself for it, with godly sorrow, detestation of it, and self-abhorrency, praying for pardon and strength of grace, with a purpose and endeavor by supplies of the Spirit to walk before God unto all well-pleasing in all things.

4. As repentance is to be continued through the whole course of our lives upon the account of the body of death and the motions

thereof, so it is every man's duty to repent of his particular known sins, particularly.

5. Such is the provision which God hath made through Christ in the covenant of grace for the preservation of believers unto salvation, that, although there is no sin so small but it deserves damnation, yet there is no sin so great that it shall bring damnation on them that repent, which makes the constant preaching of repentance necessary.

XVI. Of Good Works

1. Good works are only such as God hath commanded in his holy Word, and not such as without the warrant thereof are devised by men, out of blind zeal or upon any pretense of good intentions.

2. These good works, done in obedience to God's commandments, are the fruits and evidences of a true and lively faith; and, by them, believers manifest their thankfulness, strengthen their assurance, edify their brethren, adorn the profession of the gospel, stop the mouths of the adversaries, and glorify God, whose workmanship they are, created in Christ Jesus thereunto, that having their fruit unto holiness they may have the end eternal life.

3. Their ability to do good works is not at all of themselves, but wholly from the Spirit of Christ; and that they may be enabled thereunto, besides the graces they have already received, there is necessary an actual influence of the same Holy Spirit to work in them to will and to do of his good pleasure; yet are they not hereupon to grow negligent, as if they were not bound to perform any duty, unless upon a special motion of the Spirit, but they ought to be diligent in stirring up the grace of God that is in them.

4. They who in their obedience attain to the greatest height which is possible in this life are so far from being able to supererogate and to do more than God requires as that they fall short of much which in duty they are bound to do.

5. We cannot by our best works merit pardon of sin or eternal life at the hand of God, by reason of the great disproportion that is between them and the glory to come, and the infinite distance that is between us and God, whom by them we can neither profit nor satisfy for the debt of our former sins; but, when we have done all we can, we have done but our duty and are unprofitable servants;

and because as they are good they proceed from his Spirit; and as they are wrought by us they are defiled and mixed with so much weakness and imperfection that they cannot endure the severity of God's judgment.

6. Yet, notwithstanding the persons of believers being accepted through Christ, their good works also are accepted in him; not as though they were in this life wholly unblamable and unreprovable in God's sight, but that he, looking upon them in his Son, is pleased to accept and reward that which is sincere although accomplished with many weaknesses and imperfections.

7. Works done by unregenerate men, although for the matter of them they may be things which God commands, and of good use both to themselves and others; yet, because they proceed not from a heart purified by faith, nor are done in a right manner according to the Word, nor to a right end of the glory of God, they are therefore sinful and cannot please God nor make a man meet to receive grace from God, and yet their neglect of them is more sinful and displeasing to God.

XVII. Of Perseverance of the Saints

1. Those whom God hath accepted in the beloved, effectually called and sanctified by his Spirit and given the precious faith of his elect unto, can neither totally nor finally fall from the state of grace, but shall certainly persevere therein to the end and be eternally saved, seeing the gifts and callings of God are without repentance (whence he still begets and nourisheth in them faith, repentance, love, joy, hope, and all the graces of the Spirit unto immortality); and, though many storms and floods arise and beat against them, yet they shall never be able to take them off that foundation and rock which by faith they are fastened upon: notwithstanding through unbelief and the temptations of Satan and the sensible sight of the light and love of God may for a time be clouded and obscured from them, yet his is still the same, and they shall be sure to be kept by the power of God unto their purchased possession, they being engraven upon the palms of his hands and their names having been written in the book of life from all eternity.

2. This perseverance of the saints depends not upon their own free will; but upon the immutability of the decree of election,

flowing from the free and unchangeable love of God the Father; upon the efficacy of the merit and intercession of Jesus Christ and union with him, the oath of God, the abiding of his Spirit, and the seed of God within them, and the nature of the covenant of grace from all which ariseth; also the certainty and infallibility thereof.

3. And though they may—through the temptation of Satan and of the world, the prevalency of corruption remaining in them, and the neglect of the means of their preservation—fall into grievous sins, and for a time continue therein (whereby they incur God's displeasure and grieve his Holy Spirit, come to have their graces and comforts impaired, have their hearts hardened and their consciences wounded, hurt and scandalize others, and bring temporal judgments upon themselves), yet they shall renew their repentance and be preserved through faith in Christ Jesus to the end.

XVIII. Of the Assurance of Grace and Salvation

1. Although temporary believers and other unregenerate men may vainly deceive themselves with false hopes and carnal presumptions of being in the favor of God and in a state of salvation, which hope of theirs shall perish, yet such as truly believe in the Lord Jesus and love him in sincerity, endeavoring to walk in all good conscience before him, may in this life be certainly assured that they are in the state of grace, and may rejoice in the hope of the glory of God, which hope shall never make them ashamed.

2. This certainty is not a bare conjectural and probable persuasion grounded upon a fallible hope, but an infallible assurance of faith founded on the blood and righteousness of Christ revealed in the gospel, and also upon the inward evidence of those graces of the Spirit unto which promises are made and on the testimony of the spirit of adoption, witnessing with our spirits that we are the children of God, and as a fruit thereof keeping the heart both humble and holy.

3. This infallible assurance doth not so belong to the essence of faith but that a true believer may wait long and conflict with many difficulties before he be partaker of it; yet, being enabled by the Spirit to know the things which are freely given him of God, he may without extraordinary revelation in the right use of means attain thereunto; and therefore it is the duty of everyone to give all

diligence to make their calling and election sure, that thereby his heart may be enlarged in peace and joy in the Holy Spirit, in love and thankfulness to God, and in strength and cheerfulness in the duties of obedience, the proper fruits of this assurance; so far is it from inclining men to looseness.

4. True believers may have the assurance of their salvation divers ways shaken, diminished, and intermitted; as by negligence in preserving of it, by falling into some special sin which woundeth the conscience and grieveth the spirit, by some sudden or vehement temptation, by God's withdrawing the light of his countenance and suffering even such as fear him to walk in darkness and to have no light; yet are they never destitute of the seed of God and life of faith, that love of Christ and the brethren, that sincerity of heart and conscience of duty out of which by the operation of the Spirit this assurance may in due time be revived, and by which in the meantime they are preserved from utter despair.

XIX. Of the Law of God

1. God gave to Adam a law of universal obedience, written in his heart, and a particular precept of not eating the fruit of the tree of knowledge of good and evil; by which he bound him and all his posterity to personal, entire, exact, and perpetual obedience; promised life upon the fulfilling and threatened death upon the breach of it, and endued him with power and ability to keep it.

2. The same law that was first written in the heart of man continued to be a perfect rule of righteousness after the fall, and was delivered by God upon Mount Sinai in Ten Commandments and written in two tables; the four first containing our duty towards God, and the other six our duty to man.

3. Besides this law, commonly called moral, God was pleased to give to the People Israel ceremonial laws, containing several typical ordinances, partly of worship (prefiguring Christ, his graces, actions, sufferings, and benefits), and partly holding forth divers instructions of moral duties; all which ceremonial laws, being appointed only to the time of reformation are by Jesus Christ (the true messiah and only lawgiver, who was furnished with power from the Father for that end) abrogate and taken away.

4. To them also he gave sundry judicial laws which expired

together with the state of that people, not obliging and now (by virtue of that institution) their general equity only being of moral use.

5. The moral law doth forever bind all, justified persons as well as others, to the obedience thereof, and that not only in regard of the matter contained in it, but also in respect of the authority of God the Creator, who gave it. Neither doth Christ in the gospel any way dissolve, but much strengthen this obligation.

6. Although true believers be not under the law as a covenant of works, to be thereby justified or condemned, yet it is of great use to them as well as to others, in that (as a rule of life informing them of the will of God and their duty) it directs and binds them to walk accordingly, discovering also the sinful pollutions of their natures, hearts, and lives; so, as examining themselves thereby, they may come to further conviction of, humiliation for, and hatred against sin, together with a clearer sight of the need they have of Christ and the perfection of his obedience. It is likewise of use to the regenerate to restrain their corruptions, in that it forbids sins, and the threatenings of it serve to show what even their sins deserve and what afflictions in this life they may expect for them, although freed from the curse and unallayed rigor thereof. The promises of it likewise show them God's approbation of obedience and what blessings they may expect upon the performance thereof, though not as due to them by the law as a covenant of works; so a man's doing good and refraining from evil, because the law encourageth to the one and deterreth from the other, is no evidence of his being under the law and not under grace.

7. Neither are the aforementioned uses of the law contrary to the grace of the gospel, but do sweetly comply with it; the Spirit of Christ subduing and enabling the will of man to do that freely and cheerfully which the will of God, revealed in the law, requireth to be done.

XX. Of the Gospel, and of the Extent of the Grace Thereof

1. The covenant of works being broken by sin and made unprofitable unto life, God was pleased to give forth the promise of Christ, the seed of the woman, as the means of calling the elect and begetting in them faith and repentance; in this promise, the gospel,

as to the substance of it, was revealed and therein effectual for the conversion and salvation of sinners.

2. This promise of Christ, and salvation by him, is revealed only by the Word of God; neither do the works of creation or providence, with the light of nature, make discovery of Christ or of grace by him, so much as in a general or obscure way; much less that men destitute of the revelation of him by the promise or gospel should be enabled thereby to attain saving faith or repentance.

3. The revelation of the gospel unto sinners, made in divers times and by sundry parts (with the addition of promises and precepts for the obedience required therein, as to the nations and persons to whom it is granted) is merely of the sovereign will and good pleasure of God, not being annexed by virtue of any promise to the due improvement of men's natural abilities by virtue of common light received without it, which none ever did make or can so do; and therefore in all ages the preaching of the gospel hath been granted unto persons and nations as to the extent or straightening of it, in great variety, according to the counsel of the will of God.

4. Although the gospel be the only outward means of revealing Christ and saving grace, and is, as such, abundantly sufficient thereunto, yet—that men who are dead in trespasses may be born again, quickened or regenerated—there is moreover necessary an effectual, insuperable work of the Holy Spirit upon the whole soul for the producing in them a new spiritual life, without which no other means will effect their conversion unto God.

XXI. Of Christian Liberty and Liberty of Conscience

1. The liberty which Christ hath purchased for believers under the gospel consists in their freedom from the guilt of sin, the condemning wrath of God, the rigor and curse of the law, and in their being delivered from this present evil world, bondage to Satan, and dominion of sin; from the evil of afflictions, the fear and sting of death, the victory of the grave, and everlasting damnation; as also in their free access to God and their yielding obedience unto him, not out of a slavish fear, but a childlike love and willing mind.

All which were common also to believers under the law for the substance of them, but under the New Testament the liberty of Christians is further enlarged in their freedom from the yoke of the ceremonial law to which the Jewish church was subjected, and in greater boldness of access to the throne of grace and in fuller communications of the free spirit of God than believers under the law did ordinarily partake of.

2. God alone is Lord of the conscience and hath left it free from the doctrines and commandments of men which are in any thing contrary to his word or not contained in it. So that to believe such doctrines or obey such commands out of conscience is to betray true liberty of conscience, and the requiring of an implicit faith and absolute and blind obedience is to destroy liberty of conscience and reason, also.

3. They who, upon pretense of Christian liberty, do practice any sin or cherish any sinful lust: As they do thereby pervert the main design of the grace of the gospel to their own destruction, so they wholly destroy the end of Christian liberty, which is that being delivered out of the hands of all our enemies we might serve the Lord without fear in holiness and righteousness before him all the days of our life.

XXII. Of Religious Worship and the Sabbath Day

1. The light of nature shows that there is a God who hath lordship and sovereignty over all, is just, good, and doth good unto all, and is therefore to be feared, loved, praised, called upon, trusted in, and served with all the heart, and all the soul, and with all the might. But the acceptable way of worshiping the true God is instituted by himself, and so limited by his own revealed will that he may not be worshiped according to the imaginations and devices of men or the suggestions of Satan under any visible representations or any other way not prescribed in the Holy Scriptures.

2. Religious worship is to be given to God the Father, Son, and Holy Spirit, and to him alone; not to angels, saints, or any other creatures; and, since the fall, not without a mediator, nor in the mediation of any other but Christ alone.

3. Prayer with thanksgiving, being one special part of natural worship, is by God required of all men. But, that it may be accepted, it is to be made in the name of the Son, by the help of the Spirit, according to his will; with understanding, reverence, humility, fervency, faith, love, and perseverance, and, when with others, in a known tongue.

4. Prayer is to be made for things lawful and for all sorts of men living or that shall live hereafter, but not for the dead, nor for those of whom it may be known that they have sinned the sin unto death.

5. The reading of the Scriptures, preaching and hearing the Word of God, teaching and admonishing one another in psalms, hymns, and spiritual songs, singing with grace in our hearts to the Lord—as also the administration of baptism, and the Lord's Supper—are all parts of religious worship of God to be performed in obedience to him with understanding, faith, reverence, and godly fear; moreover, solemn humiliation, with fastings, and thanksgiving upon special occasions, ought to be used in a holy and religious manner.

6. Neither prayer, nor any other part of religious worship is now under the gospel tied unto or made more acceptable by any place in which it is performed or toward which it is directed; but God is to be worshiped everywhere in spirit and in truth; as in private families daily and in secret each one by himself, so more solemnly in the public assemblies, which are not carelessly nor willfully to be neglected or forsaken when God by his word or providence calleth thereunto.

7. As it is of the law of nature that in general a proportion of time by God's appointment be set apart for the worship of God, so by his Word, in a positive moral and perpetual commandment binding all men in all ages, he hath particularly appointed one day in seven for a Sabbath to be kept holy unto him, which from the beginning of the world to the resurrection of Christ was the last day of the week, and from the resurrection of Christ was changed into the first day of the week which is called the Lord's day, and is to be continued to the end of the world as the Christian Sabbath, the observation of the last day of the week being abolished.

8. The Sabbath is then kept holy unto the Lord, when men after a due preparing of their hearts and ordering their common affairs aforehand do not only observe a holy rest all the day from their own works, words, and thoughts about their worldly employment and recreations, but also are taken up the whole time in the public and private exercises of his worship and in the duties of necessity and mercy.

XXIII. Of Singing Psalms, Etc.

We believe that singing the praises of God is a holy ordinance of Christ and not a part of natural religion or a moral duty only, but that it is brought under divine institution (it being enjoined on the churches of Christ to sing psalms, hymns, and spiritual songs), and that the whole church in their public assemblies, as well as private Christians, ought to sing God's praises according to the best light they have received. Moreover, it was practiced in the great representative church by our Lord Jesus Christ with his disciples, after he had instituted and celebrated the sacred ordinance of his Holy Supper as a commemorative token of redeeming love.

XXIV. Of Lawful Oaths and Vows

1. A lawful oath is a part of religious worship, wherein the person swearing in truth, righteousness, and judgment, solemnly calleth God to witness what he sweareth and to judge him according to the truth or falseness thereof.

2. The name of God only is that by which men ought to swear, and therein it is to be used with all holy fear and reverence; therefore to swear vainly or rashly by that glorious, and dreadful name, or to swear at all by any other thing, is sinful and to be abhorred; yet, as in matter of weight and moment for confirmation of truth and ending all strife an oath is warranted by the word of God, so a lawful oath, being imposed by lawful authority in such matters, ought to be taken.

3. Whosoever taketh an oath warranted by the word of God, ought duly to consider the weightiness of so solemn an act and therein to avouch nothing but what he knoweth to be the truth, for that by rash, false, and vain oaths the Lord is provoked, and for them this land mourns.

4. An oath is to be taken in the plain and common sense of the words, without equivocation or mental reservation.

5. A vow, which is not to be made to any creature, but to God alone, is to be made and performed with all religious care and faithfulness, but Popish monastical vows of perpetual single life, professed poverty, and regular obedience are so far from being decrees of higher perfection that they are superstitious and sinful snares in which no Christian may entangle himself.

XXV. Of the Civil Magistrate

1. God, the supreme Lord and King of all the world, hath ordained civil magistrates to be under him, over the people, for his own glory and the public good; and to this end hath armed them with the power of the sword for defense and encouragement of them that do good and for the punishment of evildoers.

2. It is lawful for Christians to accept and execute the office of a magistrate when called thereunto, in the management whereof, as they ought especially to maintain justice and peace according to the wholesome laws of each kingdom and commonwealth, so for that end they may lawfully now under the New Testament wage war upon just and necessary occasions.

3. Civil magistrates being set up by God for the ends aforesaid, subjection in all lawful things commanded by them ought to be yielded by us in the Lord, not only for wrath but for conscience' sake; and we ought to make supplications and prayers for kings and all that are in authority, that under them we may live a quiet and peaceable life in all godliness and honesty.

XXVI. Of Marriage

1. Marriage is to be between one man and one woman; neither is it lawful for any man to have more than one wife, nor for any woman to have more than one husband at the same time.

2. Marriage was ordained for the mutual help of husband and wife, for the increase of mankind, with a legitimate issue, and for preventing of uncleanliness.

3. It is lawful for all sorts of people to marry who are able with judgment to give their consent; yet it is the duty of Christians to marry in the Lord, and therefore such as profess the true religion should not marry with infidels or idolators; neither should such as are godly be unequally yoked by marrying with such as are wicked, in their life, or maintain damnable heresy.

4. Marriage ought not to be within the degrees of consanguinity or affinity forbidden in the Word; nor can such incestuous marriage ever be made lawful by any law of man or consent of parties, so as those persons may live together as man and wife.

XXVII. Of the Church

1. The catholic or universal church, which (with respect to

internal work of the spirit and truth of grace) may be called invisible, consists of the whole number of the elect, that have been, are, or shall be gathered into one, under Christ the head thereof; and is the spouse, the body, the fullness of him that filleth all in all.

2. All persons throughout the world, professing the faith of the gospel and obedience unto God by Christ according unto it, not destroying their own profession by any errors everting the foundation or unholiness of conversation, are and may be called visible saints; and of such ought all particular congregations to be constituted.

3. The purest churches under heaven are subject to mixture and error, and some have so degenerated as to become no churches of Christ, but synagogues of Satan; nevertheless Christ always hath had and ever shall have a kingdom in this world, to the end thereof, of such as believe in him and make profession of his name.

4. The Lord Jesus is the head of the church, in whom by the appointment of the Father all power for the calling, institution, order, or government of the church is invested in a supreme and sovereign manner; neither can the Pope of Rome in any sense be head thereof, but is that Antichrist, that man of sin and son of perdition that exalteth himself in the church against Christ and all that is called God, whom the Lord shall destroy with the brightness of his coming.

5. In the execution of his power wherewith he is so entrusted, the Lord Jesus calleth out of the world unto himself through the ministry of his word, by his Spirit, those that are given unto him by his Father, that they may walk before him in all ways of obedience which he prescribeth to them in his Word. Those thus called he commandeth to walk together in particular societies or churches for their mutual edification and the due performance of that public worship which he requireth of them in the world.

6. The members of these churches are saints by calling, visibly manifesting and evidencing (in and by their profession and walking) their obedience unto that call of Christ, and do willingly consent to walk together according to the appointment of Christ, giving up themselves to the Lord and one to another by the will of God, in professed subjection to the ordinances of the gospel.

7. To each of these churches thus gathered according to his mind,

declared in his Word, he hath given all that power and authority which is any way needful for their carrying on that order in worship and discipline which he hath instituted for them to observe, with commands and rules for the due and right exerting and executing of that power.

8. A particular church gathered and completely organized according to the mind of Christ consists of officers and members; and the officers appointed by Christ—to be chosen and set apart by the church (so called and gathered) for the peculiar administration of ordinances and execution of power or duty which he entrusts them with or calls them to, to be continued to the end of the world—are bishops or elders and deacons.

9. The way appointed by Christ for the calling of any person, fitted and gifted by the Holy Spirit, unto the office of bishop or elder in a church is that he be chosen thereunto by the common suffrage of the church itself, and solemnly set apart by fasting and prayer, with imposition of hands of the eldership of the church (if there be any before constituted therein); and of a deacon that he be chosen by the like suffrage and set apart by prayer and the like imposition of hands.

10. The work of pastors being constantly to attend the service of Christ in his churches in the ministry of the word and prayer, with watching for their souls as they that must give an account to him, it is incumbent on the churches to whom they minister not only to give them all due respect but also to communicate to them of all their good things according to their ability, so as they may have a comfortable supply without being themselves entangled in secular affairs, and may also be capable of exercising hospitality towards others; and this is required by the law of nature and by the express order of our Lord Jesus who hath ordained that they that preach the gospel should live of the gospel.

11. Although it be incumbent on the bishops or pastors of the churches to be instant in preaching the Word by way of office, yet the work of preaching the Word is not so peculiarly confined to them, but that others also gifted and fitted by the Holy Spirit for it, and approved and called by the church, may and ought to perform it.

12. As all believers are bound to join themselves to particular

churches, when and where they have opportunity so to do, so all that are admitted unto the privileges of a church are also under the censures and government thereof, according to the rule of Christ.

13. No church members upon any offense taken by them, having performed their duty required of them toward the person they are offended at, ought to disturb any church order or absent themselves from the assemblies of the church or administration of any ordinances, upon the account of such offense at any of their fellow members, but to wait upon Christ in the further proceeding of the church.

14. As each church and all the members of it are bound to pray continually for the good and prosperity of all the churches of Christ in all places, and upon all occasions to further it (every one within the bounds of their places and callings, in the exercise of their gifts and graces), so the churches (when planted by the providence of God so as they may enjoy opportunity and advantage for it) ought to hold communion amongst themselves for their peace, increase of love, and mutual edification.

15. In cases of difficulties or differences, either in point of doctrine or administration, wherein either the churches in general are concerned or any one church in their peace, union, and edification—or any member or members of any church are injured, in or by any proceedings in censures not agreeable to truth and order—it is according to the mind of Christ that many churches holding communion together do by their messengers meet to consider and give their advice in or about that matter in difference to be reported to all the churches concerned; howbeit, these messengers assembled are not entrusted with any church power properly so called, or with any jurisdiction over the churches themselves, to exercise any censures either over any churches or persons, or to impose their determination on the churches or officers.

XXVIII. On the Communion of Saints

1. All saints that are united to Jesus Christ their head by his spirit and faith, although they are not made thereby one person with him, have fellowship in his graces, sufferings, death, resurrection, and glory; and, being united to one another in love, they have communion in each other's gifts and graces, and are obliged to the performance

of such duties, public and private, in an orderly way as do conduce to their mutual good, both in the inward and the outward man.

2. Saints by profession are bound to maintain a holy fellowship and communion in the worship of God and in performing such other spiritual services as tend to their mutual edification, as also in relieving each other in outward things according to their several abilities and necessities; which communion (according to the rule of the gospel, though especially to be exercised by them in the relations wherein they stand whether in families or churches, yet as God offereth opportunity) is to be extended to all the household of faith, even all those who in every place call upon the name of the Lord Jesus; nevertheless their communion one with another as saints doth not take away or infringe the title or propriety which each man hath in his goods and possessions.

XXIX. Of Baptism and the Lord's Supper

1. Baptism and the Lord's Supper are ordinances of positive and sovereign institution, appointed by the Lord Jesus, the only lawgiver, to be continued in his church to the end of the world.

2. These holy appointments are to be administered by those only who are qualified and thereunto called according to the commission of Christ.

XXX. Of Baptism

1. Baptism is an ordinance of the New Testament, ordained by Jesus Christ, to be unto the party baptized a sign of his fellowship with him in his death and resurrection; of his being engrafted into him, of remission of sins, and of his giving up unto God through Jesus Christ to live and walk in newness of life.

2. Those who do actually profess repentance towards God, faith in and obedience to our Lord Jesus, are the only proper subjects of this ordinance.

3. The outward element to be used in this ordinance is water, wherein the party is to be baptized in the name of the Father and of the Son and of the Holy Spirit.

4. Immersion, or dipping of the person in water, is necessary to the due administration of this ordinance.

XXXI. Of Laying On of Hands

We believe that laying on of hands (with prayer) upon baptized believers, as such, is an ordinance of Christ, and ought to be submitted unto by all such persons that are admitted to partake of the Lord's Supper; and that the end of this ordinance is not for the extraordinary gifts of the Spirit but for a further reception of the Holy Spirit of promise or for the addition of the graces of the Spirit and the influences thereof, to confirm, strengthen, and comfort them in Christ Jesus, it being ratified and established by the extraordinary gifts of the Spirit in the primitive times, to abide in the church. As meeting together on the first day of the week was (that being the day of worship, or Christian Sabbath, under the gospel), and as preaching the Word was, and as baptism was, and prayer was, and singing Psalms, etc. was, so this of laying on of hands was; for as the whole gospel was confirmed by signs and wonders and divers miracles and gifts of the Holy Ghost in general, so was every ordinance in like manner confirmed in particular.

XXXII. Of the Lord's Supper

1. The Supper of the Lord Jesus was instituted by him, the same night wherein he was betrayed, to be observed in his churches unto the end of the world, for the perpetual remembrance and showing forth the sacrifice in his death, confirmation of the faith of believers in all the benefits thereof, their spiritual nourishment and growth in him, their further engagement in and to all duties which they owe unto him, and to be a bond and pledge of their communion with him and each other.

2. In this ordinance Christ is not offered up to his Father, nor any real sacrifice made at all for remission of sin of the quick or dead, but only a memorial of that one offering up of himself, by himself, upon the cross, once for all, and a spiritual oblation of all possible praise unto God for the same; so that the Popish sacrifice of the Mass (as they call it) is most abominable, injurious to Christ's own sacrifice, the alone propitiation for all the sins of the elect.

3. The Lord Jesus hath in this ordinance appointed his ministers to pray and bless the elements of bread and wine, and thereby to set them apart from a common to a holy use; and to take and break the

bread, to take the cup, and (they communicating also themselves) to give both to the communicants.

4. The denial of the cup to the people, worshiping the elements, the lifting them up, or carrying them about for adoration, and reserving them for any pretended religious use are all contrary to the nature of this ordinance and to the institution of Christ.

5. The outward elements in this ordinance, duly set apart to the uses ordained by Christ, have such relation to him crucified as that truly (although in terms used figuratively) they are sometimes called by the name of the things they represent, to wit body and blood of Christ; albeit in substance and nature they still remain truly and only bread and wine, as they were before.

6. That doctrine which maintains a change of the substance of bread and wine into the substance of Christ's body and blood (commonly called transubstantiation) by consecration of a priest, or by any other way, is repugnant not to Scripture alone, but even to common sense and reason, overthroweth the nature of the ordinance, and hath been and is the cause of manifold superstitions, yea, of gross idolatries.

7. Worthy receivers, outwardly partaking of the visible elements in this ordinance, do then also inwardly by faith really and indeed, yet not carnally and corporally but spiritually, receive and feed upon Christ crucified and all the benefits of his death: the body and blood of Christ, being then not corporally or carnally, but spiritually present to the faith of believers in that ordinance, as the elements themselves are to their outward senses.

8. All ignorant and ungodly persons, as they are unfit to enjoy communion with Christ, so are they unworthy of the Lord's Table and cannot without great sin against him, while they remain such, partake of these holy mysteries or be admitted thereunto: yea whosoever shall receive unworthily are guilty of the body and blood of the Lord, eating and drinking judgment to themselves.

XXXIII. Of the State of Man after Death and of the Resurrection of the Dead

1. The bodies of men after death return to dust and see corruption, but their souls (which neither die nor sleep), having an immortal subsistence, immediately return to God who gave them; the souls

of the righteous, being then made perfect in holiness, are received into paradise where they are with Christ and behold the face of God in light and glory, waiting for the full redemption of their bodies; and the souls of the wicked are cast into hell where they remain in torment and utter darkness, reserved to the judgment of the great day; besides these two places for souls separated from their bodies, the Scripture acknowledgeth none.

2. At the last day, such of the saints as are found alive shall not sleep but be changed, and all the dead shall be raised up with the selfsame bodies and none other, although with different qualities, which shall be united again to their souls forever.

3. The bodies of the unjust shall by the power of Christ be raised to dishonor; the bodies of the just by his spirit into honor, and be made comfortable to his own glorious body.

XXXIV. Of the Last Judgment

1. God hath appointed a day wherein he will judge the world in righteousness by Jesus Christ, to whom all power and judgment is given of the Father; in which day not only the apostate angels shall be judged, but likewise all persons that have lived upon the earth shall appear before the tribunal of Christ to give an account of their thoughts, words, and deeds, and to receive according to what they have done in the body, whether good or evil.

2. The end of God's appointing this day is for the manifestation of the glory of his mercy in the eternal salvation of the elect, and of his justice in the eternal damnation of the reprobate, who are wicked and disobedient; for then shall the righteous go into everlasting life and receive that fullness of joy and glory, with everlasting reward in the presence of the Lord; but the wicked, who know not God and obey not the gospel of Jesus Christ, shall be cast into eternal torments and punished with everlasting destruction, from the presence of the Lord and from the glory of his power.

3. As Christ would have us to be certainly persuaded that there shall be a day of judgment, both to deter all men from sin and for the greater consolation of the godly in their adversity, so will he have that day unknown to men, that they may shake off all carnal security and be always watchful, because they know not at what

hour the Lord will come; and may ever be prepared to say, "Come, Lord Jesus, Come quickly, Amen."

The New Hampshire Confession

The New Hampshire Confession was of slow growth, as most enduring standard documents have been. Its origin dates back to 1830, when the New Hampshire Baptist State Convention, holding its session at Concord, June 24, authorized the preparation of a "declaration of faith" that might secure the approval and serve the purpose of all the Baptist churches in that state. The proposition met with general approval, and a committee of three was appointed to do the work, and report. As the convention met only annually the matter was finally referred to the board. The committee underwent various changes, and it was not until 1833, after many modifications from the first draft, that the "Declaration" was approved, article by article, and unanimously adopted as their standard of faith.

When, in 1889, Hiscox was contemplating the preparation of a new and much enlarged edition of the *Baptist Church Directory*— or, rather, a new and larger work on the same plan—he sought in vain for definite information as to the origin of the New Hampshire Confession. It has been generally supposed that the late Rev. J. Newton Brown, D.D., was the author, as it was known he held some connection with its preparation and had in more recent years issued a copy under his own name.

As first published, there were sixteen articles. Subsequently Dr. Brown added two: one on repentance and faith, and one on sanctification. When Hiscox prepared them for his *Standard Manual* in 1890, he divided the article on baptism and the Lord's Supper, making two, and increasing the number to nineteen. Some verbal changes were also made, which seemed to be improvements, and a few of the proof texts, which did not appear pertinent, were omitted. For the *New Directory* a further change was made by dividing the article on repentance and faith, giving one to each subject, and adding an article on adoption, which seems to deserve a place in such a document. It is to be noted, however, that none of these changes have modified, or in any way altered, the doctrinal substance or teaching of the confession.

Text of the New Hampshire Confession

I. The Scriptures

We believe that the Holy Bible was written by men divinely inspired, and is a perfect treasure of heavenly instruction; that it has God for its author, salvation for its end, and truth without any mixture of error for its matter; that it reveals the principles by which God will judge us; and therefore is, and shall remain to the end of the world, the true center of Christian union, and the supreme standard by which all human conduct, creeds, and opinions should be tried.

II. The True God

We believe the Scriptures teach that there is one, and only one, living and true God, an infinite, intelligent Spirit, whose name is Jehovah, the Maker and Supreme Ruler of heaven and earth; inexpressibly glorious in holiness, and worthy of all possible honor, confidence and love; that in the unity of the Godhead there are three persons, the Father, the Son, and the Holy Ghost; equal in every divine perfection, and executing distinct but harmonious offices in the great work of redemption.

III. The Fall of Man

We believe the Scriptures teach that man was created in holiness, under the law of his Maker; but by voluntary transgression fell from that holy and happy state; in consequence of which all mankind are now sinners, not by constraint but choice; being by nature utterly void of that holiness required by the law of God, positively inclined to evil; and therefore under just condemnation to eternal ruin, without defense or excuse.

IV. God's Purpose of Grace

We believe the Scriptures teach that *election* is the eternal purpose of God, according to which he graciously regenerates, sanctifies and saves sinners; that being perfectly consistent with the free agency of man, it comprehends all the means in connection with the end; that it is a most glorious display of God's sovereign goodness, being infinitely free, wise, holy, and unchangeable; that it utterly excludes boasting, and promotes humility, love, prayer, praise, trust in God, and active imitation of his free mercy; that it encourages the use of means in the highest degree; that it may be ascertained by its effects in all who truly believe the Gospel; that it is the foundation of Christian assurance; and that to ascertain it with regard to ourselves demands and deserves the utmost diligence.

V. The Way of Salvation

We believe the Scriptures teach that the salvation of sinners is wholly of grace; through the mediatorial offices of the Son of God; who according to the will of the Father, assumed our nature, yet without sin; honored the divine law by his personal obedience, and by his death made a full atonement for our sins; that having risen from the dead, he is now enthroned in heaven; and uniting in his wonderful person the tenderest sympathies with divine perfections, he is every way qualified to be a suitable, a compassionate and an all-sufficient Savior.

VI. Of Regeneration

We believe the Scriptures teach that *regeneration*, or the new birth, is that change wrought in the soul by the Holy Spirit, by which a new nature and a spiritual life, not before possessed, are imparted, and the person becomes a new creation in Christ Jesus; a holy disposition is given to the mind, the will subdued, the dominion of sin broken, and the affections changed from a love of sin and self, to a love of holiness and God; the change is instantaneous, effected solely by the power of God, in a manner incomprehensible to reason; the evidence of it is found in a changed disposition of mind, the fruits of righteousness, and a newness of life. And without it salvation is impossible.

VII. Of Repentance

We believe the Scriptures teach that repentance is a personal act, prompted by the Spirit; and consists in a godly sorrow for sin, as offensive to God and ruinous to the soul; that it is accompanied with great humiliation in view of one's sin and guilt, together with prayer for pardon; also by sincere hatred of sin, and persistent turning away from, and abandonment of, all that is evil and unholy. Since none are sinless in this life, repentance needs to be often repeated.

VIII. Of Faith

We believe the Scriptures teach that *faith*, as an evangelical grace wrought by the Spirit, is the medium through which Christ is received by the soul as its sacrifice and Savior. It is an assent of the mind and a consent of the heart, consisting mainly of belief and trust; the testimony of God is implicitly accepted and believed as true, while Christ is unreservedly trusted for salvation; by it the believer is brought into vital relations with God, freely justified, and lives as seeing him who is invisible. Faith cannot save, but it reveals Christ to the soul as a willing and sufficient Savior, and commits the heart and life to him.

IX. Of Justification

We believe the Scriptures teach that the great Gospel blessing which Christ secures to such as believe in Him is *justification*; that justification includes the pardon of sin, and the promise of eternal life on principles of righteousness; that it is bestowed, not in consideration of any works of righteousness which we have done, but solely through faith in the Redeemer's blood; by virtue of which faith his perfect righteousness is freely imputed to us of God; that it brings us into a state of most blessed peace and favor with God, and secures every other blessing needful for time and eternity.

X. Of Adoption

We believe the Scriptures teach that *adoption* is a gracious act, by which the Father, for the sake of Christ, accepts believers to the estate and condition of children, by a new and spiritual birth; sending the Spirit of adoption into their hearts, whereby they become members of the family of God, and entitled to all the rights, privileges, and promises of children; and if children, then heirs, heirs of God, and joint-heirs with Jesus Christ, to the heritage of saints on earth, and an inheritance reserved in heaven for them.

XI. Of Sanctification

We believe the Scriptures teach that sanctification is the process by which, according to the will of God, we are made partakers of his holiness; that it is a progressive work; that it is begun in regeneration; that it is carried on in the hearts of believers by the presence and power of the Holy Spirit, the Sealer and Comforter, in the continual use of the appointed means—especially the Word of God, self-examination, self-denial, watchfulness, and prayer;

and in the practice of all godly exercises and duties.

XII. The Perseverance of Saints

We believe the Scriptures teach that such as are truly regenerate, being born of the Spirit, will not utterly fall away and finally perish, but will endure unto the end; that their persevering attachment to Christ is the grand mark which distinguishes them from superficial professors; that a special Providence watches over their welfare; and they are kept by the power of God through faith unto salvation.

XIII. The Law and the Gospel

We believe the Scriptures teach that the Law of God is the eternal and unchangeable rule of his moral government; that it is holy, just, and good; and that the inability which the Scriptures ascribe to fallen men to fulfill its precepts arises entirely from their sinful nature; to deliver them from which, and to restore them through a Mediator to unfeigned obedience to the holy Law, is one great end of the Gospel, and of the means of grace connected with the establishment of the invisible Church.

XIV. A Gospel Church

We believe the Scriptures teach that a visible Church of Christ is a congregation of baptized believers, associated by covenant in the faith and fellowship of the Gospel; observing the ordinances of Christ; governed by his laws; and exercising the gifts, rights, and privileges invested in them by his word; that its only scriptural officers are bishops or pastors and deacons, whose qualifications, claims, and duties are defined in the Epistles to Timothy and Titus.

XV. Christian Baptism

We believe the Scriptures teach that Christian Baptism is the immersion in water of a believer in Christ, in the name of the Father, and Son, and Holy Ghost; to show forth, in a solemn and beautiful emblem, our faith in the crucified, buried, and risen Savior, with its effect, in our death to sin and resurrection to a new life; that it is prerequisite to the privileges of a church relation, and to the Lord's Supper.

XVI. The Lord's Supper

We believe the Scriptures teach that the Lord's Supper is a provision of bread and wine, as symbols of Christ's body and blood, partaken of by the members of the Church, in commemoration of the suffering and death of their Lord; showing their faith and participation in the merits of his sacrifice, and their hope of eternal life through his resurrection from the dead; its observance to be preceded by faithful self-examination.

XVII. The Christian Sabbath

We believe the Scriptures teach that the first day of the week is the Lord's Day; and is to be kept sacred to religious purposes, by abstaining from all secular labor, except works of mercy and necessity, by the devout observance of all the means of grace, both private and public; and by preparation for that rest that remaineth for the people of God.

XVIII. Civil Government

We believe the Scriptures teach that civil government is of divine appointment, for the interest and good order of human society; and that magistrates are to be prayed for, conscientiously honored and obeyed, except only in things opposed to the will of our Lord Jesus Christ, who is the only Lord of the conscience, and the Prince of the kings of the earth. But that civil rulers have no rights of control over, or of interference with, religious matters.

XIX. Righteous and Wicked

We believe the Scriptures teach that there is a radical and essential difference between the righteous and the wicked; that such only as through faith are justified in the name of the Lord Jesus, and sanctified by the Spirit of our God, are truly righteous in his esteem; while all such as continue in impenitence and unbelief are, in his sight, wicked and under the curse; and this distinction holds among men both in this life and after death.

XX. The World to Come

We believe the Scriptures teach that the end of the world is approaching; that at the last day, Christ will descend from heaven, and raise the dead from the grave for final retribution; that a solemn separation will then take place; that the wicked will be adjudged to endless sorrow, and the righteous to endless joy; and this judgment will fix forever the final state of men in heaven or hell, on principles of righteousness.

Covenant

Having been, as we trust, brought by divine grace to embrace the Lord Jesus Christ, and to give ourselves wholly to him, we do now solemnly and joyfully covenant with each other, to walk together in him, with brotherly love, to his glory, as our common Lord. We do, therefore, in his strength, engage—

That we will exercise a Christian care and watchfulness over each other, and faithfully warn, exhort, and admonish each other as occasion may require:

That we will not forsake the assembling of ourselves together, but will uphold the public worship of God, and the ordinances of his house:

That we will not omit closet [private] and family religion at home, nor neglect the great duty of religiously training our children, and those under our care, for the service of Christ, and the enjoyment of heaven:

That, as we are the light of the world, and salt of the earth, we will seek divine aid to enable us to deny ungodliness, and every worldly lust, and to walk circumspectly in the world, that we may win the souls of men:

That we will cheerfully contribute of our property, according as God has prospered us, for the maintenance of a faithful and evangelical ministry among us, for the support of the poor, and to spread the Gospel over the earth:

That we will in all conditions, even till death, strive to live to the glory of him who hath called us out of darkness into his marvelous light.

"And may the God of Peace, who brought again from the dead our Lord Jesus, that great shepherd of the sheep, through the blood of the everlasting covenant, make us perfect in every good work, to do his will, working in us that which is well pleasing in his sight through Jesus Christ; to whom be glory, forever and ever. Amen."

NOTES

1. Erastians were followers of Erastus, a German divine and physician of the sixteenth century, who taught that the church ought to be wholly dependent on the state for its support, government, and discipline.

A Treatise on Baptism

Introductory Comments

No issue or practice has been at the center of Baptist definition more consistently than the Baptist means and circumstances of the rite of baptism. This is ironic, in part, because the earliest Baptists focused on other concerns in their original formation, notably the independence of the local congregation, the priesthood of individual believers, and issues of taxation, church support, persecution by the state, and similar matters.

Nevertheless, baptism by immersion soon became a Baptist hallmark, and the name "Baptists" was derived from that practice. Soon debate among Baptists on this issue became heated (and continues in some form until now), and defense of the practice by Baptists has often been an important means of defining Baptist distinctives.

The following treatise on Baptism has been constructed from several writings by Hiscox, most significantly from a condensation of chapters XV and XVII of *The New Directory for Baptist Churches*. Other Hiscox writings and publications provided materials for clarification and revision of that primary source. The following material is included here as a classic Baptist apologia for baptism by immersion. The modern reader will note its thoroughness, detail, passion, and, occasionally, its polemical style.

A Treatise on Baptism

Part I. The Form of Baptism

The subject of baptism constitutes one of the primary points of discussion between Baptists and other Christian denominations, with reference to the form and uses of that ordinance. The following propositions set forth the Baptist position on the form of baptism:

1. The baptism that John administered, Jesus received and enjoined, and the apostles practiced was immersion, a dipping, an entire submergence of the person baptized, in water, on a profession of repentance and faith in Christ.

2. The same baptism of immersion was used by the apostles and the disciples of our Lord and by the primitive churches, without any known exception, for more than two hundred years after Christ.

3. The first recorded departure from the practice of immersion of baptism was about A.D. 250, in the case of Novatian, who received pouring on his sickbed, being, as was supposed, incapable of baptism.

4. From this time pouring, or sprinkling, for baptism was occasionally resorted to as a substitute, and in cases of sick persons, called clinic baptism.

5. For more than thirteen hundred years immersion was the prevailing practice of Christian churches throughout the world in the administration of baptism.

6. The Greek and other oriental churches have never abandoned the primitive mode but still practice immersion, whether in the case of adults or of infants, in all climates and at all seasons of the year.

7. The substitution of sprinkling for immersion was one of the corruptions of the papal church, transmitted to, and accepted by, the Protestant Christians in later times.

8. After the Reformation, sprinkling for baptism came into general use among Protestant Christians in Europe, by whom it was transmitted to Protestant churches in America.

9. The leading scholarship of the world declares that the meaning of the Greek word *baptizo* is "to immerse" and that immersion was the original scriptural baptism, while sprinkling and pouring are conceded substitutes, used for convenience only, and are without divine authority.

10. More than half the nominal Christians in the world still practice immersion in baptism, denying the validity of any other form, while all Christians, the world over, hold such baptism to be valid, primitive, and scriptural.

What Is Christian Baptism?

It is of primary importance to know what constitutes baptism itself. That point, once settled, will decide the form of its administration. To say it is a ceremony in which water is the element used, and by which persons are admitted to the Christian church, does not answer the question. What *is* baptism? As a gospel ordinance, the New Testament must define it.

Baptists answer the question by saying that baptism is the immersion or dipping of a candidate in water, on a profession of faith in Christ, administered in the name of the Father, Son, and Spirit.

Pedobaptists answer the question by saying it is either the sprinkling or pouring of water upon the person, touching the forehead with a wet finger, or dipping the candidate into water, in either case in the name of the Father, Son, and Spirit, and that it may be administered to one on his or her own profession of faith, or to an infant on the professed faith of some other person. This would make four forms of the ordinance, administered to two classes of subjects.

Baptists hold to a unity in the ordinance, as in the faith, believing that as there is but one Lord and one faith, so there is but one baptism and not four. And the one baptism is the immersion in water, in or into the name of the Father, Son, and Spirit. Neither pouring nor sprinkling water upon, nor any other application of water to a person, is baptism, though it may be called such ever so often, and ever so earnestly.

Meaning of "Baptizo"

The word *baptize*, a Greek word *(baptizo)* adapted to the English language, is the word used by the sacred writers to express and define the ordinance. What does this word mean as originally used? It is certain that divine wisdom, in commanding an ordinance to be observed by believers of all classes, in all lands, and through all ages, would use a word of positive and definite import, and one whose meaning would admit of no reasonable doubt.

What, then, does *baptizo* mean? Let us ask Greek scholars—those familiar with and skilled in the use of Greek words.

Grimm's *Lexicon of the New Testament*, which in Europe and America stands confessedly at the head of Greek lexicography, as translated and edited by Prof. Joseph Henry Thayer of Harvard University, thus defines *baptize*:

> (1) To dip repeatedly, to immerge, submerge . . . (2) To cleanse by dipping or submerging . . . (3) To overwhelm . . . In the New Testament it is used particularly of the rite of sacred ablution; first instituted by John the Baptist, afterwards by Christ's command received by Christians and adjusted to the contents and nature of their religion, vis., an immersion in water performed as a sign of the removal of sin, and administered to those who, impelled by a desire for salvation, sought admission to the benefits of the Messiah's kingdom.

Of the noun *baptisma*, the only other word used in the New Testament to denote the rite, this writer says: "A word peculiar to the New Testament and ecclesiastical writers; used . . . of John's baptism . . . and . . . of Christian baptism. This, according to the view of the Apostles, is a rite of sacred immersion commanded by Christ."

A roll call of eminent non-Baptist scholars would emphasize the accuracy of Thayer's interpretation of the meaning of the word. John Calvin said: "The word *baptize* signifies *to immerse*; and the rite of immersion was observed by the ancient church" *(Institutes,* IV, 15.19). Martin Luther is said to have stated: "The term *baptism* is a Greek word. It may be rendered *a dipping*, when we dip something in water, that it may be entirely covered with water" (cited by Du Veile on Acts 8:38.) Moses Stuart, one of the ablest scholars America has produced, says: "*Baptize* means to *dip*, plunge, or immerse into any liquid. All lexicographers and critics of any note are agreed in this" *(Essay on Baptism, 51; Bib. Repos., 1833, p. 298).*

Other noted writers who have offered similar definitions include

Frederic Schleusner (Lutheran), Cornelius Schrevelius (Dutch Reformed), John Parkhurst (Episcopal), William Greenfield (Episcopal), John Henry Alstidius (Reformed Lutheran), Christian Schoettgen (Lutheran), Edward Robinson (Congregational), Charles Anthon (Episcopal), John George Rosenmuller (Lutheran), John James Wetstein (Lutheran), Edward Leigh (Presbyterian), John Alph Turretin (Presbyterian), Theodore Beza (Presbyterian), Herman Witsius (Dutch Reformed), Gerhard Vossius (Episcopal), and George Campbell (Presbyterian).

Very many other competent scholars and critics familiar with the Greek language might be cited to the same effect. There can be no reasonable question that the true, indeed the only proper, meaning of *baptizo* is to dip, plunge, immerse, or bury in water.

Significant Use of the Word

Our Lord, in commanding baptism, evidently used such words as conveyed his meaning in no doubtful terms. And the sacred writers in transmitting his command to posterity, as well as his apostles in preaching his gospel to the nations, chose from all the words of the Greek language that one that accurately and truthfully conveyed his meaning to those who should believe upon his name. The Greek language is rich in terms to express all positive ideas and all varying shades of thought. Why was this one word, and no other, selected to describe an ordinance of great significance, intended to be observed by all believers, to the end of the world?

Baptizo is found eighty times in the New Testament and is a derivative from *bapto*. In nearly all it is used to designate this ordinance—and no other word is ever used for that purpose. *Baptisma*, a baptism, an immersion, is found twenty-two times, and *baptismos*, the act of baptizing or immersing, four times, both formed from *baptizo*. Scholars have abundantly proven that this word means "to dip, plunge, or immerse," and that, primarily and properly, it means nothing else. Our Savior, in leaving a command universally binding on his disciples, meant doubtless to express it so plainly and so positively, that none could misunderstand him. Therefore, this particular word and no other has been used because it means just what he intended.

Bapto is found three times in the New Testament and also means "to dip," but it is never used to describe baptism. Why not? Because it has other meanings, as well as that of dipping; and with this word the nature of the ordinance might be misunderstood.

Louo is found six times and means "to wash, to wash the whole body, to bathe." If baptism means "to wash," as some hold, here was just the word to express it. But this word is never applied to the ordinance because washing is not baptism, and baptism is not washing.

Nipto is found seventeen times and means also "to wash, to wash the extremities, as the face, hands, or feet, as distinguished from bathing the entire body." But this word is never used to express baptism. Why not, if a little water applied to the face may be baptism, as some teach?

Breko is found seven times and means "to wet, to moisten, to rain upon," but is never used to designate the rite of baptism; therefore to touch or moisten the forehead with wet fingers is not baptism, though frequently declared to be such.

Rantizo is found four times and means "to sprinkle." If baptism could have been performed by sprinkling, as is at present so widely believed, this would have been the word above all others to describe the ordinance. But this word is in no case so used, simply because sprinkling is not baptism.

Keo is found many times in its various combinations, and means "to pour," but it is never used to designate baptism. But if baptism may be performed by pouring water on a candidate, why was not this word sometimes used to indicate the act?

Katharizo is found thirty times and means "to purify," but it is never used to signify the act of baptizing. If the ordinance means "to purify," as some claim, this word would have expressed it much better than the one used.

We again ask, why did the sacred writers, from all the words in the Greek language, select only and always that one that strictly means "to dip or immerse," to express the act by which the sacred ordinance that Christ had commanded, and his disciples administered, should be performed? The only consistent answer is: Because baptism means immersion, and nothing else—and nothing but immersion is baptism.

The Baptism of Christ

Of the baptism of Jesus in the Jordan, it is said: "And when Jesus was baptized, he went up immediately from the water" (Matthew 3:16). Again it is recorded that Jesus "was baptized by John in the Jordan. And when he came up out of the water . . ." (Mark 1:9-10).

Does not the very fact of his going down into the water, so as to come up out of the water, show, if not positively, yet presumptively, that his baptism was an immersion, or burial, in the water? For to say he went down into the river for the purpose of having a small quantity of water poured, or a few drops sprinkled on him, is quite too trifling to have weight with candid minds.

Turning again to the Scriptures, we find an emphasis on the amount of water required: "Then Jesus came from Galilee to the Jordan to John, to be baptized by him" (Matthew 3:13). "John also was baptizing at Aenon [or Enon], near Salim, because there was much water there" (John 3:23).

Thoughtful persons will ask why should they have resorted to places expressly because these furnished large supplies of water, if baptism was performed by sprinkling. A very small quantity would have answered the purpose in that case.

John Lightfoot (Episcopal), the most distinguished and influential member of the Westminster Assembly, summarized the case in these words: "That the baptism of John was the *immersion* of the body, in which manner both the ablutions of unclean persons and the baptism of proselytes was performed, seems evident from those things which are related of it; namely, that he baptized in the Jordan, and in Enon, because there was much water; and that Christ, being baptized, went up out of the water" (Matthew 3:6).

Or, in the words of Matthew Poole, the illustrious English Presbyterian: "It is apparent that both Christ and John baptized by *dipping* the body in the water, else they need not have sought places where had been a great plenty of water" *(Annot. John 3:23).*

Likewise, Stephen Curcellaeus (Dutch Reformed), professor of divinity at Amsterdam, said: "Baptism was performed by *plunging* the whole body into water, and not by sprinkling a few drops, as is now the practice. For John was baptizing in Enon, near to

Salim, because there was *much* water there" *(Relig. Ch. Inst., cited Booth, Ped. Ex. ch. 4, p. 50).*

Philip and the Ethiopian

Why should Philip and the Ethiopian eunuch have gone down into the water, if a mere sprinkling or pouring of water, and not immersion in water, was to be used? "And they both went down into the water, both Philip and the eunuch, and he baptized him. And when they came up out of the water, the Spirit of the Lord caught up Philip" (Acts 8:38-39).

Dr. Gabriel Towerson (Episcopal), commenting on this passage, wrote: "For what need would there have been of Philip and the eunuch going *into* this the water, were it not that the baptism was to be performed by *immersion?*" *(Com. Acts 8:38).*

Likewise, Dr. Herman Vencma (Dutch Reformed), professor in the University of Franeker, Friesland, declared: "It is without controversy, that baptism in the primitive Church was administered by *immersion* into water, and not by sprinkling, seeing that John is said to have baptized in Jordan, and where there was *much water*, as Christ also did by his disciples in the neighborhood of those places. Philip, also, going down into the water, baptized the eunuch" *(Eccl. Hist., ch. I, sec. 138. See Booth, Ped. Ex., ch. 4, sec. 76).*

The Testimony of Expositors

The great questions with every candid mind should be: "What is truth? What is right?" But as the Scriptures are our only and sufficient standard in matters of religious faith and practice, we ask, "What do the Scriptures teach?" In order to ascertain this point, we inquire of those pious men, eminent for learning and a devout study of the Bible, who have prepared able commentaries on the sacred text, as to what they understood to be the nature of baptism, and the form of its original administration. What have expositors said? Here is a sampling:

Jerome Zanchius, professor of theology at Heidelberg, whose opinion, De Courcy declared, "is worth a thousand others": "The proper signification of *baptizo* is to *immerse*, plunge under, to overwhelm in water" *(Works, Vol. VI, p. 217, Geneva 1619).*

Herman Witsius, professor of divinity at Franeker, Utrecht, and Leyden: "It cannot be denied that the native signification of the *baptein,* and *baptizein,* is to plunge or dip" *(Econ. Covenants, p. 1213).*

Jeremy Taylor, distinguished English bishop and author: "The custom of the ancient churches was not sprinkling, but *immersion*" *(Duct. Dubit, B. III, ch. 4, R. 15).*

Martin Luther, the great German reformer: "The term *baptism* is Greek; in Latin it may be translated *immersio*; since we *immerse* anything into water, that the whole may be covered with water" *(Works, Vol. I, p. 74, Wit. Ed., 1582).*

Phillip Melanchthon, Luther's learned associate: "Baptism is *immersion* into water, which is made with this admirable benediction" *(Melancht. Catec., Wit., 1580).*

William Cave, eminent English scholar and author: "The party to be baptized was *wholly immersed,* or put under water" *(Prim. Chris., P. I., ch. 10, p. 320).*

Thomas Sherlock, bishop of Bangor, Salisbury, and London: "Baptism, or an *immersion* into water, according to the ancient rite of administering it, is a figure of our burial with Christ, and of our conformity to his death" *(Bloom, Crit. Dig., Vol. V, p. 537).*

Theodore Beza, professor of theology at Geneva, and associate of John Calvin: "Christ commanded us to be baptized; by which word it is certain *immersion* is signified" *(Epis. ad. Thom. Tillium, Annot. on Mark 7:4).*

Matthew Poole, learned English divine and commentator: "He seems here to allude to the manner of baptizing in those warm Eastern countries, which was to *dip* or plunge the party baptized, and, as it were, to bury him for a while under water" *(Annot. on Romans 6:4).*

James Bossuet, Catholic bishop of Meaux, and state counselor of France: "To baptize signifies to *plunge,* as is granted by all the world" *(Stennett against Russen, p. 174).*

John Calvin, the great reformer: "The word *baptize* signifies *to immerse*; and it is certain that immersion was the practice of the ancient Church" *(Institutes, IV, 15.19).*

Adam Clark, a leading Methodist commentator: "Alluding to the *immersions* practiced in the case of adults, wherein the person appeared to be buried under the water, as Christ was buried in the heart of the earth" *(Comment on Colossians 2:12).*

Philip Schaff, eminent scholar and historian, professor on the faculty of Union Theological Seminary, New York: *"Immersion,* and not sprinkling, was unquestionably the original form. This is shown by the very meaning of the words *baptizo, baptisma* and *baptismos,* used to designate the rite" *(Hist. Apos. Ch., p. 488. Merc. ed., 1851. See also Noel on Bapt., ch. 3, sec. 8).*

Johann August Wilhelm Neander, great German scholar and ecclesiastical historian, professor in the Universities of Heidelberg and Berlin: "The usual form of *submersion* at baptism, practiced by the Jews, was passed over to the Gentile Christians. Indeed, this form was the most suitable to signify that which Christ intended to render an object of contemplation by such a symbol: the *immersion* of the whole man in the spirit of a new life" *(Planting and Training, p. 161).*

To the same effect might be adduced many others from among the most able and distinguished of biblical scholars and commentators of the Pedobaptist communions.

Apostolic Allusions

The idea that Paul had of both the form and purpose of baptism is very manifest from the manner in which he refers to it in his Epistles. To the Romans he said: "We were buried therefore with him by baptism into death" (Romans 6:4). To the Colossians, using nearly the same language, he said: *"Buried* with him in baptism" (Colossians 2:12). His concept must have been that of a burying, a covering of the subject entirely in the water, by a sinking into it. No other form could have been true to a figure here used. And this fact has been generally acknowledged.

For instance, John Tillotson, Archbishop of Canterbury, wrote: "Anciently those who were baptized were *immersed,* and *buried* in the water, to represent their death to sin; and then did rise up out of the water to signify their entrance upon a new life. And to these customs the Apostle alludes" *(Works, Vol. I, p. 179).*

The great Swiss reformer, Huldreich Zwingli, stated: "When ye were *immersed* into the water by baptism, ye were ingrafted into the death of Christ" *(Annot. Romans 4:4. See Conant's Append. to Matthew).*

In the writings of John Wesley, the founder of Methodism, we read: "Buried with Him—alluding to the ancient manner of baptizing by *immersion" (Note on Romans 4:4).*

In similar vein, Wesley's associate, George Whitefield, wrote: "It is certain that in the words of our text (Romans 6:3-4) there is an allusion to the manner of baptism, which was by immersion" *(Eighteen Sermons, p. 297).*

Likewise Bishop John Fell of Oxford, vice chancellor of the university, wrote: "The primitive fashion of *immersion* under the water, representing our death, and elevation again out of it, our resurrection or regeneration" *(Note on Romans 6:4).*

Such opinions, expressed by these learned and pious men, do not surprise us. It is difficult to see how they could have expressed any others.

Historical Evidence

The writings of the so-called Church Fathers, those who helped to shape the course of Christianity in the first few centuries after Christ, placed great emphasis on immersion.

Barnabas, the companion of Paul, in an epistle ascribed to him, and which must have been written very early (whoever was the real author), spoke of baptism as a "going down into the water." He said: "We go down into the water full of sin and filth, but we come up bearing fruits."

Hermas, writing about A.D. 95, in the "Shepherd," a work ascribed to him, spoke of the apostles as having gone "down into the water with those they baptized," and "come up again."

Justin Martyr, writing about A.D. 140, spoke of those baptized as "washed in the water, in the name of the Father, Son, and Spirit."

Tertullian, about A.D. 204, said the person to be baptized "is let down into the water, and, with a few words said, is *dipped.*"

Hippolytus, about A.D. 225: "For he who goes down with faith into the bath of regeneration, is arrayed against the evil one, and on the side of Christ. He comes up from the baptism bright as the sun, flashing for the rays of righteousness."

Gregory, A.D. 360: "We are *buried* with Christ by baptism,

that we may also rise with him."

Ambrose, A.D. 374: "Thou saidst, I do believe, and wast *immersed* in water; that in thou wast buried."

Cyril, A.D. 374: "Candidates are first anointed with consecrated oils; they are then conducted to the laver, and asked three times if they believe in the Father, Son, and Holy Ghost; then they are *dipped* three times into the water, and retire by three distinct efforts."

Chrysostom, A.D. 398: "To be baptized and *plunged* in the water, and then emerge and rise again, is a symbol of our descent into the grave, and our ascent out of it."

Not only was immersion the original form of baptism, as received by Christ, administered by his apostles, and practiced by the earliest Christians, but it was that form that was retained in use by all Christian churches, with few exceptions, for about thirteen centuries. Following are some statements on this point:

Daniel Whitby, Anglican divine and commentator: "And this immersion being religiously observed by all Christians for thirteen centuries, and approved by our Church"—referring to the Church of England—*(Annotations on Romans 6:4)*.

Thomas Stackhouse, English expert on Bible history: "Several authors have shown and proved that this manner of immersion continued, as much as possible, to be used for thirteen hundred years after Christ" *(History of the Bible, B. VIII, ch. I)*.

Frederick Brenner, a distinguished Catholic writer: "Thirteen hundred years was baptism generally and orderly performed by immersion of the person under water, and only in extraordinary cases was sprinkling, or affusion, permitted. These later methods of baptism were called in question, and even prohibited" *(Hist. Exhibit. Bapt., p. 306)*.

Daniel von Colen, professor of theology at Breslau: "Immersion in water was general until the thirteenth century among the Latins; it was then displaced by sprinkling, but retained by the Greeks" *(Hist. Doct., Vol. II, p. 303)*.

While these testimonials do not exhaust historical evidence on this point, they are sufficient to satisfy unbiased minds as to the primitive and long-continued use of immersion for baptism in the Christian world.

Usage of the Greek Church

While it may not be an unanswerable argument in favor of the position taken by Baptists that the Eastern Orthodox Church has always practiced, and does still practice, immersion, yet the fact is too significant to be overlooked.

Alexander Stourdza, the Russian scholar and diplomat, said: "The Church of the West [Rome] has, then, departed from the example of Jesus Christ; she has obliterated the whole sublimity of the exterior sign. Baptism and immersion are identical. Baptism by aspersion is as if one should say, immersion by aspersion; or any other absurdity of the same nature" *(Consid. Orthodox Ch., p. 87; Conant's Append., p. 99)*.

Sir Paul Ricaut, English consul at Smyrna, commented with regard to the Eastern church: "Thrice dipping, or plunging, this Church holds to be as necessary to the form of baptism, as water is to the matter" *(State of Greek Church, p. 163)*.

Dr. William Wall, whose learned and laborious researches into the history of baptism left little for others to discover, said: "The Greek Church in all its branches does still use immersion, and so do all other Christians in the world, except the Latins. All those nations that do now, or formerly did submit to the authority of the Bishop of Rome, do ordinarily baptize their infants by pouring or sprinkling. *But all other Christians in the world*, who never owned the Pope's usurped power, do, and ever did, *dip* their infants in the ordinary use. All the Christians in Asia, all in Africa, and about one-third in Europe, are of the last sort" *(Hist. Inf. Bap., Vol. II, p. 376; ed. 3)*.

The Testimony of Baptisteries

It will cast some further light on this subject to know what places were used for this ordinance during the early ages of Christianity. Early Christians never would have frequented rivers, pools, cisterns, and other large bodies of water for the mere purpose of sprinkling the baptismal candidates.

We know that John the Baptist and the disciples of Jesus resorted to the Jordan for the purpose of baptizing, and to Enon, near Salim, "*because* there was much water there."

Tertullian said:

"There is no difference whether one is baptized in the sea or in a lake, in a river or in a fountain; neither was there any difference between those whom John baptized in Jordan, and those whom Peter baptized in the Tiber. *(De Bapt., ch. 4; Bing. Antiq., B. VIII, ch. 8, sec. I.)*

Dr. Doddridge said:

"John was also at the same time baptizing at Enon; and he particularly chose that place because there was a great quantity of water there, which made it very convenient for his purpose" *(Fam. Expositor on Matthew 3:16).*

As Christianity spread and converts multiplied, in many places, especially in large cities, there were few opportunities for the convenient and agreeable administration of the ordinance. Other cities were not so well supplied with pools as was Jerusalem. Then began to be erected *baptisteries*, expressly designed for this use. These, at first, were constructed in the simplest manner; but, in process of time, large, costly, and imposing edifices were built for this purpose.

"The place of baptism was at first unlimited, being some pond or lake, some spring or river, but always as near as possible to the place of public worship. Afterward they had their *baptisteries*, or (as we call them) fonts, built at first near the church, then in the church porch, and, at last, in the church itself. . . . The baptistery was, properly speaking, the whole house or building in which the font stood, which later was only the fountain or pool of water in which the *immersion* was performed" *(Thomas Broughton, Hist. Dict., Arts. Baptism and Baptistery).*

Professor Karl Rudolph Hagenbach, of the University of Basle, offered a similar description: "That baptism in the beginning was administered in the open air, in rivers and pools, and that it was by *immersion* we know from the narratives of the New Testament. In later times there were prepared great baptismal fonts or chapels. The person to be baptized descended several steps into the reservoir of water, and then the whole body was *immersed* under the water" *(Hist. Christ. Church, ch. 19, p. 324).*

Some of these structures are still preserved, and others are well known to have existed—as that of Florence, Venice, Pisa, Naples, Bologna, and Ravenna. That of the Lateran, at Rome, is considered the oldest now existing, having been erected A.D. 324.

That at Pisa was completed A.D. 1160, the entire structure being 115 feet in diameter, by 172 feet in height, and of a circular form. That at Florence is an octagonal building, 90 feet in diameter, with a lofty dome. That of St. Sophia, at Constantinople, erected by Constantine A.D. 337, was capable of accommodating a numerous council, whose sessions were held in it. Most of these structures are large, elaborate, and costly edifices.

The baptistery proper, or pool for baptizing, was an open cistern in the center of the large hall, or main part of the building.

Can anyone suppose these buildings would have been provided if sprinkling and not immersion had been the manner of administering baptism?

The Meaning of Baptism

It is not difficult to ascertain from the New Testament what was intended by baptism. It was clearly this: to show forth the death, burial, and resurrection of Christ, who died for our sins, and rose again for our justification. And every candidate who receives the ordinance professes thereby faith in the merits of Christ's death as the ground of one's own hope and salvation, fellowship also with Christ's sufferings, and a declaration of one's own death to sin, and a rising to newness of life in Christ. It also typifies the washing of regeneration, and the renewing of the Holy Spirit, and declares the candidate's hope of a resurrection from the dead, even as Christ, into the likeness of whose death he or she is buried, was raised up by the glory of the Father.

Immersion alone can meet this demand and serve its purpose. Sprinkling, or pouring water on a candidate, has no force in the direction of this sacred symbolism. It cannot show the death, burial, or resurrection of Christ nor the disciple's death to sin and his or her rising to a new life. If immersion, therefore, be abandoned, the entire force of the ordinance will be destroyed, and its design will be obliterated.

Sprinkling sets forth no great doctrine of the gospel. Only when the disciple is buried beneath the water, and raised up again, do the beauty, force, and meaning, which divine wisdom intended, appear in that sacred ordinance.

The Water Supply

Among the weak arguments used, and the indefensible positions assumed by the weakest, and least defensible—that the Jordan had not sufficient depth of water for immersing the multitudes said to have been baptized by John and the disciples of Jesus; and that there were no conveniences in Jerusalem for immersing the large number of early converts who were baptized there. Consequently, they say, those converts must have had water sprinkled on them instead.

Puerile as may seem this objection, it has been seriously put forth by not a few of the advocates of aspersion, even in the face of Scripture testimony and against scholarship and history. Such assertions indicate the ignorance or the recklessness of those who make them, and show how prejudice may unfit even good people for a just discussion of grave subjects. The objection is too trifling to merit serious regard, and yet the testimony on this point is so abundant, and so conclusive—and that, too, from Pedobaptist sources—as to make it both pleasant and fitting to adduce some of it in this connection.

Lieutenant Lynch, of the United States Navy, was, in 1848, sent out by his government in charge of an expedition to explore the river Jordan and the Dead Sea. This, of course, had no connection with polemic discussions, and least of all was it to settle the baptismal question. It was done for antiquarian research and for the advancement of science.

The expedition passed down the entire length of the Jordan, in boats, from the Sea of Galilee to the Dead Sea; they made frequent and careful surveys, which were accurately recorded and officially published. The river was found to vary in width from 75 to 200 feet and in depth from 3 to 12 feet. At Bethabara, where tradition has fixed the place of our Savior's baptism, and where John baptized the multitudes, Lieutenant Lynch gives the width as 120 feet and the greatest depth as 12 feet. There certainly is no lack of water there, since one-quarter of 12 feet would be sufficient for burying converts in baptism.

It is a well-known fact that thousands of Christian pilgrims from adjacent countries visit this spot at a certain season annually to bathe in the waters, held sacred by them because of Christ's baptism there. The expedition witnessed one of these scenes and had their boats in readiness to prevent accidents, which it was feared might occur in so great a crowd of fanatical devotees, in so great a depth of water. Had the advocates of sprinkling been present, they might have found an argument as perilous as it would have been convincing for a sufficient depth of water for the immersion of Christian believers. Scarcely an occasion of this kind transpires without some fatal accidents by drowning in the deep and rapid current.

The Substitution of Sprinkling

We may now properly inquire, When and why was sprinkling introduced and accepted as a substitute for the original scriptural form of dipping in baptism? The question has its interest and its importance, and is fully and satisfactorily answered by Pedobaptists themselves. We accept their testimony as a complete justification of our position in respect to this ordinance.

For 250 years after Christ we have no evidence of any departure from the primitive practice of immersion—the first authenticated instance of such a departure being about the middle of the third century, or A.D. 250. This was in the case of Novatian. Eusebius, the historian, told us that Novatian was dangerously ill, and believing himself about to die, he greatly desired to be baptized, not having as yet received that ordinance. As the case seemed urgent, and he was thought too feeble to be immersed, it was decided to try a substitute as nearly resembling baptism as possible. Water was poured profusely over him as he lay on his bed, so as to resemble as much as possible a submersion.

It is evident that such a substitute for baptism was, at the time, generally considered as unscriptural and improper. But, having been introduced, and by some accepted, from that time the practice of pouring or sprinkling was resorted to in cases of sickness; hence, called "clinic baptism," from *clina*, a couch or bed, on which it was received.

In the Roman church, pouring for baptism was tolerated by Pope Stephen II in the eighth century, sanctioned as an option by the

Council of Ravenna in the fourteenth, and in the sixteenth century generally adopted as a matter of convenience. It was adopted first in France, then in other Catholic countries.

John Calvin, in the Genevan church, prepared directions for "administering the sacrament" through pouring, whereupon the churches of the Reformation adopted it also in large measure. By 1600, pouring had become quite general on the continent. It gained official sanction in England in 1643, by a majority of one vote against baptizing by immersion. The year following, Parliament sanctioned this decision and decreed that sprinkling should be the legal mode of administering baptism. Both immersion and sprinkling had been in common use. This action ruled out immersion and made sprinkling sufficient.

The following is the form finally decided and fixed by the assembly for the minister to use in baptism: "He is to baptize the child with water, which, for the manner of doing, is not only lawful, but also sufficient and most expedient to be by pouring or sprinkling water on the face of the child without any other ceremony" *(Pittman and Lightfoot's Works, Vol. XIII, p. 300).*

Thus we have given, briefly but accurately, the rise, progress, and final prevalence of this perversion—the substitution of sprinkling for immersion in the administration of Christian baptism.

Part II: Infant Baptism

The baptism of unconverted children and unconscious infants has become common through the Christian world. Yet Baptists condemn it as unscriptural, unreasonable, and pernicious. They believe that repentance and faith should always precede baptism. Without these, baptism has no significance and serves no religious purpose. Infants incapable of faith are, therefore, unfit for baptism.

Baptists defend the following propositions:

1. There is in the New Testament neither precept nor example to sanction infant baptism. Nor, indeed, is there even an allusion to it in the Scriptures.

2. Christ did not institute it, nor did either the apostles or early Christians practice it.

3. It was a part of the corruption which in subsequent ages crept into the churches, having its basis in the belief of a saving power

exerted by baptism on the soul of the child.

4. The practice is unauthorized, presumptuous, and censurable on the part of parents, sponsors, and administrators, and it produces evil both to the child who receives it and the church that allows and practices it.

5. It perverts the design of the church as the spiritual body of Christ by introducing to its membership an element of unconverted persons.

Not of Scriptural Authority

Nearly all the learned and scholarly supporters of infant baptism have, with commendable candor, admitted that it was not instituted by Christ nor practiced either by his apostles or their immediate successors.

Dr. William Wall, of the English church, who wrote a *History of Infant Baptism*, a work so thorough and able that the clergy, assembled in convocation, gave him a vote of thanks for his learned defense of this custom, nevertheless said: "Among all the persons that are recorded as baptized by the Apostles, there is no express mention of infants" *(Hist. Inf. Bapt., Introd., pp. 1, 55)*.

Similar statements are to be found in the writings of Richard Baxter (Presbyterian), Philip Limborch (Dutch Reformed), Johann August Wilhelm Neander (Lutheran), Hermann Olshansen (Lutheran), William Penn (Quaker), Karl Rudolph Hagenbach (Lutheran), and many other non-Baptists.

Household Baptisms

Some, however, have supposed that the "household baptisms" mentioned in the New Testament must have included children, and thus constitute a warrant for the baptism of such.

This argument, like the others in its support, is founded on the faintest and most illogical inference. It is inferred that these households certainly had infant children in them, and that such children certainly were baptized; both of which are wholly gratuitous. There probably are but few Baptist churches in the world of any considerable standing and numbers that do not have one or more entire households in their communion, each member of which was baptized on a profession of faith.

The case of Lydia, baptized at Philippi, mentioned in Acts 16:14-15, is especially relied on as a strong case. Now observe, Lydia was a merchant woman, "a seller of purple goods," from "the city of Thyatira," and was at Philippi, some three hundred miles from home, on business, when she heard Paul preach, was converted, and then "she was baptized, and her household." There is not the least evidence that she had either husband or children. If she had a husband, why was *she* so far from home on mercantile business? If she had infant children, they would not likely have been with her on such a journey, so far away, and for such a purpose. Her "household," doubtless, were adults, and employed by her in her business—her company. The most reckless sophism alone could build infant baptism on such a case. A poor cause it must be that relies for support on such evidence as this.

The case of the Philippian jailer and his household, also mentioned in Acts 16, is often referred to as of force by the advocates of this practice. Observe, however, that Paul and Silas, being released from their confinement, spoke the word of the Lord to the jailer "and to all that were in his house" (v. 32). Whether adults or infants, anyone can judge; the gospel was preached to them. And the jailer "was baptized at once, with all his family" (v. 33). Then "he rejoiced with all his household that he had believed in God" (v. 34). Observe, the jailer's family was baptized; but first they listened to the preaching of the Word; then they believed in God; and then they rejoiced with him in their newfound hope. Who believes that such a record as this could ever have been made of unconscious infants? There is not the remotest allusion to children, and the narrative does not fit them at all. Those who were baptized were those who believed and who rejoiced. It was therefore "believers' baptism," beyond which fact the particular age of the subjects is of no consequence whatever.

Paul spoke, in 1 Corinthians 1:16, of having baptized "the household of Stephanas." This is also quoted as giving some support to the infant baptismal theory. The course of argument, or inference, is the same. It is supposed that the household contained children and that these children were baptized. How entirely gratuitous! Households are constantly being baptized and admitted to the fellowship of our churches without infants in them. Doddridge, Guise, Hammond, Macknight, and others consider this case as giving no countenance to the custom of baptizing infants.

This family of Stephanas were "the first converts of Achaia," according to Paul (1 Corinthians 16:15); "they have devoted themselves to the service of the saints." This could not have been spoken of baptized infants, but it well describes the Christian activities of adult believers. No infants can be found in the household of Stephanas.

Rise of Infant Baptism

If the baptism of infants and unconverted children was not appointed by Christ nor practiced by his apostles nor known in the primitive age, how did it arise, and when did it come into use?

Tertullian was the first writer who mentioned it in history, and he opposed it. This was at the close of the second century, or about A.D. 200. His opposition proves two things: (1) that it was in occasional use, at least, and (2) that it was of recent origin, and not generally prevalent. For it must have been in use to be discussed and opposed, and had it been long prevalent, it would have been earlier mentioned.

In the first half of the third century, Hippolytus, bishop of Pontus, mentioned infant baptism in these words: "We, in our days, never defended the baptism of children, which had only begun to be practiced in some regions." Bunsen, the learned translator of Hippolytus, declared that infant baptism, in the modern sense, "was utterly unknown to the early church, not only down to the end of the second century, but, indeed, to the middle of the third century" *(Hippol. and His Age, Vol. III, p. 180)*.

It should be added that when the baptism of children did begin to be practiced, it was not the baptism of infants at all, but, as Bunsen said, of "little growing children, from six to ten years old." He declared that Tertullian, in his opposition to infant baptism, did not say a word of newborn infants. Cyprian, an African bishop, at the close of the third century urged the baptism of infants proper because of the regenerating efficacy that the ordinance was supposed to exert. He and his associates were the first to take this ground.

From What Cause Did It Spring?

It is well known that at a very early period in Christian history, the notion began to prevail that the ordinances possessed some magical virtue. It was believed that baptism conveyed saving grace to the soul; that by it sins were washed away and the spirit fitted for heaven. For example, John Chrysostom, writing about A.D. 398, said: "It is impossible without baptism to obtain the kingdom. It is impossible to be saved without it. . . . If sudden death seize us before we are baptized, though we have a thousand good qualities there is nothing to be expected but hell." This is a clear statement of the doctrine of baptismal regeneration.

Thus the sick were thought to be prepared for death, and salvation secured, or made more certain by its efficacy. Anxious parents therefore desired their dying children to receive baptism and thus, "washed in the laver of regeneration," be secured against the perils of perdition. Such was one of the errors of a superstitious age. Hence arose infant baptism as one of the many perversions that early corrupted the doctrines and ordinances of Christianity. It received formal approval by the Milevitan Council in A.D. 418, which declared pedobaptism to be a necessary rite.

Reasons for Infant Baptism

Now, since this rite was not instituted by Christ nor practiced by the apostles nor known among Christians until about A.D. 200, how is it justified as a Christian ordinance by those who practice it? And by what reasons is it sustained and defended?

1. Some good and honest people really believe, after all, that infant baptism is taught in the Bible and are greatly astonished, if they examine the subject, not to find it there. A very little effort will show how utterly without foundation is such a supposition. Read the sacred records through, from beginning to end, and no allusion to such a practice appears.

2. Its antiquity commends it to some. It has been a long time in vogue and very generally practiced by various Christian communions. But does that make it right? Is a usage necessarily good and true because it is old? Heathenism is older than the institutes of Christianity. Shall we adopt and practice all the absurd superstitions

of the early corrupted churches—the worship of images, invocation of saints, prayer to the Virgin, oblations for the dead, baptism of bells, and many others—not a few of which came into use about the same time as this, and some of which are still older, and any one of which has as much scriptural authority as infant baptism? Why do Protestants preserve this relic of popery alone and reject the others?

Not what is *old* but what is *true* should be our rule. Not what is antiquity but what the Bible commends should we obey. Not tradition but, as Chillingworth declared, "the Bible only is the religion of Protestants." As Basil said, so should we say, "It is a manifest mistake in regard to faith, and a clear evidence of pride, either to reject any of those things which the Scripture contains, or to introduce anything that is not in the sacred pages."

3. There are some who confess that there is neither clear precept nor example in the New Testament to commend this practice, yet they hold that the general spirit of the gospel favors it. This is a strange mode of reasoning, surely. If we may, by remote deduction and vague inference, originate ceremonies, call them gospel ordinances, and impose them on the consciences of men, then the whole Jewish ceremonial, and, indeed, the ritual of the Roman Catholic church entire may be adopted, used, and taught as of divine authority, binding on believers.

But what a reflection is this on the wisdom and goodness of God: that he should have left positive institutions, designed for universal observance in his churches, to be vaguely inferred from supposed general principles rather than to have been plainly and explicitly taught in his Word! Such reasoning will not serve in matters of religion.

4. Some have claimed that baptism came in the place of *circumcision*. Hence, it is inferred—only *inferred*—that as all the male Jewish children were to be circumcised, so all the children of Christians, both male and female, should be baptized. What connection there is between these two institutions would require a philosopher to discover. And yet this has been the argument chiefly relied on by theologians, scholars, and divines in this country especially, for generations past, to prove the divine authority of infant baptism. More recently this stronghold of the tradition has

been less confidently resorted to by learned men, and it may be said the tradition itself is being slowly abandoned. It cannot well endure the light of Christian intelligence.

Baptism did not come in the place of circumcision nor in the place of any other previously existing institution. It has no connection with, and no reference to, circumcision whatever. The following considerations will make this plain:

a. If baptism, a Christian ordinance, was designed to take the place of circumcision, a Mosaic rite, would not Christ have so stated, or the apostles have mentioned the fact? But no allusion is to be found to any such design.

b. Circumcision was applied to males alone. If baptism was its substitute, why are females baptized?

c. Circumcision was an external sign of an external union with a national congregation, to secure the separation of the Jews from all other nations and races and their unity as a people. Baptism is an external sign of an inward spiritual work of grace already wrought in the heart. It indicates not the separation of races but the unity of the true people of God, of all races, as believers in Christ, without distinction of blood or tongue.

d. If baptism did take the place of circumcision, as is claimed, evidently the apostles did not know it, else they would have made some mention of it in the conference at Jerusalem, in epistles written for the guidance of the churches, or on other occasions when both these subjects were under discussion and directions given respecting them. But no allusion is anywhere made to such a substitution.

e. Jewish Christians for a time insisted on the practice of *both* circumcision and baptism, which proves they did not understand the one to have displaced the other. With their strong Jewish predilections they wished to retain circumcision as the sign and seal of their fellowship with the house of Israel; at the same time they received baptism as a sign and seal of their adoption into the faith and fellowship of Christ and his kingdom.

Objections to Infant Baptism

1. It is founded on a falsehood. It claims to be a gospel ordinance when it is an invention of men. Christ did not appoint it; the apostles did not practice it; the Scriptures did not sanction it.

2. It impugns divine wisdom and insults the divine authority because it claims to be needful, or useful, to religion; though Christ, by not appointing it when he instituted the church, virtually decided it to be neither needful nor useful. Also, by binding the service on the consciences of Christian parents, as of religious obligation when God has not commanded it, there is an unwarrantable assumption of authority, and a grievous wrong is committed. Divine wisdom knew best what institutions to ordain and what commands to lay upon God's people.

3. It deprives Christian converts of the pleasure and privilege of believers' baptism. For having received this rite in their infancy without their consent or knowledge, if later they become regenerate and truly united to Christ, they cannot go forward in the discharge of this duty and be baptized on a profession of their faith without discrediting their earlier baptism—if baptism it may be called.

4. It appears like a solemn mockery for parents and sponsors to become sureties for the child about to be baptized and declare for him or her that they believe in God's holy Word and in the articles of the Christian faith.

5. It requires the officiating minister to declare what is false, in the very performance of what should be a most sacred service. He declares what is false when he says, "I baptize thee," since he "rantizes" or sprinkles and does not baptize at all. Worse yet, when he asserts that in this act the child "is regenerated and grafted into the body of Christ's church," the child is in fact *not* regenerated, *nor* adopted of God, *nor* incorporated into the church of Christ by this act. The service falsifies the facts most flagrantly.

6. But perhaps worst of all, infant baptism still teaches, to an extent, *baptismal regeneration*. It is more than a false statement; it is a pernicious and destructive error. What could be more reckless than to assert, even by inference, that a few drops of water on the face can make one regenerate and a child of God? If children, when grown, believe all this—and why should they not believe it when thus solemnly taught by parents and minister?—they believe themselves heirs of heaven, sealed and sanctified by the Spirit, while blind to the fact that they are still unsaved.

7. Infant baptism, in some sense—though its advocates are not agreed in what sense—makes the child a church member and thus

introduces an unsanctified element into the nominal body of Christ. It thus destroys the distinction that the Divine Founder of the church designed should be maintained between it and the world. "A regenerated church membership" cannot be the motto or the watchword of the advocates of pedobaptism.

Other objections than these mentioned may be urged against this unscriptural practice. But these would seem sufficient to deter any candid and conscientious Christian, who takes the Bible as the guide for living, from giving it any countenance or support.

Rules of Order

Whenever possible, the process of church business will be best accomplished by informal processes and by the achievement of consensus. This is particularly true when either the congregation or the authorized body is small in number. In such contexts, the chairperson should seek to resolve matters when consensus seems achieved by asking, "Is there consensus on this action?" At first glance this process may seem more laborious and less decisive. However, it often produces decisions in which the whole congregation is invested and which will not need to be repeatedly reconsidered.

On other occasions, however, especially when a group is large or when matters of controversy, diversity of opinion, or multiple perspectives are to be considered, more formal rules of order will facilitate effective decisions. It is important for a church to establish in advance the rules by which such meetings will be guided. The classic, often-used guide for meetings is one variation or another of *Roberts' Rules of Order*. Because these rules guide many organizations in their procedures, they will most likely be most familiar in a church context. Nevertheless, this resource can be complex and, to some, intimidating, except in its most simplified form. While good order may be required to preserve the health of the body, complex rules may encourage frustration or resentment among those who do not frequently use them. The following rules, therefore, are offered as an elementary guide useful to most churches in most situations.

Regardless of the specific rules chosen, business meetings should always be approached as part of the whole life of the church.

That is, the spirit of worship should pervade the meetings, and the outcome of meetings should be consistent with the purpose of the church and its witness. Meetings should be opened with singing, Scripture, and prayer, and the moderator, whether it be the pastor or an elected lay leader, should approach his or her task of conducting a meeting of the congregation as a responsibility of great spiritual, as well as procedural, importance.

A Simplified Rule

Reports

1. Reports are offered as a means of officially communicating information, activities, proposals, or other matters to the body, usually from an officer or committee.

2. To be included in the minutes, reports should be reviewed by the body by means of a motion to receive or accept.

3. Action arising from a report must be considered by means of a motion, whether offered by the person responsible for the report or another member of the body.

4. A report containing actions or activities accomplished on behalf of the body should be affirmed by the body. If not affirmed, then other action required of the committee or individual sponsoring the report should be situated by motion or other means.

5. The moderator or other presiding officer shall establish the sequence of reports and their place in the meeting. Reports from church officers (clerk, treasurer, church-school superintendent, etc.) should generally be scheduled at the beginning of the meeting or assembly, unless specifically deferred or relocated by the moderator or by request of the meeting. Other reports may be scheduled as an item for business under old or new business, or as an item of special consideration.

Motions

1. All business shall be presented by a *motion*, made by one member, and seconded by another, and presented in writing by the mover, if so required.

2. No discussion can properly be had until the motion is made, seconded, and stated by the chairperson.

3. A motion cannot be withdrawn after it has been discussed, except by the unanimous consent of the body.

4. A motion, having been discussed, must be put to vote, unless withdrawn, laid on the table, referred, or postponed.

5. A motion lost should not be recorded, unless so ordered by the body at the time.

6. A motion lost cannot be renewed at the same meeting, except by unanimous consent.

7. A motion should contain but one distinct proposition. If it contains more, it must be divided at the request of any member, and the propositions acted on separately.

8. Only one question can properly be before the meeting at the same time. No second motion can be allowed to interrupt one already under debate, except a motion to amend, to substitute, to refer to committee, to postpone, to lay on the table, for the previous question, or to adjourn.

9. These subsidiary motions just named cannot be interrupted by any other motion; nor can any other motion be applied to them, except that to amend, which may be done by specifying some time, place, or purpose.

10. Nor can these motions interrupt or supersede each other; only that a motion to adjourn is always in order, except while a member has the floor, or a vote is being taken, and, in some bodies, even then.

Amendments

1. Amendments may be made to resolutions in three ways: by omitting, by adding, or by substituting words or sentences.

2. An amendment to an amendment may be made, but is seldom necessary, and should be avoided if possible.

3. No amendment should be made which essentially changes the meaning or design of the original resolution.

4. But a *substitute* may be offered, which may change entirely the meaning of the resolution under debate.

5. The amendment must first be discussed and acted on, and then the original resolution as amended.

Speaking

1. Any member desiring to speak on a question should rise in his place and address the moderator, confining his remarks to the question.

2. A speaker using improper language, introducing improper subjects, or otherwise out of order, should be called to order by the chairperson, or any member, and must either conform to the regulations of the body, or take his or her seat.

3. A member while speaking can allow others to ask questions, or make explanations; but if that member yields the floor to another, he or she cannot claim it again as his or her right.

4. If two members rise to speak at the same time, preference is usually given to the farthest from the chair, or to the one opposing the motion under discussion.

5. The fact that a person has several times arisen and attempted to get the floor gives him or her no claim or right to be heard. Nor does a call for the question deprive a member of his or her right to speak.

Voting

1. A question is put to vote by the chairperson, having first distinctly restated it, that all may vote intelligently. First, the *affirmative*, then the *negative* is called, each so deliberately as to give all an opportunity of voting. The chairperson then distinctly announces whether the motion is *carried* or *lost*.

2. Voting is usually done by "aye" and "no," or by raising the hand; in a doubtful case by standing and being counted; on certain questions by ballot.

3. If the vote, as announced by the chairperson, is doubtful, it is called again, usually by standing to be counted.

4. All members should vote, unless for reasons excused; or unless under discipline, in which case they should take no part in the business.

5. The moderator does not usually vote, except the question be taken by ballot; but when the meeting is equally divided, the moderator is expected, but is not obliged, to cast the deciding vote.

6. When the vote is to be taken by ballot, the chairperson appoints tellers to distribute, collect, and count the ballots.

Committees

1. Committees are nominated by the chairperson, if so directed by the body, or by any member, and the nomination is confirmed by a vote of the body. More commonly the body directs that all committees shall be *appointed* by the chairperson, in which case no vote is needed to confirm.

2. Any matter of business, or subject under debate, may be *referred* to a committee, with or without instructions. The committee make their *report*, which is the result of their deliberations. The body then takes action on the report, and on any recommendations it may contain.

3. The report of a committee is *received*, by the act of listening to it, with or without a vote of the body. The report is *accepted* by a vote, which acknowledges their services, and places the report before the body for its action. Afterward, any distinct *recommendation* contained in the report is acted on, and may be *adopted* or *rejected*.

4. Frequently, however, when the recommendations of the committee are of a trifling moment or likely to be generally acceptable, the report, having been *received*, is *accepted* and *adopted* by the same vote.

5. A report may be *recommitted* to the committee, with or without instructions, or that committee discharged and the matter referred to a new one for further consideration, so as to present it in a form more likely to meet the general concurrence of the body.

6. A committee may be appointed *with power* for a specific purpose. This gives them power to dispose conclusively of the matter, without further reference to the body.

7. The first named in the appointment of a committee is, by courtesy, considered the *chairperson*. But the committee has the right to name its own chairperson.

8. The member who moves the appointment of a committee is usually, though not necessarily, included among those appointed to the committee.

9. Committees of arrangement, or for other protracted service, *report progress* from time to time, and are continued until their final report, or until their appointment expires.

10. A committee is *discharged* by a vote when its business is done and its report accepted. But usually, in routine business, a committee is considered discharged by the acceptance of its report.

Standing Committee

A committee appointed to act for a given period, or during the recess of the body, is called a standing committee. It has charge of a given department of business assigned by the body, and acts either with power, under instructions, or at discretion, as may be ordered. A standing committee is substantially a minor board, and has its own chairperson, secretary, records, and times of meeting.

Appeal

The moderator announces all votes, and decides all questions as to rules of proceeding and order of debate. But any member who is dissatisfied with his or her decisions may *appeal* from them to the body. The moderator then puts the question, "Shall the decision of the chair be sustained?" The vote of the body, whether negative or affirmative, is final. The right of appeal is undeniable but should not be resorted to on trivial occasions.

Previous Question

Debate may be cut short by a vote to take the *previous question*. This means that the question currently under discussion be immediately voted on, without further debate. Usually a *two-thirds* vote is necessary to order the previous question.

1. If the motion for a previous question be *carried*, then the question must be immediately put to a vote without further debate.

2. If the motion for the previous question be *lost*, the debate proceeds as though no such motion had been made.

3. If the motion for the previous question be *lost*, it cannot be renewed with reference to the same question during the same session.

To Lay on the Table

Immediate and decisive action on any question under discussion may be deferred by a vote to *lay on the table* the resolution pending.

This disposes of the whole subject for the present, but any member has the right subsequently to call it up, and the body will decide by vote whether or not it shall be taken from the table.

1. Sometimes, however, a resolution is laid on the table for the present, our until a specified time, to give place to other business.

2. A motion to lay on the table must apply to a resolution or other papers. An abstract subject cannot be disposed of in this way.

Postponement

A simple *postponement* is for a specified time or purpose, the business to be resumed when the time or purpose is reached. But a question *indefinitely postponed* is considered as finally dismissed.

Not Debatable

Certain motions, by established usage, are *not debatable*, but when once before the body, must be taken without discussion.

These are: the *previous question*, for *indefinite postponement*, to *commit*, to *lay on the table*, to *adjourn*.

But when these motions are modified by some condition of *time*, *place*, or *purpose*, they become debatable, and subject to the rules of other motions, but debatable *only in respect to* the time, place, or purpose that brings them within the province of debate.

A body is, however, competent, by a vote, to allow debate on all motions.

To Reconsider

A motion to *reconsider* a motion previously passed must be made by one who voted *for* the motion when it passed. Likewise, a motion to reconsider a motion previously rejected must be made by one who voted *against* it.

If the body votes to reconsider, then the motion or resolution being reconsidered stands before them as previous to its passage, and may be discussed, adopted, or rejected.

A vote to reconsider should be taken at the same session at which the vote reconsidered was passed, and when there are as many members present. But this rule, though just, is frequently disregarded.

Not to Be Discussed

If, when a question is introduced, any member objects to its discussion as foreign, profitless, or contentious, the moderator should at once put the question, "Shall this motion be discussed?" If this question be decided in the negative, the subject must be dismissed.

Order of the Day

The body may decide to take up some definite business at the specified time. That business therefore becomes *the order of the day* for that hour. When the time mentioned arrives, the chairperson calls the business, or any member may demand it, with or without a vote, and all pending questions are postponed in consequence.

Point of Order

Any member who believes that a speaker is out of order, or that discussion is proceeding improperly, may at any time *rise to a point of order*. He or she must distinctly state his or her question or objection, which the moderator will decide.

Privileges

Questions relating to the *rights and privileges* of members are of primary importance, and, until disposed of, take precedence of all other business and supersede all other motions, except that of adjournment.

Rule Suspended

A rule of order may be *suspended* by a vote of the body to allow the transaction of business necessary, but which could not otherwise be done without a violation of such rule.

Filling Blanks

Where different members are suggested for filling blanks, the *highest number, greatest distance,* and *longest time* are usually voted on first.

Adjournment

1. A simple motion to *adjourn* is always in order, except while a member is speaking, or when taking a vote. It takes precedence of all other motions, and is not debatable.

2. In some deliberate bodies a motion to adjourn is in order while a speaker has the floor or a vote is being taken. On reassembling, the business stands precisely as when adjournment took place.

3. A body may adjourn to a specific time, but if no time be mentioned, the fixed or usual time of meeting is understood. If there be no fixed or usual time of meeting, then an adjournment without date is equivalent to a dissolution.

Forms and Certificates

Certain forms and certificates may frequently be required or useful in observing significant achievements, milestones, or business in the life of Baptist churches and their members. Examples include letters of transfer or dismission, baptismal certificates, calls for ordination councils, ordination certificates, and many others. Customs of churches may differ, as well as tastes. Modern word processing and desktop publishing allow churches to customize such materials, and, indeed, to create forms for special occasions. Models for such material can be found in many church and religious bookstores, as well as in catalogs from commercial suppliers. The following samples and versions of such materials are printed here as suggestions that may be suitable and are subject to adaptation and alteration as individual circumstances may require.

1. Letter of Dismission

From the _____ Baptist Church of

_____
                    City   State

To the _____ Baptist Church of

_____
                    City   State

Dear Brethren:

This is to certify that_____

is a member of this church in good and regular standing and is, at

his/her own request, hereby dismissed from us to unite with you.

When he/she shall have so united with you, of which you will

please inform us, then his/her connection with us will cease.

May the richest blessing of God rest on him/her and on you.

Done by order and in behalf of the church, _____, 19____.

Church Clerk _____

_____
                    Address

                                        This letter is valid for six months.

2. Letter of Notification

_____, 19____

To the _____Church

_____
                City   State

Dear Brethren:

You are hereby notified that we have received _____

into our fellowship in accordance with the letter of dismission

from your church dated _____, 19_____.

_____, Church Clerk

of the _____Church

3. Request for Letter of Dismission

_____, 19____

To the _____Baptist Church

_____
                                            Address

M_____, presently residing at

_____,

has indicated to us a desire to unite with us upon the transfer of

his/her membership from your church. If this action meets with

your approval, we will appreciate receiving a suitable letter of

dismission at your convenience.

_____
                                  Pastor or Clerk

_____Baptist Church
                                            Address

4. Record of Christian Decision

____ I accept Jesus Christ as my Savior and Lord.

____ I purpose to follow him in baptism and the Christian life, in
the fellowship of his church.

____ I reaffirm my faith in Jesus Christ as my Savior and Lord,
and purpose to renew my fellowship in the church by

____ Statement of Christian experience.

____ Transfer of letter. Write to the _____Church at

_____. My name is on record there as _____.

____ I will present myself to the church on _____.
                                                    Date

____ I will attend a class in Christian life and church membership.

Name _____

Address _____

5. Certificate of Baptism

This certifies that

on the _____ day

of _____, 19____,

_____

was baptized by

Pastor _____

of _____.
                              Church

6. Certificate of Church Membership

This certifies that

_____

was received into membership

in the _____ Church

of _____

coming by _____

on the _____ day of _____, 19____.

_____
Minister

7. Certificate of Baptism and Church Membership

This certifies that following baptism

on the _____ day of _____, 19____

_____

was received into membership

in the _____ Church

of _____.
Minister

8. Call for an Ordination Council

_____, 19 ____

To the _____ Baptist Church of _____

You are requested to send your pastor and two other members together with those of the other churches of the _____ Association _____, 19 ____, at _____ p.m., to consider and advise as to the wisdom of publicly setting apart to the work of the gospel ministry our brother/sister,

_____ .

The council will meet in

_____ .

By order of the church.

_____
Church Clerk

_____ Baptist Church

_____
Address

9. Certificate of License

This is to Certify

that at a meeting of the _____ Baptist Church,

_____, on the _____ day of _____, 19____,

having given evidence that he/she possesses gifts for the work

of the gospel ministry, was licensed to preach the gospel as

he/she may have opportunity, and to exercise his/her gifts in

the work of the ministry for the period from this date

to_____, 19____, when his/her status will be reviewed

by the church (in cooperation with the Associational Committee

on Ordinations).

When acting as pastor of a Baptist church and authorized

by that church to do so, he/she shall be considered eligible to

administer the ordinances of baptism and the Lord's Supper

and to officiate at funerals and weddings, when compatible

with the laws of the state.

_____
Moderator (if a layperson)

_____
Pastor

_____
Church Clerk

10. Certificate of Ordination

This is to certify that, after satisfactory examination regarding his/her Christian experience, call to the ministry, and personal and educational qualifications,

_____

was duly ordained to the work of the Christian ministry by the _____ Church of _____, on the _____ day of _____, 19____, upon the recommendation of a duly called council composed of delegates from _____ churches of the _____ Association.

_____
Clerk of the Church

_____
Clerk of the Council

_____
Moderator of the Council

11. Deacon's Certificate

This is to certify that, after a satisfactory relation of his/her

Christian experience and views of Bible doctrine, _____

was publicly set apart to the office and work of deacon on the

_____ day of _____, 19 _____, by the _____

Church at _____.

_____

Pastor

_____

Clerk

12. Infant Dedication Certificate

On _____

Date

_____

Name of Child

was brought to the house of God at the _____

Church by _____

Parents, Sponsor, Other

to be there publicly dedicated to God, remembering the

admonition of the Lord Jesus Christ, who said,

"Let the children come unto me."

_____

Pastor

13. Certificate of Appreciation

With great appreciation for effective leadership and diligent serv-

ice on behalf of the _____ Church, this certificate

is presented to _____

for _____.

Nature of Service

_____

Pastor, Moderator, Other

14. Certificate of Course Completion

This certifies that _____

Name

has successfully completed

_____.

Name of Training Event or Course

By this achievement his/her skills are enhanced for the greater

service of Christ's kingdom.

_____

Teacher, Pastor or Other Official

_____

Date

Church Covenants

Church covenants are important reminders of the essential spirit and meaning of the corporate life of faith in a church. Often they are used on a regular basis, such as part of the preparation for the Lord's Supper, on church anniversaries, or on other significant occasions to renew the commitments of the members to one another and to their Lord. Covenants may be composed to suit the specific circumstances of each church or may be copied or adapted from covenants used by other churches.

The following examples are merely suggested models that some churches have found effective. The first is a covenant included in the New Hampshire Confession. It has been the source from which many church covenants have been derived. The second is typical of many covenants developed by churches in the twentieth century. The third is a covenant developed by a particular church. It serves both as a mission statement and a covenant.

Historic Baptist Covenant

(This covenant is attributed to or associated with the New Hampshire Confession. Because of its attribution and long-standing influence on Baptist churches, it has long served as a model for church covenants. Some of its phrasing is therefore quite familiar to many.)

Having been, as we trust, brought by divine grace to embrace the Lord Jesus Christ, and to give ourselves wholly to him, we do now solemnly and joyfully covenant with each other, to walk together in him, with brotherly love, to his glory, as our common Lord. We do, therefore, in his strength, engage:

That we will exercise a Christian care and watchfulness over each other, and faithfully warn, exhort, and admonish each other as occasion may require:

That we will not forsake the assembling of ourselves together, but will uphold the public worship of God, and the ordinances of his house:

That we will not omit closet [private] and family religion at home, nor neglect the great duty of religiously training our children, and those under our care, for the service of Christ and the enjoyment of heaven:

That, as we are the light of the world, and salt of the earth, we will seek divine aid to enable us to deny ungodliness, and every worldly lust, and to walk circumspectly in the world, that we may win the souls of men:

That we will cheerfully contribute of our property, according as God has prospered us, for the maintenance of a faithful and evangelical ministry among us, for the support of the poor, and to spread the Gospel over the earth:

That we will in all conditions, even till death, strive to live to the glory of him who hath called us out of darkness into his marvelous light.

"And may the God of Peace, who brought again from the dead our Lord Jesus, that great shepherd of the sheep, through the blood of the everlasting covenant, make us perfect in every good work, to do his will, working in us that which is well pleasing in his sight through Jesus Christ; to whom be glory, forever and ever. Amen."

A Traditional Covenant

We believe that we have been led by the Spirit of God to receive the Lord Jesus Christ as our Savior, and on the profession of our faith, having been baptized in the name of God, and of his Son, and of the Holy Spirit, we do now, in the presence of God and this assembly, joyfully enter into covenant with one another, as one body in Christ. By our profession, and with the aid of the Holy Spirit, we commit ourselves to walk together in Christian love; to strive for the advancement of this church, in knowledge, holiness, and comfort; to promote its prosperity and spirituality; to sustain its worship, ordinances, discipline, and doctrines; to contribute cheerfully and regularly to the support of the ministry, the expenses of the church, the relief of the poor, and the spread of the gospel through all nations.

We also engage to maintain family and private devotion; to provide religious instruction for our children; to seek the salvation of our kindred and acquaintances; to walk circumspectly in the world; to be just in our dealings, faithful in our engagements, and exemplary in our deportment; to avoid all tattling, backbiting, and excessive anger; to abstain from the sale and use of addictive substances; and to be faithful in our efforts to advance the kingdom of our Savior.

We further engage to watch over one another in Christian love; to remember each other in prayer; to aid each other in sickness and distress; to cultivate Christian sympathy in feeling and courtesy in speech; to be slow to take offense but always ready for reconciliation, and, mindful of the rules of our Savior, to secure it without delay. We moreover engage that, if and when we move from this community, we will as soon as possible unite with some other church where we can carry out the spirit of this covenant and the principles of God's Word.

A Contemporary Covenant/Mission Statement

We are a community of faith united in exploring what it means to follow the way of Jesus Christ, to be a people of God and to love and care for our neighbors. As a church we will know no circles of exclusion, no boundaries we will not cross, and no loyalties above those which we owe to God.

Appendix G

For Further Reading

Resources on the history, development, principles, experiences, missions, churches, preachers, and activities of Baptists are numerous. Below are several suggested avenues for further exploration, presented in the knowledge that each suggested resource will provide new doors to open and new resources to discover.

Historical scholarship about the origins of Baptists, and particularly their struggle to define their principles and purposes, has been growing. Much has been written in the past generation. B. R. White's *The English Separatist Tradion* (Oxford: Oxford University Press, 1971) will help locate the earliest origins of Bapists. For the English origins of Baptist life, Champlin Burrage, *The Early English Dissenters in the Light of Recent Research (1550–1641)*, 2 vols. (1912; Reprinted New York: Russell & Russell, 1967) also remains a valuable source, as does Wilbur K. Jordan, *The Development of Religious Toleration in England*, 4 vols. (Cambridge: Harvard University Press, 1932–1940). For a work that parallels Hiscox's approach to Baptist essentials from an English perspective, including a view of the church, its ministry, and its ordinances, Ernest A. Payne's *The Fellowship of Believers: Baptist Thought and Practice Yesterday and Today* (London: The Kingsgate Press, 1944) is an admirable source. A uniquely English perspective on believer's baptism is available in H. Wheeler Robinson's *Baptist Principles* (London: The Kingsgate Press, 1945). More recently several volumes by the Baptist Historical Society of the Baptist Union of Great Britain and Ireland have expanded on the development of particular English Baptist churches, institutions, and personalities. The volumes in the series *History of the English Baptists* are especially helpful. For Americans, B.R. White's *The English Baptists of the Seventeenth Century* (London: Baptist Historical Society, 1983) will be helpful. Brian Stanley's *The History of the Baptist Missionary Society: 1792–1992* (Edinburgh: T & T Clark, 1994) will reward readers interested in the early English origins of Baptist missions.

In the American experience of Baptist formation, early Baptist historian Isaac Backus left us with *A History of New England with Particular Reference to the Denomination of Christians called Baptists*, 2 vols. (Newton, Mass.: Backus Historical Society, 1871). For a specific focus on Backus and his times, William G. McLoughlin's *Isaac Backus and the American Pietist Tradition* (Boston: Little, Brown, & Co., 1967) is a valuable resource. For those interested in expanding their knowledge of early Baptist life and views in the American colonies, several works by Edwin S. Gaustad will be particularly helpful. They include *Faith of Our Fathers: Religion in the New Nation* (Grand Rapids, Mich.: Wm. B. Eerdmans Publishing Co., 1993), *The Great Awakening in New England* (New York: Harper and Row, 1957), and *Dissent in American Religion* (Chicago: University of Chicago Press, 1973). In addition, Gaustad edited a volume of essays written by several authors published first in *Foundations* and then later under the title *Baptists, the Bible, Church Order and the Churches* (New York: Arno Press, 1980), which will provide helpful insights. His *Baptist Piety: The Last Will and Testimony of Obadiah Holmes* (Valley Forge, Pa.: Judson Press, 1994) provides a clear perspective into an individual Baptist's life and faith, including primary as well as interpretive material.

William G. McLoughlin's *New England Dissent, 1630–1833: The Baptists and the Separation of Church and State*, 2 vols. (Cambridge: Harvard University Press, 1971) brought scholarship about Baptist contributions to the separation of church and state, as well as the formation of a Baptist ethos and institutional style to a new and high level. The introduction to the same author's *Soul Liberty: The Baptists' Struggle in New England, 1630–1833* (Hanover, N.H.: University Press of New England, 1991) provides a brief and brilliant summary of the same subject. Edwin S. Gaustad's

Liberty of Conscience: Roger Williams in America (Grand Rapids, Mich: Wm. B. Eerdmans Publishing Co., 1991) provides a focus on the iconoclastic and titular "father" of the Baptist movement in America and the earliest stages of Baptist liberty issues.

For an overview of Baptist development, H. Leon McBeth's *The Baptist Heritage: Four Centuries of Baptist Witness* (Nashville: Broadman Press, 1987) offers wide, helpful categorizations of various movements within Baptist life, and the companion *Sourcebook for Baptist Heritage* by H. Leon McBeth, et al., has added immeasurable riches to Baptist history. For my introduction to the development of Baptist institutional life and others' perspectives on the issues and concerns which presently shape and threaten Baptist life see Everett C. Goodwin (ed.), *Baptists in the Balance: The Tension between Freedom and Responsibility* (Valley Forge, Judson Press, 1997).

For a greater understanding of the formation of the African American or black-church Baptists, two works are especially to be recommended: Michael Sobel's *Trabelin' On: The Slave Journey to an Afro-Baptist Faith* (Princeton, N.J.: Princeton University Press, 1988) focuses specifically on the early development of black worship and institutional traditions, and C. Eric Lincoln's *The Black Church in the African American Experience* (Durham, N.C.: Duke University Press, 1990) discusses the role of the black church more broadly in the flow of American cultural life.

Two works that provide excellent resources to trace and interpret the growth of the "Baptist way" and to enlarge a general understanding of Baptist purposes are Winthrop S. Hudson, ed., *Baptist Concepts of the Church* (noted below) and Walter Shurden, *Baptist Identity: Four Fragile Freedoms* (noted below). *The Dictionary of Baptists in America* by Bill Leonard, ed. (Downers Grove, Ill.: InterVarsity Press, 1994) also provides a wealth of information, history, and perspectives on Baptist life and institutions. A specific analysis of the polarizations that have occurred in the Southern Baptist Convention is available in Bill J. Leonard, *God's Last and Only Hope: The Fragmentation of the Southern Baptist Convention* (Grand Rapids, Mich.: Wm. B. Eerdmans Publishing Co., 1990).

Though not himself a Baptist, Martin Marty has written widely on the nature of faith experience in America and is the editor of *Modern American Protestantism and Its World* (New York: K.G.

Saur), a multivolume work. See especially in volume 3 (*Civil Religion, Church and State*, 1992) the article entitled *Baptists and Church-State Issues in the Twentieth Century*, which provides a helpful introduction to the continuing and often controversial role Baptists have played in championing First Amendment causes. Other works by Marty are well worth investigating to expand general knowledge of churches and church organizations in the American cultural and social experience.

The subject of church organization, management, and leadership of churches in general has been the focus of much comment and publication in the last generation. Some of the best and most helpful has been offered by Lyle Schaller and the Yokefellow Institute and by the Alban Institute in Washington, D.C. (Alban Institute materials are published under a variety of authors and subjects). Likewise, a veritable industry now exists in materials devoted to the subject of church growth. The offerings are too numerous to mention here, but investigation of these sources will reward readers who wish to expand their understanding of growth-oriented programs, leadership styles and skills, changes, and opportunities.

The following additional list of books is essentially a list of long-standing works that address from differing perspectives many of the subjects of this book. A few are recent additions to Baptist bibliography or represent recent editions of older works. Many were listed in the 1964 edition of the *Hiscox Guide*. Of these, some may be out of print, but all are valuable either as continuing sources of information or as historical points of reference for Baptist church development and leadership.

Asquith, Glenn H. *Church Officers at Work*. Valley Forge, Pa.: Judson Press, 1963.

Ayer, Joseph C. *A Source Book for Ancient Church History*. New York: Charles Scribner's Sons, 1913.

Bettenson, Henry. *Documents of the Christian Church*. Rev. ed. London: Oxford University Press, 1963.

Browne, Benjamin P. *Tales of Baptist Daring*. Valley Forge, Pa.: Judson Press, 1961.

Cattan, Louise A., and Helen C. Schmitz. *One Mark of Greatness*. Valley Forge, Pa.: Judson Press, 1962.

Clark, Wayne C. *The Meaning of Church Membership*, Valley Forge, Pa.: Judson Press, 1963.

Cober, Kenneth L. *The Church's Teaching Ministry*. Valley Forge, Pa.: Judson Press, 1964.

Estep, William R. *Revolution within the Revolution*. Grand Rapids, Mich.: Wm. B. Eerdmans Publishing Co., 1990.

Gilbert, Clarence B. *The Board of Christian Education at Work*. Valley Forge, Pa.: Judson Press, 1962.

Gilmore, A., ed. *Christian Baptism*. Valley Forge, Pa.: Judson Press, 1959.

Harrison, Paul M. *Authority and Power in the Free Church Tradition*. Princeton, N.J.: Princeton University Press, 1959.

Hudson, Winthrop Still. *American Protestantism*. Chicago: University of Chicago Press, 1961.

Hudson, Winthrop Still, ed. *Baptist Concepts of the Church*. Valley Forge, Pa.: Judson Press, 1959.

Hudson, Winthrop Still. *Baptist Convictions*. Valley Forge, Pa.: Judson Press, 1963.

Knight, Allan R., and Gordon H. Schroeder. *The New Life*. Valley Forge, Pa.: Judson Press, 1960.

Knudsen, Ralph E. *Theology in the New Testament*. Valley Forge, Pa.: Judson Press. 1964.

Latourette, Kenneth Scott. *A History of Christianity*. New York: Harper and Row, 1953.

Lumpkin, William L. *Baptist Confessions of Faith*. Valley Forge, Pa.: Judson Press, 1959.

McCall, Duke K., ed. *What Is the Church? A Symposium of Baptist Thought*. Nashville: Broadman Press, 1958.

McConnell, F. M. *McConnell's Manual for Baptist Churches*. Valley Forge, Pa.: Judson Press, 1958.

McNutt, William R. *Polity and Practice in Baptist Churches*. Valley Forge, Pa.: Judson Press, 1959.

Maring, Norman H., and Winthrop S. Hudson. *A Baptist Manual of Polity and Practice*. Valley Forge, Pa.: Judson Press, 1963.

Mullins, Edgar Y. *Baptist Beliefs*. Valley Forge, Pa.: Judson Press, 1962.

Yearbook of American Churches. The National Council of the Churches of Christ in the U.S.A. New York. Published annually.

Nichols, Harold. *The Work of the Deacon*. Valley Forge, Pa.: Judson Press, 1962.

Payne, Ernest A. *The Fellowship of Believers: Baptist Thought Yesterday and Today*. London: The Kingsgate Press, 1944.

Roberts, Alexander, and James Donaldson, eds. *The Ante-Nicene Christian Library*. 24 vols. Edinburgh: T & T Clark, 1867–1872.

Robinson, H. Wheeler. *Baptist Principles*. London: The Kingsgate Press, 1925.

Rowe, Henry K., and Robert G. Torbet. *The Baptist Witness*. Valley Forge, Pa.: Judson Press, 1953.

Schaff, Philip. *The Creeds of Christendom*. 3 vols. 6th Ed. New York: Harper and Row, 1919.

Schaff, Philip. *History of the Christian Church*. 8 vols. Rev. ed. Grand Rapids, Mich.: Wm. B. Eerdmans Publishing Co., 1960.

Shurden, Walter B. *The Baptist Identity: Four Fragile Freedoms*. Macon, Ga: Smyth & Helwys, 1993.

Shurden, Walter B., ed. *Proclaiming The Baptist Vision: The Priesthood of All Believers*. Macon, Ga: Smyth & Helwys, 1993.

Torbet, Robert G. *A History of the Baptists*. Rev. ed. Valley Forge, Pa.: Judson Press, 1963.

Torbet, Robert G. *The Baptist Story*. Valley Forge, Pa.: Judson Press, 1957.

Torbet, Robert G. *The Baptist Ministry Then and Now*. Valley Forge, Pa.: Judson Press, 1954.

Vedder, Henry C. *A Short History of the Baptists*. Valley Forge, Pa.: Judson Press, 1960.

Walker, Williston. *A History of the Christian Church*. Rev. ed. New York: Charles Scribner's Sons, 1985.

Walker, Williston. *Creeds and Platforms of Congregationalism*. New York: Pilgrim Press, 1991.

Index